THE Big
BOOK OF
Details

Foreword by
Harvey "Smokey" Daniels

46 Moves for Teaching Writers to Elaborate

ROZLYN LINDER

HEINEMANN • PORTSMOUTH, NH

Heinemann
361 Hanover Street
Portsmouth, NH 03801–3912
www.heinemann.com

Offices and agents throughout the world

The author and publisher wish to thank those who have generously given permission to reprint borrowed material:

Page 4: Photograph of Judy Blume and Rozlyn Linder. Copyright ©2013 by Judy Blume. Reprinted with permission from William Morris Endeavor Entertainment, LLC. All rights reserved.

Library of Congress Cataloging-in-Publication Data
Names: Linder, Rozlyn, author.
Title: The big book of details : 46 moves for teaching writers to elaborate / Rozlyn Linder.
Description: Portsmouth, NH : Heinemann, [2016] | Includes bibliographical references.
Identifiers: LCCN 2015042708 | ISBN 9780325077666
Subjects: LCSH: English language—Composition and exercises—Study and teaching. | Description (Rhetoric)—Study and teaching.
Classification: LCC LB1576 .L532 2016 | DDC 372.62/3—dc23
LC record available at http://lccn.loc.gov/2015042708

Editor: Tobey Antao
Production: Victoria Merecki
Cover and interior designs: Suzanne Heiser
Typesetter: Kim Arney
Manufacturing: Steve Bernier

Printed in the United States of America on acid-free paper

20 19 18 17 VP 2 3 4 5

*I dedicate this book to Judy Blume and
Beverly Cleary, my first writing teachers.*

Contents

*Y*ikes, I cringe when I think of all the times I scrawled *add more detail* in the margin of some student's paper (usually not in red ink, I wasn't that mean, but still). OK, no excuses, but I was a victim of the benighted times, nobody told me any different, and I hadn't met Roz Linder yet.

This lively and practical book addresses a persistent problem in our profession. We still don't *show kids how to write.* More broadly, we don't demonstrate how literate people think. Sure, we're great at assigning, demanding, and commanding literacy activities of all kinds: "Read Chapter 7 for Friday." "Write an essay on this article." "Take a position on this controversy and support it with evidence from the text." But when it comes to the how-to part, where we ought to demonstrate how such mental work gets done, we too often abandon our students and let them *guess* how a skilled reader or writer might tackle the task. Sometimes we even withhold further "teaching" until assessment time, when we tally up the wrong answers on the comprehension quiz or drench kids' papers with red ink.

On the reading side, this gap has been slowly closing. We have learned from the ground-breaking research of David Pearson (percolating up since 1983, what a slow system!) how to show kids ways of making sense of text. We now recognize a handful of specific thinking strategies that proficient readers (like us) use to comprehend—moves that can be named, explained, and explicitly taught. So we open up our own heads and share those mental processes though powerful modeling lessons like think-alouds.

In writing, the *showing* piece has been slower to develop. It's rare for teachers to open up their own heads and demonstrate their own writing, let alone simultaneously explain what mental moves they are using along the way. And there's an extra challenge: we teachers may feel less confident about ourselves as model writers than we do as readers. As Jim Vopat says in *Writing Circles,* almost everyone in America, adult or child, marches among "the writing wounded" after the bruising kind of writing instruction typically offered in school.

Into this fraught and urgent situation steps Roz Linder, kid wise, whip smart, and brimming with ready-to-use ideas. Roz gently pushes us forward, handing out tools we can actually use and showing us clear-cut writing strategy lessons we can confidently and comfortably offer our students. Writing doesn't have to be a mysterious black box that only "good writers" are able to activate. On the

—should be purpose of ea. lesson

contrary, the mechanisms of skillful writing can be put on open display for all to see and test-drive.

It worked for me. As a person who's written a bunch of books (and modeled my own writing for kids of many ages), Roz's resource was an eye-opener. Smugly, I began *The Big Book of Details* thinking that I was hyperaware of my own mental moves as a writer. Did I get a lesson! As I kept reading, Roz named many strategies I do regularly use but never knew I did. What I mean is, I frequently employed these moves but did so automatically, below the level of awareness, without conscious intent. They just "came to me."

I could not have taught these moves to students, because I wasn't aware enough of what was happening in my head as I wrote. But here was Roz, pointing out, naming, and showing me how to share dozens of my own subconscious moves: "zoom in," "INGS up front," "pop culture references," "think and act," "invisible tags," and "adverb commas." Who knew?

What Roz offers us in writing instruction parallels what we have been doing with reading. Until David Pearson (and Steph Harvey, Ellin Keene, Debbie Miller, Cris Tovani, Kelly Gallagher, and Tanny McGregor) came along, even veteran teachers didn't consciously understand their own reading/thinking processes well. So it was hard for them to demonstrate their thinking explicitly. But now we're getting there. Roz is doing the same thing for writing; helping us better understand our own writing-as-thinking strategies, so we can *show them to kids*.

Roz Linder traffics in teaching ideas that are "sticky"—that grab you right away, that are memorable, usable, and reliable. This book is just about the stickiest teacher resource you'll ever dip into. Watch out! It won't let go of you.

—Harvey "Smokey" Daniels
Santa Fe, New Mexico

Acknowledgments

Many authors tend to thank their editors somewhere near the bottom of their acknowledgments. For me, it is the opposite. This book would not exist without the hard work of Tobey Antao. Thank you for being the best coauthor, editor, shoulder to cry on, problem fixer, cheerleader, encourager, and all-around awesome person. I love all of our conversations and value your talent and expertise. You are my best writing friend in the whole wide world!

There are so many people responsible for making this book a reality. None of this would exist without the wonderful work of all of the teachers and students who welcomed me into their classrooms. I am forever grateful to the students and staff at Mountain Park Elementary School in Roswell, Georgia. Stacy Perlman, thank you for letting me work with your dynamic staff and students. You guys are so talented, and you remind me of how much fun it is to be a teacher!

Most of the middle school work in this book comes from the hardworking students at East Coweta Middle School in Senoia, Georgia. Thank you, Dr. Jackson, for letting me work with your staff and students. Sarah Klein, your students were a delight to work with. They kept me on my toes and constantly laughing. They were a great group, with big personalities and tons of great ideas. Karhma Novak—wow—can I be like you when I grow up? Your class was amazing and made me want to go back to middle school. Finally, Karen Smith—thank you for letting me feel like a superstar with your creative, funny, and wonderfully talented sixth graders.

Last, but definitely not least, are the teachers at Lithia Springs Elementary in Lithia Springs, Georgia. Spending the year working with you guys was a blast. I have to say, you take the cake for personality, hard work, and a willingness to venture into unknown territory, even when at times it felt a bit uncomfortable. William Marchant and Pam Bates—wow! You both participated in every professional development session, right there with the classroom teachers. Your commitment and willingness to learn with your staff is amazing and should be the norm for all administrators. Eugene Glover, Tiffanie Cartie, Althea Carter, and Will Alexander—thank you for going the extra mile and letting me work additional sessions with your students. Anay Barajas—it was amazing watching you teach in English and Spanish. Mr. Carr, if I ever go back to elementary school, I want to be in your class. You are great at making writing come alive and seem fun (even if sometimes it wasn't).

Thank you to my Georgia State University crew. You guys helped keep me sane when I was close to the edge: Kelly Sowerbrower, Sarah Klein, and Nicole Dukes. I might thank each of you in every book that I write! Each of you is wonderfully fabulous and always helps me to remember what is most important in life.

I am grateful to all of the wonderful people who have influenced my thinking about writing and writing instruction. Dr. Sarah Robbins, thank you for opening doors for me to be a part of the National Writing Project and begin to network with other teachers about writing best practices. Dr. Nadia Behizadeh—I appreciate all of our conversations about writing assessment and instruction, and thank you for introducing me to a whole new body of literature on what writing is, how we assess it, and what really matters in authentic writing. I cannot have an acknowledgement section without mentioning Dr. Michelle Zoss. Over the past year of writing this book, I always felt like I was trying to juggle way too many things at the same time. Thank you for supporting me and letting me know that it was okay to simply put some of those things down and take a breath.

I love and appreciate my family for putting up with me as I shed some tears, screamed at the computer, and buried myself in student work and charts. Thank you for letting this book borrow Mommy for a few months. Chris, Sydney, and Brooke—I adore and love each of you. You all are my favorite authors, and I love everything that you guys write.

Finally, thank you to the team at Heinemann. You all are amazing! I stand in awe at the talent under that one roof. Thank you for showering me with love, and believing that I had something to say that could help teachers and students.

1

THE

Power

OF

Details

*a*s a teacher of writing and as a reader, you know that details are the lifeblood of texts, whether they be video, audio, print, essays, arguments, stories, or poems. You've felt the hairs on the back of your neck stand up as you watched Diane Keaton's unflinching glare in the closing seconds of *The Godfather*. Four sentences into *To Kill a Mockingbird*, you loved Jem and you trusted Scout's eye for presenting things just as she sees them. An author's selected details have the power to create believable worlds, bring readers to tears, or incite anger. Rich details are power.

Our students are no less aware of the details in their worlds. Think about the questions we field every day from students about the details of our school and staff members. "Why does the principal say *kinny garten* instead of *kindergarten*?" "Why are the walls on the left side painted with murals, but the walls on the right side are just plain white?" "Why does that teacher always wear skirts, never pants?" Kids get that details can lead them to new understandings.

But if we can all agree that details are important, why is it so difficult for students to craft meaningful details in their own writing?

Perhaps this story will sound familiar to you: I remember conferencing with one of my fifth-grade students who had written a paper arguing for better food choices in the school cafeteria. Shannon had written several paragraphs about the poor quality of the food and offered suggestions for the changes she sought. Her paper read like a list. She made a point, offered a brief explanation, and moved on to the next point. She did not elaborate much at all. My directive to her was to add more details to her paper. "You have to elaborate more. Your reader needs to know more about this," I told her. I even wrote asterisks next to all of the places that lacked adequate detail.

I felt good about our conference. I thought that I had given her pretty specific guidance to improve her essay. When we conferenced again later, she had indeed added many more sentences to her paper. It made it longer, but not any better. I repeated the process and we even crafted a few sentences together that she could add to her essay. This time, I was certain that I had really set her off in the right direction. When she finished, she had a lengthier paper, but it still wasn't any better. Her paper listed information. It was filled with facts and sentences, but the lack of meaningful elaboration left the paper lifeless and without voice. She needed tools to create and describe the events in an intentional way, not just to add more words. Writing more is not the same as creating more powerful descriptions, images, and explanations.

I mistakenly thought that I had taught Shannon about details. In fact, I hadn't really taught her how to do anything. I named places that lacked details. I explained that her paragraphs needed more elaboration. I even pointed to where that elaboration should happen. I didn't teach her a skill that she could take and apply to any other type of writing, though. I, like many teachers, was not explicit about how to select details, why they could improve writing. I just stressed that good writing features rich details and elaboration. The concepts of *rich details* and *elaboration* means nothing to a fifth grader. It just says: write more! But, why are we adding more? Is it to meet some arbitrary length requirement? Is it because longer is better?

Here's what I needed to teach: Why add details? Why should you add more words and what type of words should you add? I lost a teaching moment by telling rather than teaching. To help our students use details effectively, we need to find out what our students want their writing to do, and then show them *explicit* moves, or strategies, to make that happen. Detailing the different writing moves that authors rely on changed the focus of my instruction. Imagine what my work with Shannon might have looked like if I had made her intentions the focus of our conference: Did she want to make the reader feel sad for the students who had to eat the current food selections? Did she want the readers to visualize the current food choices? Did she want to imply that something else was going on that impacted the food choices?

Here's what the power of writing with details *can* look like: When I taught tenth-grade English, I had a group of students who were reluctant writers. They took little pride in their work and produced the bare minimum for any writing assignment. By the time I taught them, I knew that I had to explicitly teach different types of details and how to craft them. I taught my students that details were the key to making the reader see what you wanted them to see.

We spent much of our time exploring types of details. We worked on not just how to craft them, but how and when to use different types of details and recognize them in text. My students began to enjoy writing more and recognized the power that they had each time they put pen to paper. They began to understand that they could create and define what they wanted to with the right details. I felt successful, but wondered if this instruction had been "sticky." Did students really internalize this? Would this carry over into their writing after they left my classroom?

I got confirmation that this message had indeed been sticky with my students in the most unexpected and unlikely manner. One morning, two students were arguing outside of our classroom before the bell rang. The argument was heated and looked like it could escalate into a fight. My entire class saw what happened between the two students. In an effort to investigate, the principal asked all of my students to write down what happened. He was very explicit that this was to be independent and that no students should share or talk to each other. These were supposed to be independent accounts.

Later that day, I was summoned to the principal's office. Filled with the same fear I would have had as a child, I headed to the office during my lunch break. On his desk were my students' statements about the confrontation in the hall. The principal read aloud from some of the papers. He wanted to know what was going on. These did not sound like the reluctant writing that usually reached his desk.

As I read over the papers, I couldn't help but smile. I recognized the moves that they were making. I could tell who wanted to create a sense of sympathy for one of the students. I could see who wanted to stretch out a particular part of the argument. I could see who wanted to appear distant and objective. The details were intentional. They read much more like prose than the normal lists of what happened in an incident. They were so intentionally crafted that my principal thought that they had been coached or guided. *He was accusing me of helping them write their statements!*

At first I was offended at the suggestion, but that offense quickly changed to pride. The rich details and intentional creation of different moods or points of view were fantastic. The next day I asked my students to share not what they had written, but what they did. Students explained that they had a point of view and that they knew what type of moves they had to make to communicate their versions of what happened. They recognized the power that they had and relied on their toolbox of moves to create what they wanted to on paper. A call to the principal's office never felt so good.

The Connection Between Powerful Details and the Standards-Based Classroom

We recognize that details are both powerful and omnipresent. They are also emphasized in the Common Core State Standards (CCSS). Many states have adopted these standards or developed very similar standards of their own. Although the standards can seem unwieldy, there is a common thread that is woven throughout the standards: details! There is a heavy reliance and reoccurring focus on details within the reading and writing standards that seems to go unspoken, but should be front and center. Teaching students to read details critically and to use details purposefully in their own writing lays the foundation for both the reading and writing standards. All of the work that the Common Core and similar state standards require in reading—close reading; making inferences; citing evidence; determining central ideas or themes; analyzing development across a text; analyzing word choices; assessing point of view, purpose, and style; evaluating texts; comparing texts—requires students to dive into the rich details of a text to make sense of the text as a whole. In writing, all three of the genres prescribed by the CCSS—arguments, informative/explanatory texts, and narratives—rely on well-used details. Students have been making arguments, explaining, and telling stories all of their lives. Where might their writing in these genres need work? Probably in creating meticulously developed details and reasons to support their thinking. They have the content; they just need to know the moves to convince, to explain, and to draw readers in.

Learning from the Experts

My first writing teachers were Beverly Cleary and Judy Blume. As a young child, I read almost every title that both of these women released. I shared Beezus and Ramona's life experiences and learned all about mean girls from Blume's *Blubber,* decades before Lindsey Lohan popularized the term. The content of these books helped me to grow, but I was also in awe of the authors' ability to re-create the type of world that I knew and understood. Through these books, I taught myself how to punctuate dialogue and use dialogue tags (other than *said*). I learned that characters think in their heads a lot during a book and that one way authors show this is with italics. I learned how cool it is to read analogies that help you picture the world authors wanted to introduce. I learned that dependent clauses make sentences sound complex and rich. I loved how they packed character description right in the middle of a sentence, couched between commas (appositive phrases and descriptive clauses). I didn't know the name of any of those things, but I had models of them, courtesy of Mrs. Blume and Mrs. Cleary, to teach me. One day, I sat at our home computer, 1986 edition, and began to write. I was going to craft my own novel. I wrote for two days before I felt brave enough to share my writing with my mother. My mom, not a woman to mince words, read a few pages, then looked at me and said, "You can't just sit and copy from other books. You've got to make up your own." Puzzled, I explained to her that this was my story and that I wrote it. She went on to explain that she knew it was copied because of the dialogue and the names, the way I typed the dialogue, the type of dialogue tags I used, and the way that each line of dialogue was indented. "That's just like those books you read." I was crushed. I stuck my story in my desk and figured it wasn't any good.

I was finally face to face with my original writing teacher, Judy Blume.

Decades later I realized that my writing must have been pretty good. It was so good that my own mother was certain that it was copied. At nine, I had learned writing moves that were good enough to make a grown-up think that what I have written couldn't possibly have come from a nine year old. Retroactive score!

Despite being discouraged, I still kept reading, learning, and growing. Those rich lessons from those two authors helped me to develop my own writing chops without a writing workshop or even a writing teacher. I was a student with rich literacy resources. Today, educators actively seek books that will help their students to learn to write. You may know these as mentor texts, touchstone texts, model texts, exemplar texts, literature models—the list is endless. As my experience as a child shows, finding a name for this practice doesn't matter as much as the power and learning that comes from it. What I got from those books was a clear example of how words can work together. My reading experiences provided lots of examples of the kind of moves that writers make.

As a teacher, I wanted my students to do the same thing. They should also read like writers. This way, they can discover different moves that writers make. My hopeful desire for this, unfortunately, ignores two types of students: the reluctant reader and the struggling reader. Reluctant readers (not always poor readers) have yet to develop a love and appreciation of the written word. These are students who don't have the desire to look at text critically and consume books as writers. Although I want to change this, I don't want this lack of interest in reading to serve as the roadblock to critical and varied writing moves. Struggling readers face different obstacles: they don't read well and may be focusing on below-level comprehension or decoding strategies. Their current reading ability shouldn't get transferred to their writing ability. So, although I want my students to read like writers and uncover moves, I don't want their reading to serve as the only or primary means to learn different ways to elaborate and add detail to their writing. If we wait until students find these moves on their own, reluctant and struggling readers will be at a disadvantage in writing as well as in reading. We should, as teachers, bring the moves to students to try on for size. Does this mean that students reading like writers is never on our agenda? Of course not! Just don't fall into the trap of assuming that each student will embrace this path to learn more about writing.

With this in mind, I decided that I had to bring the models to my writers. I would neatly categorize the moves that writers made, share them with my students, and encourage them to recognize these models when we read and wrote. My students and I don't re-create the wheel: we learn the moves that writers make and consider how we could adopt them as our own. This approach also helps the strong readers: they begin to read books not just as readers, but as writers, too. The strongest readers love to test-drive the moves I teach and to identify and share new moves that they notice in books.

Reading Like a Writing Teacher: Discovering Moves

"**Reading** like a writing teacher" is a term coined by Katie Wood Ray. In her book *What You Know by Heart: How to Develop Curriculum for Your Writing Workshop* (2002), Katie explains that teachers should be on the lookout for interesting sentences and paragraphs. She describes the world as being "full of writing that makes us slam on our brakes when we're reading and think, *Ooo . . . look at that, I need to show that to my students. That's really good writing*" (90).

Reading like a writer is what I did as a child; reading like a writing teacher is what I do now. I cannot look at a website, commercial, article, novel, basal passage, or book jacket without eyeing a juicy sentence or detail that I feel I need to show my students. I joke with my husband that it is hard for me to read for pleasure because I have become consumed with looking at the moves that writers make: I don't want to miss anything that could be brought back into the classroom. Text is all around me with lessons and ideas that my students can integrate into their writing. Over the years, I started to catalog these different details. Sometimes, I would forget where they came from or mix up the titles. It started not to matter as much, though. Once I knew a move, I could easily search for it again. Writers use some of the same things—the same *moves*—over and over. If I couldn't find the move as I remembered it, I would sit and type up a paragraph to show the detail move I was thinking of. Then, I shared the found or created model with my students to give them access to that move so they could use it in their own writing. As my lists grew, I began organizing the moves by type. Just like I did with Judy Blume and Beverly Cleary, I started noticing some patterns that writers used.

For example, I noticed Judy Blume often relied on recounts of conversations, instead of the actual conversations, in her books. She didn't always use dialogue tags to tell readers what was said. Sometimes she just remembered the conversation for the read. In her classic, *Tales of a Fourth Grade Nothing*, Blume writes:

> *My father said he invited Mr. and Mrs. Yarby to stay with us. My mother wanted to know why they couldn't stay at a hotel like most people who come to New York. My father said that they could. But he didn't want them to. He thought they'd be more comfortable staying with us. My mother said that was about the silliest thing she'd ever heard. (2007, 8)*

This move became one of my details that talk. Writers didn't always have to replay a conversation with quotation marks at all.

In *Alice's Adventures in Wonderland*, Lewis Carroll writes:

> *"What is the use of a book," thought Alice, "without pictures or conversations?"*
>
> *So she was considering, in her own mind (as well as she could, for the hot day made her feel very sleepy and stupid), whether the pleasure of making a daisy-chain would be worth the trouble of getting up and picking the daisies. (2015, 7)*

Carroll let the reader have a peek into the character's mind in two different ways. First, he offers what I call a *Thought Bubble*: he quotes the exact thinking of the character. Next, he switches tactics: he just explains what else the character is thinking. If he had shared Alice's thinking using direct quotations, this section would have been much clunkier, and the pace would have easily slowed.

In *The Giver*, Lois Lowry writes:

> *Instantly, obediently, Jonas dropped his bike on its side on the path*
> *behind his family's dwelling. (2014, 2)*

Lowry describes how Jonas drops the bike in a very specific way here. She offers the readers two adverbs before she names the character or the action. This move, used frequently by writers, helps to situate the action very specifically. The writer automatically knows the nature of the action before the rest of the sentence unfolds. This feels different than adding them after naming the subject or the verb in the sentence.

This is what I wanted for my students: to use details in their writing in a meaningful way that conveyed their ideas and their purpose. I knew that my students couldn't learn this from a bland assignment; they needed to learn from great writers. This obsession catapulted me into a summer of reading at the library. I sat in the children's section and pulled titles off the shelves. Once I had about twenty books, I found a quiet corner and read. When I saw a sentence or detail that appealed to me or stood out, I copied it down on a note card. Then, I moved to the nonfiction section of the library. My daily visits to the library resulted in an unwieldy stack of index cards. When I wasn't in the library, I was cutting out editorial columns and articles from any newspaper I could get my hands on, perusing first-year composition manuals, and stockpiling every magazine from *Time* to *Vogue*. I was building a collection of details.

To read like a writing teacher in a time of accountability also meant reading the types of essays that kids wrote for the standardized writing assessments with that same type of lens. Because most states post writing samples and exemplars from past writing tests online, it was easy for me to access tons of student writing samples. I started to browse different state websites and print out the papers that the states identified as exceeding the writing standard. I printed dozens of papers from fourth through eighth grade. I couldn't just limit my writers to the moves we found in books in our classroom: these essays offered direction and advice and were written in the same timed, highly rigid environment that my students would eventually need to perform well in. These students were, in fact, writers.

The Wall of Crazy: Naming the Moves

I wanted to notice what these writers did to elaborate and explain. I pulled out highlighters, and began underlining sentences that seemed particularly powerful. I spread the papers on my living room floor and walked around the carpet of paper I had created. There was a lot there. I couldn't possibly show my students each of these moves. We did have *every* other subject to cover as well! I decided to group the details into categories. I grabbed a pair of scissors and began cutting out the sentences that had been highlighted. My apartment was filled with shreds of paper and cutouts. As I walked (and sometimes crawled) among the paper, I pulled out sentences that seemed to do the same thing; though the authors had written about something different, they relied on the same strategy.

I taped each sentence and note card onto the wall, creating different columns for each group. Slowly I added new categories and watched other categories grow longer. After days of work, I admired my wall of details and gave a name to each category. I had a column for moves that compared, moves that described, moves that showed action, and a wide variety of other moves. My wall may have looked crazy, but it reminded me of something that Barry Lane, author of *After the End* (1993), said at a conference I attended: we shouldn't give kids strict formulas that they have to follow; instead, we should show them all of the possibilities. My writers just needed to see the actual possibilities for their writing.

I decided to create minilessons around these different moves. Each lesson needed to be a sampling of a possibility that students could include in their writing. I decided that not only did I need to teach my students concrete, explicit moves, but they needed to talk about them, laugh about them, and have fun with them. They needed to feel that these moves were tools at their fingertips, and they needed to know how each tool worked and why they might choose to use it. I needed to make all of these writing possibilities available to my students.

In my classes, and in the classrooms of teachers whom I coach, I introduce a move by name. Then, I share examples of what that move looks like and give my students some fun ways to explore the move and give it a test-drive. As a class, we would look for these moves in real texts and begin to have intentional conversations about our craft. Our conversations were not just about the move itself, but how the move could help students do what they wanted in their writing. I wanted students not just to recognize details, but to see how different details could work for them. This made those seemingly abstract writing moves much more concrete. In *Comprehension Connections*, Tanny McGregor (2007) shares a conversation with Donna King, who describes reading comprehension as abstract. Donna says, "It's all so abstract to the kids. I always thought that kids learn best when it's concrete for them, at least at first" (xii). Donna nails it on the head, not just for reading, but writing as well. Writing is also extremely abstract. This list of explicit moves was tangible and explicit. This was concrete and real.

Teaching Details with Purpose

You don't have to build a wall of crazy like I did to discover the concrete moves for writing details: you are holding my collection in your hand. This book doesn't just represent the moves that I gleaned from those papers, news articles, books, and magazines, but it has been revised and revisited for more than a decade. I have added to the details, collected more examples of how writers use these moves, and deleted moves that seemed to confuse or fail kids over time. I have taught hundreds of teachers to use these moves successfully in grades K–8 and worked in classrooms to do this with every grade level. I have been most excited to find that teachers with their own school-age children have used these strategies not only to teach their classes, but to help their own children craft essays for school, contests, and admissions into academic programs. It doesn't matter what program your school follows, you can benefit from these writing strategies because these do not replace curriculum, they augment it. This book is the writing wall from my living room, shrunk down and bound together. I hope you can take it, add to it, and make it your own. No scissors or tape required.

The writing lessons in this book are organized to quickly unpack the detail, explain when and why the strategy works well, share how I have taught it to my students in a way that emphasizes its effect on meaning in their writing, and offer ways to practice with your students and make these your own. Practice opportunities reinforce what the different detail moves do. The *Make It Your Own* ideas are methods to reinforce the different strategies in ways that are concrete but small and don't require writing a full essay or lengthy writing assignment. Once your students have practiced a strategy, they will be able to store it in their mental writing toolkits. This is where they pull from when they craft their own essays.

Throughout this book, I share excerpts of students' writing that use the different detail moves. These offer bite-size examples to help you conceptualize what each move might look like in different grade levels. These excerpts can even serve as examples to share with your students.

I'm proud of these lessons and the help that they've given students over the years. However, I want to be clear about what these lessons are *not*: they are not unit plans, curriculum, or a complete writing program. The resources and teaching ideas found here are not meant to be taught cover to cover, nor do they represent a particular scope and sequence for teaching details and elaboration. There are multiple ways to make the most of the teaching ideas and resources in this book. The three most common ways that I have noticed in schools are outlined below. Hopefully, one of these methods works for you and your writers.

1. Use this book to help you troubleshoot during writing conferences. When you conference with students and notice a weakness in a particular area, pull a detail lesson that you can use one-on-one with that student. For example, if that student keeps writing weak descriptions that continue to list or parrot your models, share some of the description moves in this book.

2. Treat this book as a go-to manual. When you plan your minilessons, pick and choose the moves that you want to teach your whole class. Read my teaching ideas, then plan the lesson to align with your writing program or curriculum. Integrate what you need, leave out what you don't. Check Chapter 7 for some example lesson clusters—groups of moves that address particular genres, writing traits, and situations.

3. If your school has adopted a commercial or scripted writing program, but students still don't fully develop their writing, pull the section you need from this toolkit and layer it on top. For example, most programs encourage students to elaborate their ideas and support their opinions. Rarely do these programs outline enough moves to actually do the elaboration and provide specific details; they just encourage students to add them. The minilessons here are designed to model explicit examples of different strategies. Pull specific moves from this book that make the instruction more concrete and provide a scaffold for students.

Of course, introducing a move once doesn't mean that students will automatically put a move to use in their own writing. See Chapter 7 for suggestions about how to help students not only remember the moves you teach but apply them when needed. If you've ever encountered a blank stare from a student when you've asked him or her to "include more detail" in a piece, you know that trying to help students can feel like an enormous task. It reminds me of a joke that one of my students, a delightful third grader named Kiyoko, once told me: "How do you eat an elephant?" she asked. I shrugged and told her that I didn't know. "One bite at a time!" She laughed and I did, too. Today Kiyoko is all grown up and probably doesn't remember this joke. I, on the other hand, kept that joke in mind. I have heard many variations of this saying over the past decade. Each time I hear it, I think about writing instruction. The ability to elaborate and craft rich details, whether students are writing over the course of weeks or in a timed setting, seems so big and wild, just like eating an elephant. To get really good at it, you have to just focus on one tiny part at a time. It is my hope that this book will help you to do just that.

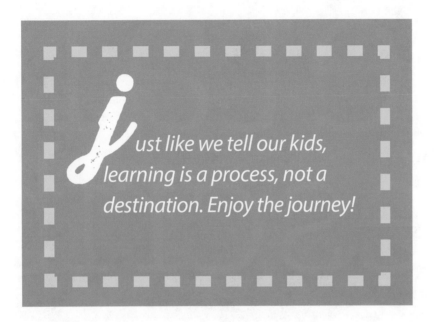

just like we tell our kids, learning is a process, not a destination. Enjoy the journey!

2

Details
THAT
Describe

People, Places, Mood, Emotions, and Things

When an author uses details that describe well, readers are transported into the text. Consider the vivid descriptions to the right. What do you feel? See? Think?

How is it that these descriptions are so powerful, yet when many of our students try to include details that describe, they fall flat? Our student writers have had experiences and feelings as rich as those in the examples shown. They have many topics that they understand inside and out. However, if they don't know how to use descriptive details effectively, they cannot completely convey the information, make the argument, or share the experience that they aim for. As a result, readers cannot connect with their writing, and, in turn, students may not feel that writing is a useful tool for them.

The *Details That Describe* moves paint a picture, helping readers to visualize people, places, and experiences. These types of details are usually the ones that are taught early on in school. In elementary school, students begin to learn that sensory language is powerful, and they cling to their favorite adjectives and adverbs. This primary focus on description continues in middle and high school as well. By the time students have reached the upper grades, they have studied figurative language and can typically identify similes, analogies, and a wide variety of other descriptive elements. Despite being able to name these types of describing details, students often ignore them when it comes time to craft their own writing. Often students believe that

Caleb's expression is placid as the bus sways and jolts on the road. The gray robe falls from his arm as he clutches a pole for balance. I can tell by the constant shift of his eyes that he is watching the people around us—striving to see only them and forget himself.

—Veronica Roth, from Divergent

He prodded the corner of her backpack with the stock of his rifle. Annemarie trembled. "What is in here?" he asked loudly. From the corner of her eye, she saw the shopkeeper move quietly back into the shadows of the doorway, out of sight.

—Lois Lowry, from Number the Stars

His straw-colored haired flapped hard against his forehead, and his arms and legs flew out every which way. He had never learned to run properly, but he was long-legged for a ten-year-old, and no one had more grit than he.

—Katherine Paterson, from
Bridge to Terabithia

these styles of description are the property of literature or professional writers. To fix this problem, we, as teachers, sometimes set arbitrary requirements for the use of description. Instructions such as: "You need at least five adjectives in your paragraph" or "Include at least two analogies and one type of figurative language" are not uncommon. I, too, have been guilty of providing this type of guidance. This type of directive actually does the opposite of what we intend. Instead of encouraging students to see the beauty and usefulness of different types of description, we make details seem arbitrary and cumbersome. Students believe that the number of details, not the quality or the purpose of details, is what is important. The writing becomes formulaic and bland. Instead of teaching that a specific number of descriptive moves be included in a text, we can teach students multiple possibilities for crafting details, give them practice with each one, and let them navigate what they use and do not use.

When Do Writers Make These Moves?

Whether students are crafting an argument, narrative, or explanatory text, description has its place. I tell students that anytime they have a noun or a verb, there is a space to add description. Although this directive is simplified (because we can describe anything), it is short enough to be sticky with kids. They can look at a paper that has been deemed guilty of "not enough detail" and find homes for a descriptive detail. The students themselves need to decide when adding a detail is useful and when it contributes to the reader's visualization. Questions readers might ask themselves regarding description:

- Do I want my readers to feel a certain way? Will this piece, as I've written it, help them to feel that way?
- Did I tell my story, but it still feels flat or boring?
- Do my sentences sound a lot like each other?
- Did I show what is most important here?
- Did I write in a way that convinces my reader?
- Can readers close their eyes and play this scene in their minds?
- Did I just stretch this out too much? Did I use a lot of words to say very little?

Modeling These Moves

Because descriptive details are about visualization, consider images and film as tools to model how to add rich description. Although your students will write and read increasingly complex text throughout the year, when you model specific writing moves, you want something accessible and kid-friendly to demonstrate and connect with students. Don't begin with George Orwell's 1984 and ask students to describe Winston Smith. Take small, highly visible subjects to write about. Look for images of interesting people, locations, or objects. Consider sharing commercials, movie trailers, or short excerpts from movies or television with students. Talk about different ways to describe the events, people, and settings found in these. Your goal is to spend time letting students test out different ways to craft descriptive details so that they remember them and can pull them out of their toolkits later when needed.

To model any writing move, you have to write. You have to write. I repeat this to stress the importance. I visit English classes all the time where teachers assign writing, but they don't actually write much themselves. Students need to watch you write and hear you think out loud about your writing. I begin this by simply asking myself questions out loud. I don't expect my students to answer. They are simply asked as a model of what I want students to do when they begin to think about the details and words that they choose. I ask myself things like, "Do I want them to just have a hint about this character or topic, but not give a peek at the full picture just yet? Do I want to make this description front and center? Is this the big part of my writing here or do I just want to drop it in and keep moving fast in my writing? What is my goal? What is my intention?" I want students to see and hear me question and consider different options and finally express my specific intentions for my writing. Then, I introduce the writing move for that lesson. I show how it helps me achieve the effect that I want in my own writing. I always craft a few sentences that model the move as my students look on and continue to hear my thinking. As I write, I keep questioning and checking to see if my intentions are being realized on paper. Each time you introduce any move, consider doing the same. Students will adopt your practice and begin to question the role of the type of details they craft as you help them to build a bank of different details and styles.

Spend several lessons where you write a short description (while thinking out loud) based on your image or movie clip. After your writing, invite the class to help you repeat this process again with a different image, movie trailer, or clip. After you have had time to model and write together, shift gears and ask students to try the move. Repeat this activity until you have introduced a wide variety of different moves. Then, when students are writing longer pieces, guide them to use the moves they think are most effective for the piece. The goal is exposure to lots of choices and ideas for crafting details. If you simply model one or two, your students won't have enough options, and their writing choices will be limited.

Details That Describe: The Writing Moves

Each of the *Details That Describe* moves in this chapter is listed on the following page. When you read students' writing and notice different things that you would like them to elaborate on or revise, this chart provides direction to help move students to consider different possibilities.

Details That Describe

If you see this in the student's writing . . .	>	Try this . . .
Overused adjectives and/or purposeless description	>	*State the Obvious* (page 19) *Just Like That* (page 23) *Right in the Middle* (page 31)
No description	>	*Just Like That* (page 23) *Right in the Middle* (page 31) *Zoom In* (page 36) *Set It Up* (page 51)
Details shoved into clunky sentences or unnecessary extra sentences	>	*Right in the Middle* (page 31) *Repeaters* (page 40)
Text that doesn't "grab" the reader	>	*Action Clues* (page 27) *Zoom In* (page 36) *Pop Culture References* (page 44) *Personify It* (page 48)
Too little focus on setting or mood	>	*Zoom In* (page 36) *Set It Up* (page 51)
Lack of student voice in text	>	*Right in the Middle* (page 31) *Pop Culture References* (page 44) *Personify It* (page 48) *Thought Bubbles* (page 55)
Limited sentence variety and repetitive structure	>	*Just Like That* (page 23) *Right in the Middle* (page 31) *Repeaters* (page 40)

This chart is a tool to help *students* think about different ways to use *Details That Describe* effectively in their writing. Based on student goals, this chart can direct students to some possibilities. This is not all-inclusive, and moves can be used to meet lots of different writing goals. This chart just offers a beginning set of possibilities.

Details That Describe

If you want to . . .		Try this . . .
I have too many adjectives and want to replace them with other types of description.	〉	*State the Obvious* *Just Like That* *Right in the Middle*
My writing just lists and tells. I want to describe more.	〉	*Just Like That* *Right in the Middle* *Zoom In* *Set It Up*
I have lots of long sentences that feel clunky or slow down my writing. I want to make my sentences shorter, but still include description.	〉	*Right in the Middle* *Repeaters*
I want to have vivid and more complex description in my writing. I want descriptions that will wow or surprise my readers.	〉	*Action Clues* *Zoom In* *Pop Culture References* *Personify It*
I want to paint a picture of the setting or location for my reader. I really want them to have a mental image where my writing is situated.	〉	*Zoom In* *Set It Up*
I want readers to hear my voice. I want to include details that sound like me.	〉	*Right in the Middle* *Pop Culture References* *Personify It* *Thought Bubbles*
I don't want my sentences to sound or look just like one another. I want sentences that are organized in lots of different ways.	〉	*Just Like That* *Right in the Middle* *Repeaters*

A Word About the Moves

In the descriptions of the moves, I share some of the ways that I have modeled these different descriptive detail moves with students. Each snapshot explains the specific description move, includes examples from real authors that you can share with students, and outlines a fun, easy-to-follow way to introduce the moves to your students. After each lesson are some simple ways that you can tailor the learning to meet the needs of novice or more experienced writers. These lessons are *not* templates. Instead, they are examples to spark your own thinking as you develop different lessons to teach description.

I teach students nine different description moves. I find that the moves need to have names to provide a common language for writing conferences: students can sit with me and say things like: "I wanted to use a *Repeaters* sentence here to make that point stand out," or "I used a *Pop Culture Reference* to describe this character's way of speaking." Using the same names that I've given these moves isn't necessary: feel free to rename them to fit your own teaching style and the personality of your classroom.

Move 1

State the Obvious

many students overly describe objects because they have been taught that the more description they include, the better. This results in lengthy descriptions of every object in a scene. Sometimes it is appropriate to simply tell the description.

I begin with this move because it is the least challenging one for kids to grasp. I have learned to lead with moves that students can easily latch onto: if they feel a sense of ease and familiarity, they tend to be more willing to hear what's next. If you begin with the most abstract or complex move, students may shut down before you have a chance to really go deeper.

What Does This Move Look Like in Writing?

The year was 1847. The winter was cold and snowy. The place was a little town in Ohio.

> —Frank Murphy, *from* Always Inventing: The True Story of Thomas Alva Edison

The kids cheered. Somebody ran for the ball. They were anxious for more.

> —Jerry Spinelli, *from* Maniac Magee

There were four of us children. Hild, the eldest; then Bea; I was the third and the only son; Tzipora was the youngest. My parents ran a store. Hilda and Bea helped with the work.

> —Elie Wiesel, *from* Night

In all three of these examples, the authors state the obvious of what they know and see. These examples don't attempt long, flowery descriptions. These authors are capable of writing with rich detail, and other portions of each of these books show that beautifully. In these sections, however, the authors are trying to propel the story forward: stating just what the readers need to know rather than building a scene or painting a picture.

When Writers Make This Move

There are three primary reasons that authors use this move. First, authors use *State the Obvious* after using rich or lengthy description. Alternating between telling and showing offers an even balance of text. Authors also use this move when making a point and stopping to add too much description would slow down the writing or break up the flow of the text. Finally, this move can be effective when the author is deliberately trying to minimize or marginalize something in the text. This can be to establish a certain tone, attitude, or mood toward something in the writing.

How I Introduce This Move

1. I begin by setting this move up as a "secret." I usually say something like this to my class: ***Sometimes in your writing you have to describe something. We teachers have been telling you for years to show, not tell. This means you have to use lots of words and description to get your readers to visualize your description. Well, I have a bit of a secret to share with you today. Sometimes, the opposite is true. Sometimes it is okay to just tell the reader.***

2. I create an anchor chart like the one in Figure 2.1 that outlines reasons that an author would make this move. This is important because it offers a cross-connection to reading. For example, Common Core literacy standard RL.5.6 asks students to analyze text and consider how an author's choices establish point of view. If a student is reading an argument, they can deliberately look at how the author described ideas. Did he or she use rich description to describe one side of an issue, but provide limited description for the opposing side? Students can consider why an author would do so because they can notice that the author is just stating the description. The chart lets students peek behind the curtain and talk about why authors use this move and when they might use it themselves. Students can even make inferences about the author's point of view

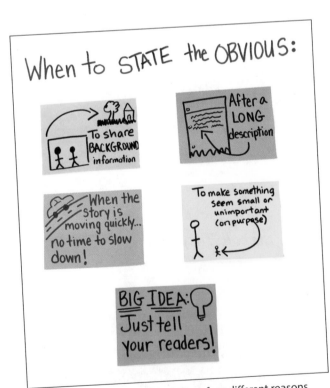

Figure 2.1 Our anchor chart outlines four different reasons for making the *State the Obvious* move.

toward each side. These types of complex decisions about text are inherent in the standards. I ask students to turn and talk about this move and consider how they might use it in the future.

3. After creating the anchor chart, I like to show students one picture from a wordless picture book. My favorite book for this lesson is Chris Van Allsburg's wordless picture book, *The Mysteries of Harris Burdick*, a great book with beautiful images that generate wonder and curiosity. I ask students to help me identify which parts of the picture might need rich, detailed description and which might just need to be named using a *State the Obvious* move.

4. Then, I simply write several sentences that describe parts of the image by just telling what they look like. For example, if I show an image that features a ship sailing on the ocean, I might write:

> The large, grey sailboat drifted across dark water.

I point out that I just state the obvious. An alternative is to write two sentences to describe the picture, one using this strategy and one with overused description. This could be something like:

> The monstrous, bulky boat slowly started to creep across the waveless ocean in the middle of the night, while everything was dark.

I like to do this to show students that longer is not always better. Sometimes students think that the more they stretch a sentence out, the better it is. The anchor chart for this lesson is used as a thinking tool to help students decide which direction to go to get the results that they want. The chart helps students to be intentional in their writing choices.

5. I repeat this with multiple images from this book. Then, we shift gears. I display another image from Van Allsburg's book and invite students to use the *State the Obvious* move to describe the picture.

6. As students share, I record some of their examples on large chart paper (Figure 2.2). I often revisit these pictures and sentences later so that I can repeat this activity with other, more elaborate and varied types of detail moves later in the year.

> Let's State the Obvious !
>
> The man held the chair over his head.
>
> A big lump was under the rug.
>
> The lamp cast a shadow on the wall.
>
> The table was covered with a white table cloth.
>
> The light reflected in his glasses.
>
> The pictures were neatly hung on the wall.

Figure 2.2 Our anchor chart features *State the Obvious* sentences based on the image called "Under the Rug" in Chris Van Allsburg's *The Mysteries of Harris Burdick*.

Guided Writing Practice Ideas

- Take a picture walk around the school. As your students travel throughout the school, armed with their own clipboards or sticky notes, have them stop to write a *State the Obvious* detail about different objects around the school. Return to class and share the detail sentences.

- Write your own *State the Obvious* details to describe objects around the room on index cards. Make sure that you make your own list that tells which cards describe which objects. (I have confused myself so many times by not doing this.) Ask pairs to pull cards and make decisions about what object the detail sentence is describing. Share as a whole group or just check in with each group and switch the cards to reuse them with different students.

- Create a *State the Obvious* anchor chart where you list different types of *State the Obvious* sentences that you craft with your class. Place the name of the object you described in parentheses next to the description.

- Select a picture book where the author uses the *State the Obvious* move. Gather students together and read several pages aloud. Ask students to listen carefully and to raise their hand if they notice the author using this move. When a student raises her hand, ask her to point out the sentence, then lead a brief discussion about why this move works in this situation—how it helps the author—and record the sentence on a sentence strip or chart paper. The *Miss Nelson* collection by Harry Allard offers lots of examples.

- Take a visit to the school media center. Challenge students to look for examples of this detail in real books. As students find examples, place a sticky note on the page. After collecting several examples, discuss the findings with the whole class: **When did authors State the Obvious? When did they give more detailed descriptions? Why?** To make this go smoothly, consider asking your media specialist to pull informational text, rather than all literature. Historical fiction and science concept books are more likely to feature multiple examples of this type of move.

- Consider examining informational text examples on the whiteboard or using a document camera. Ask students to read excerpts silently. After reading, discuss the *State the Obvious* details that students notices. Highlight or underline these.

- Don't isolate this learning to one day! When discussing or describing other books, characters, or even things in the school, stop after your description and ask students if they noticed what type of move you made. Deliberately plan a few moments when you can make this happen. Students will be amused to see that details are not confined to the written assignments that you give them.

Move 2

Just Like That

Just Like That details make comparisons. Instead of just relying on adjectives, this move compares someone or something to something else. The reader can write a simile, metaphor, or analogy to show how similar two things are. I like to use this name for this detail so that it is all-inclusive of any type of comparison method and doesn't become about identifying or classifying sentences as metaphors or similes; when that happens, this can feel like a drill-and-kill activity. The focus is on students understanding what the move can do, not matching a name for the sake of matching it correctly.

What Does This Move Look Like in Writing?

Moss and ferns, vines and orchids, hang from branches like the beards of wise wizards.

—Sy Montgomery, from Quest for the Tree Kangaroo: An Expedition to the Cloud Forest of New Guinea

It shone like silver . . . looking somehow like a tiny building rising out of the mounds of rubble and earth.

—Lynne Reid Banks, from The Mystery of the Cupboard

His face was frozen like ice.

—John Reynolds Gardiner, from Stone Fox

Mae sat there frowning, a great potato of a woman . . .

—Natalie Babbit, from Tuck Everlasting

It was one of those super-duper-cold Saturdays. One of those days that when you breathed out your breath kind of hung frozen in the air like a hunk of smoke and you could walk along and look exactly like a train blowing out big, fat, white puffs of smoke.

> —Christopher Paul Curtis, *from* The Watsons
> Go to Birmingham

He looked like a miniature, clean-shaven Neanderthal man.

> —E. L. Konigsburg, *from* From the Mixed-up Files of
> Mrs. Basil E. Frankweiler

She stood like a mountain, her big ham hands dangling helplessly at her sides.

> —Louise Fitzhugh, *from* Harriet the Spy

Each of these examples helps the reader to associate the characteristics of the subject being described or compared to something else. This move, although simple, is one that professional writers rely on time and again. Some of these examples use similes, incorporating the word *like* into the description. Others, like Natalie Babbit's, omit the word *like* and simply create a metaphor. Often we teach metaphors and similes in isolation, teaching kids to hunt for *like* or *as* and then identify the type of comparison. But when we address comparisons within the context of this description move, we take the emphasis off of the definitions of these two terms and instead focus on meaning making in the comparison.

When Writers Make This Move

Writers make this move for a variety of reasons. For instance, *Just Like That* is helpful when emphasizing particular qualities. Consider the example from *Tuck Everlasting:* Babbit wants readers to know that Mae is somewhat round and possibly dull. As a character she has lots of other features that could have been described, but Babbit used the *Just Like That* detail to compare only a specific part of this character—the part she wanted to highlight—to another object.

Just Like That can also help writers make readers visualize a scene, place, or person. Asking the reader to think of another object, then building an association tasks the reader with visualizing.

Finally, *Just Like That* can help writers vary the structure and rhythm of their writing: the comparison breaks away from descriptions built with multiple adjectives.

How I Introduce This Move

1. I describe this move to students as a fun way to add pizzazz to their writing and get readers involved in creating the description by making the connections between the objects being compared.

2. Then, I spread several objects out on a table or desk and ask students to think about one of the objects that they are just like. I have fun with this and vary the objects that I display. I have brought in toy Corvettes, Barbie dolls, jewelry, rocks, empty shoeboxes, expired credit cards, and ornaments.

3. I ask students to write down the name of the object they selected and one or two reasons why they are similar to that object.

4. I call on students to share. As they share, I write their ideas on large sticky notes and add them to a chart or stick them on a wall or space in the classroom. This creates a visual of different ways that students are like everyday objects (Figure 2.3). After recording this list, I point out that writers can make this move to describe anything that they want in whatever light they want—the objects of their comparison can bring a whole slew of connotations with them that send readers a message about the subject, even if it's not stated directly. I deliberately talk about how cool and interesting this move can be and encourage students to try it out when they notice that they are consistently relying on the same types of sentences in their writing or feel that their descriptions are falling flat.

Figure 2.3 Students named reasons why they were just like everyday objects. This list serves as a great reminder that even the simplest objects can be used as a point of comparison.

Guided Writing Practice Ideas

- Read a character-centric picture book out loud to students. I like to rely on short favorites that the students are already familiar with from primary grades. Mo Willems and David Shannon have a wide variety of choices. Ask students to help craft *Just Like That* sentences to describe the characters.

- Ask students to write *Just Like That* sentences about the school, your class, or you (if you feel brave) on sticky notes. Share the sentences, then place these notes on your classroom door to greet visitors as they enter.

- Read an excerpt from a novel with rich description out loud to students. *Sideways Stories from Wayside School* by Louis Sachar or any Roald Dahl novel works well here. Project the text overhead if possible. Ask students to talk with a neighbor or in a small group to write *Just Like That* sentences to describe any object, character, or event that they choose. Share these sentences and discuss how well this move worked (or didn't work) for that description: **Did that move help you to see the character (or object or event) in a new way? Did it help you to notice something in particular about the character? How?**

- Using individual or class literature, ask students to take a moment a reread a section where the author provided description. Challenge students to rewrite the description using a *Just Like That* detail. Share these in small groups or as a whole class. It is much more interesting if students use their individual reading books, because the topics and characters described will be more varied and will keep students more interested in hearing the rewrites.

- Students can revisit their own writing to look for places where this move might have been effective. Students can revise and discuss the impact of the move on the text. Conference with students to discuss the shifts, specifically how this move made the writing feel different from the original writing.

- Assign writing homework after introducing this move. Ask students to think of an important person, place, or event in their lives. Ask students to test-drive this move by writing a short paragraph that describes that person, place, or event. Tell students to try out this move in their papers (see Figures 2.4 and 2.5). The next day, let students work in groups to share their writing, and discuss if/how the *Just Like That* comparisons in each other's work helped them to understand the topic more clearly.

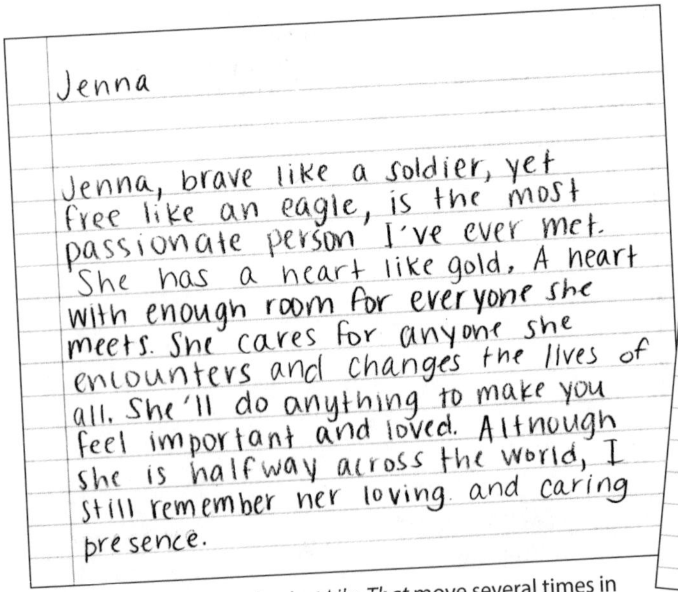

Jenna

Jenna, brave like a soldier, yet free like an eagle, is the most passionate person I've ever met. She has a heart like gold, A heart with enough room for everyone she meets. She cares for anyone she encounters and changes the lives of all. She'll do anything to make you feel important and loved. Although she is halfway across the world, I still remember her loving and caring presence.

Figure 2.4 Emilie uses the *Just Like That* move several times in her writing to compare a close friend to an eagle and a soldier.

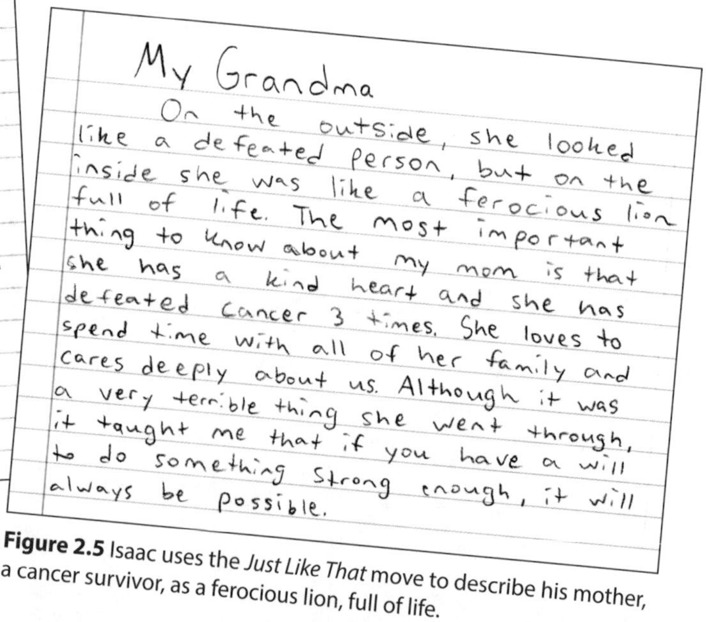

My Grandma

On the outside, she looked like a defeated person, but on the inside she was like a ferocious lion full of life. The most important thing to know about my mom is that she has a kind heart and she has defeated cancer 3 times. She loves to spend time with all of her family and cares deeply about us. Although it was a very terrible thing she went through, it taught me that if you have a will to do something strong enough, it will always be possible.

Figure 2.5 Isaac uses the *Just Like That* move to describe his mother, a cancer survivor, as a ferocious lion, full of life.

Action Clues

essentially the opposite of *State the Obvious*, the *Action Clues* move describes a series of actions that offer the reader clues to interpret and make their own inferences about.

What Does This Move Look Like in Writing?

Jerry sat on his bed and I could tell that he was losing the fight not to cry. Tears were popping out of his eyes and slipping down his cheeks.

—Christopher Paul Curtis, from Bud, Not Buddy

Even though my grandmother lived in this country for over fifty years, I can still remember her breaking out in nervous perspiration and trembling as her passport was checked at the border when we returned to the United States from a shopping trip in Tijuana.

—Pam Munoz Ryan, from Esperanza Rising

The only empty seat was next to me. That's where our teacher put Maya. And on that first day, Maya turned to me and smiled. But I didn't smile back. I moved my chair, myself, and my books a little farther away from her. When she looked my way, I turned to the window and stared out at the snow.

—Jacqueline Woodson, from Each Kindness

Each of these examples vividly describes some type of movement that offers a glimpse into what is happening in a character's mind. Consider Jacqueline Woodson's writing. She could have simply said that the narrator had no interest in Maya. Although that may be true, the actions let the readers come to that conclusion without ever telling them what to think. Although *State the Obvious* can help writers to quicken the pace of the text, the *Action Clues* move slows the reader down and makes him or her participate.

When Writers Make This Move

This strategy is most effective when writing narratives. Authors use *Action Clues* when they are building the tension or when a problem is unfolding. Typically, the writer is letting the reader in on a particular feeling or character reaction, or the reader is learning about a new shift or twist in a story.

Writers also use this move when they want to show a character's emotion, particularly when it is unexpected or a surprise to the readers. Mysteries, stories that focus on characters with internal struggles, and texts that depend on building suspense all lend themselves to this type of description.

How I Introduce This Move

1. Before introducing this move, you will need to collect a few different objects that you and your students will use to model what *Action Clues* look like in real life. The objects you choose should be (or represent) things that you will use to model particular emotions. For example:

   - For *disgust*, I typically select some type of rubber bug (the grosser, the better), a furry mouse, or any type of seemingly dreadful critter.

   - For *admiration*, I bring a photograph of a notable figure (a president, your favorite author, the principal, and so on).

   - For *fear*, I use an image or action figure representing a scary villain (my Darth Vader action figure circa 1985 always makes an appearance here).

   - For *love*, I enjoy bringing a yummy treat (an excuse to bring a cupcake to class).

   This lesson works best when students recognize the objects you select. Choose objects that students will know from class discussions, prior work, or popular culture. For example, my Darth Vader action figure was useless in the nineties: most of the elementary students I taught were just being born when *Return of the Jedi* was released in 1983. They had no idea who he was. Yet, this all changed in 2005 when *Star Wars: Episode I* was released in theatres.

2. Display one item at a time and respond to it in a very obvious, overexaggerated way. Go ahead and overdo it here; have fun! In the past I have climbed onto a chair in fear of Darth Vader and taped the image of my favorite

author on the board and blown kisses and given the photo thumbs up. Physically show your reaction to the different objects *without explaining how you feel about them.*

3. After you display each object and model your reaction to it, pause and ask students to write one or two sentences that describe your reaction to the object. Explicitly state that the sentence(s) need to describe what students saw.

4. Call on several volunteers to share their sentences with the class. Discuss how that description provides clues about how you felt about the object. Ask, **How did your sentences describe how I felt without stating it directly in the sentence?** Don't worry if students label the emotions differently: when students name a few emotions, it's an indication that the experience feels as rich and multifaceted as real life, which is the goal of our work in describing! Instead of worrying about whether students got the emotion "right," focus on the rich description of what they saw.

Guided Writing Practice Ideas

- Switch roles with students. Place one object in a paper bag. Call a student to the front of the room and ask them to peek inside of the bag. Provide a countdown for students to get their thoughts together and announce, "Action!" Ask the student to *show* the class how they felt about the object in the bag without *telling* what that emotion is. Call on volunteers to guess what emotion the action represented. On chart paper or on the board, write a sentence together that describes the reaction. Afterward, reveal the object in the bag. Discuss with students. What work did they have to do to guess the emotion? When, in their own writing, might they want to ask their readers to do similar work?

- Create a T-chart on the board. Label one side: *Action Clues.* On the other side, write: *State the Obvious.* Write sentences that use either *Action Clues* or *State the Obvious* on large 6 × 8-inch sticky notes or sentence strips. Read each one to the class. Then, ask students to place the sentences in the appropriate column, discussing whether the sentence showed a character's action/feelings or if it simply stated them.

- Consider making a permanent version of the T-chart. When you read books aloud throughout the year, stop and reread sentences that use either *State the Obvious* or *Action Clues.* Ask students what move the author was making when he or she crafted the sentence. Record that sentence and add it to the chart. Often this can become a bulletin board, fill the front of a cabinet, or simply occupy the space under your board. This brings these real-life sentences alive and gives them a sense of permanence as mentor texts for your students.

- Write several sentences that simply state an emotion. Ask students to revise each sentence into several sentences that reveal the character's emotion through their actions or reactions (see Figure 2.6). Three examples from my own classroom:

> Heather was sad that her pet fish was dead.
>
> The first day of middle school was terrifying for Josephine.
>
> Tyler stood nervously, waiting for his next spelling bee word.

- Challenge students to select a book or article of their choice and find an example where the author used *Action Clues*. In small groups, ask students to share their examples and to decide which example to share with the class. Discuss each example: **How did the author craft the reaction by showing, versus telling? What effect did this have on the readers in your class?**

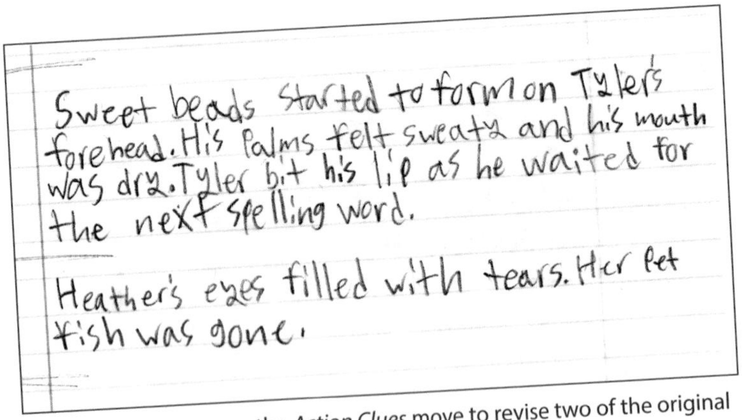

Sweet beads started to form on Tyler's forehead. His palms felt sweaty and his mouth was dry. Tyler bit his lip as he waited for the next spelling word.

Heather's eyes filled with tears. Her pet fish was gone.

Figure 2.6 Sydney uses the *Action Clues* move to revise two of the original sentences.

Ask students to be on the lookout for *Action Clues* when they peer conference. Ask students to not only identify it, but to discuss whether or how it strengthens the text: **Does it draw the reader in? Does it slow down the text? Should the author keep it in or revise it?** Move the conversation away from mere identification to a discussion about how the move works.

Move 4

Right in the Middle

*t*his move is a sophisticated way to describe a subject without adding additional sentences. Technically, students are relying on descriptive phrases and appositive phrases—grammatical structures that students probably will not be introduced to by name until high school—embedded in sentences. At this stage in their writing lives, students don't have to know the grammatical terms for these moves, but they can benefit greatly from this type of sentence structure in their writing. This move allows students to vary their sentence structure and length, provide readers with more de-tailed descriptions, and really help students to create the most complete representation of their subject that they can.

What Does This Move Look Like in Writing?

In fact since Brian had come to the small airport in Hampton, New York, to meet the plane—driven by his mother—the pilot had spoken only five words to him.

—Gary Paulsen, *from* Hatchet

Tucker finished the last few crumbs of a cookie he was eating—a Lorna Doone shortbread he had found earlier in the evening—and licked off his whiskers.

—George Selden, *from* The Cricket in Times Square

31

Alexander Ramsay, known to his friends back home in New York City as Alec, leaned over the rail and watched the water slide away from the sides of the boat.

—Walter Farley, from The Black Stallion

An orphan body named Jemmy, the son of a rat-catcher, roused from his sleep.

—Sid Fleischman, from The Whipping Boy

The boy reached into his bag and produced a rainbow of gumballs—one of every color—and dropped them into my hands.

—William Kamkwamba and Bryan Mealer, from The Boy Who Harnessed the Wind: Young Readers Edition

Unlike many of the other moves in this chapter, the focus here is on the *placement* of the description. What is consistent in this move is not the content, but the sentence structure: these descriptions interrupt the sentence to insert a description, typically using either commas or dashes. This move can easily be combined with other writing strategies, offering students a different way to arrange their sentences.

When Writers Make This Move

I introduce this move when I noticed that students are relying on the predictable subject-plus-verb sentences, sprinkled with a few adjective and/or adverbs. This move shows students that they can sneak description right in the middle of a sentence.

Right in the Middle descriptions can feel like a confidential aside to the reader. If you notice that a student's writing feels voiceless or dry, this move can help his writing feel more conversational.

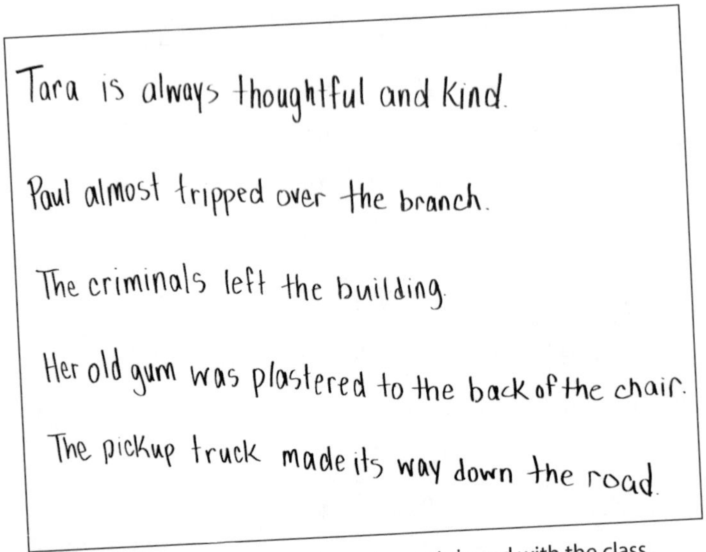

How I Introduce This Move

1. I begin by sharing a list of simple sentences on chart paper or on the whiteboard (Figure 2.7). I ask students: **Are they interesting? Do you have a rich description of the subject?**

Tara is always thoughtful and kind.

Paul almost tripped over the branch.

The criminals left the building.

Her old gum was plastered to the back of the chair.

The pickup truck made its way down the road.

Figure 2.7 These are the simple sentences I shared with the class.

2. Once students agree that these sentences are pretty basic, I introduce a set of sentence strips that have descriptions set off with commas or dashes (Figure 2.8). I hold up the strips, read them, tape them above the sentences, and use an arrow to show where I'm inserting them into the original sentence (Figure 2.9). If you have a whiteboard, you could just write on the board or add magnetic sentence strips for the revisions.

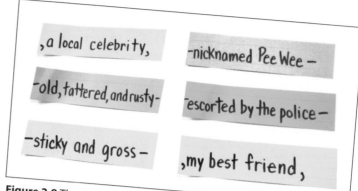

, a local celebrity,

-nicknamed Pee Wee -

-old, tattered, and rusty-

-escorted by the police -

-sticky and gross -

, my best friend,

Figure 2.8 These are the *Right in the Middle* sentence strips that I shared with students.

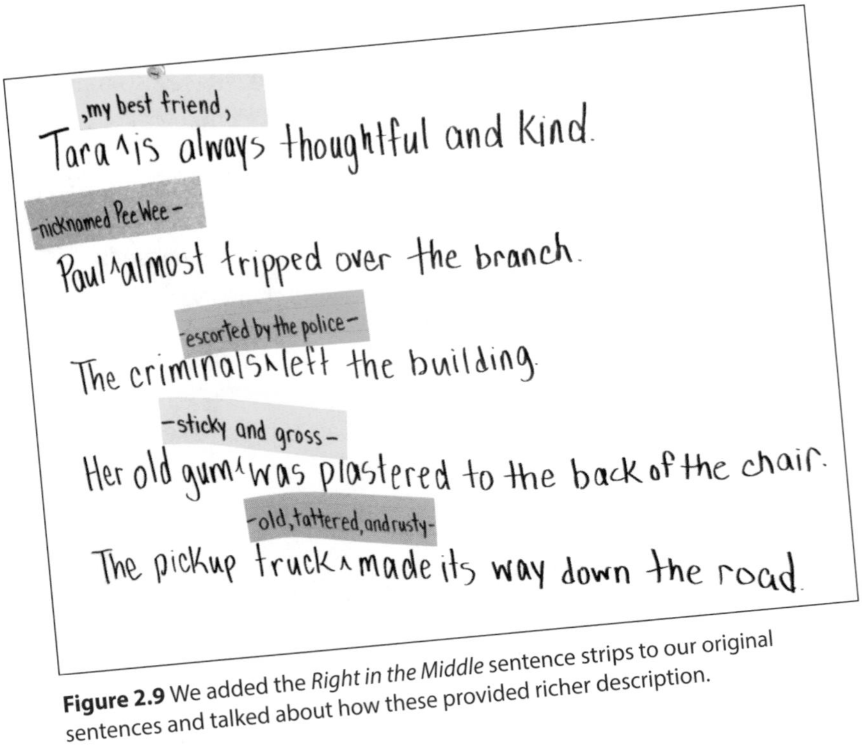

, my best friend,

Tara ^is always thoughtful and kind.

-nicknamed Pee Wee -

Paul ^almost tripped over the branch.

-escorted by the police -

The criminals ^left the building.

-sticky and gross -

Her old gum ^was plastered to the back of the chair.

-old, tattered, and rusty-

The pickup truck ^made its way down the road.

Figure 2.9 We added the *Right in the Middle* sentence strips to our original sentences and talked about how these provided richer description.

3. We reread the sentences together. I ask students: ***Do you have a better understanding of the subject? Can you picture that subject in your mind's eye? Do you have more details?***

4. Then, I write a new simple sentence. I set a timer for two to three minutes and ask the students to revise my sentence by adding a description right in the middle.

5. When the timer goes off, we share our sentences aloud. I repeat this several times with new sentences.

Guided Writing Practice Ideas

- Explain that the comma or dash "holds" the description in place. Create your own sentences that add description in the middle, but leave out the commas. Let your students identify what is wrong with your sentence and correct it.

- Picture books have a lot of simple sentences! Ask students to select a favorite picture book and revise a simple sentence using this move. Students can use large sticky notes and stick their *Right in the Middle* details on the page. Let students swap and read, or reread the picture books, inserting the changes made by students.

- Let students create *Right in the Middle* sentences about themselves. Ask them to tell you one memorable fact about themselves. To do this, they must include descriptive details in their sentence. Post these around the room or on their desks. These also make a fun label for any work that you display.

- Ask for volunteers to write their own simple sentences on the board. Let the other students revise the sentence and share their *Right in the Middle* versions.

- A great way to integrate other content areas is to make use of the social studies or science textbooks. Ask students to review a section that you are studying and find sentences that could benefit from this strategy. If you don't use textbooks, consider online articles and magazines. Content-area writing is often simplistic and relies on simple sentence structures: you will have an abundance of material to work with.

- Ask students to revisit a piece of their own writing. Ask students to find places where the *Right in the Middle* move could provide a richer description of a person or place. Invite students to revise that section of their writing (see Figures 2.10 and 2.11).

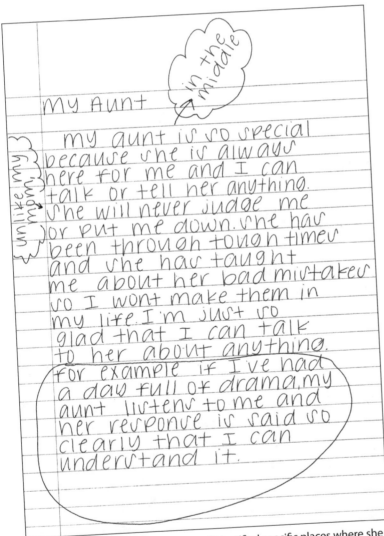

Figure 2.10 Haley reread her work and identified specific places where she could incorporate this move (along with two other moves) to offer readers a better description of her aunt.

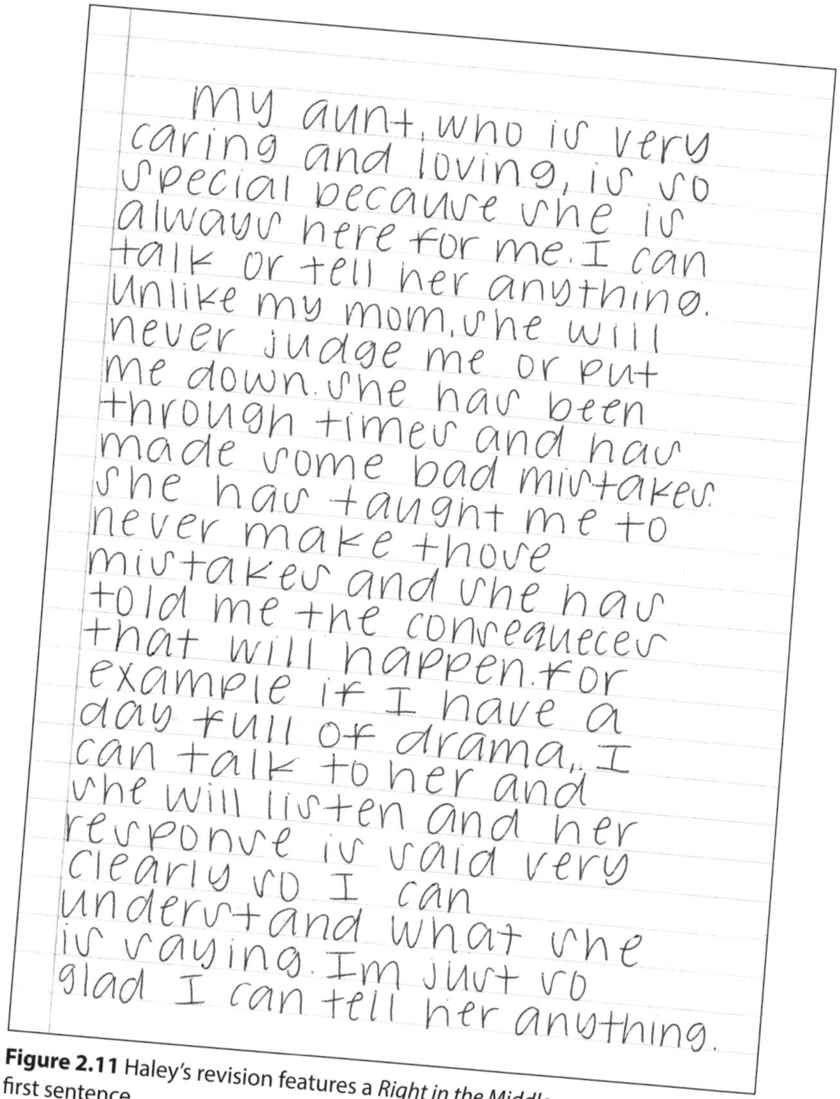

My aunt, who is very caring and loving, is so special because she is always here for me. I can talk or tell her anything. Unlike my mom, she will never judge me or put me down. She has been through times and has made some bad mistakes. She has taught me to never make those mistakes and she has told me the consequences that will happen. For example if I have a day full of drama, I can talk to her and she will listen and her response is said very clearly so I can understand what she is saying. I'm just so glad I can tell her anything.

Figure 2.11 Haley's revision features a *Right in the Middle* move in the very first sentence.

Move
5

Zoom In

*t*hese excerpts focus the reader on one object or action. The focus is so narrow that the description seems to resonate and linger a bit longer than the other parts of the text.

What Does This Move Look Like in Writing?

Caroline and Wendy started another game of Tic Tac Toe while Bruce went to work on his nose. He has a very interesting way of picking it. First he works on one nostril and then the other and whatever he gets out he sticks on a piece of yellow paper inside of his desk.

 —*Judy Blume, from* Blubber

The old lady pulled her spectacles down and looked over them about the room; then she put them up and looked out under them. She seldom or never looked through them for so small a thing as a boy; they were her state pair, the pride of her hearts, and were built for "style," not service—she could have seen through a pair of stove lids just as well.

 —*Mark Twain, from* The Adventures of Tom Sawyer

Evan lay on his back in the dark, throwing the baseball up in a straight line and catching it in his bare hands. Thwap. Thwap. The ball made a satisfying sound as it slapped his palm.

 —*Jacqueline Davies, from* The Lemonade War

Mrs. Granger kept a full set of thirty dictionaries on a shelf at the back of the room. But her pride and joy was one of those huge dictionaries with every word in the universe in it, the kind of book it takes two kids to carry. It sat on its own little table at the front of her classroom, sort of like the altar at the front of the church.

—Andrew Clements, from Frindle

Bruce's habit is seared into my mind. I know a lot about Bruce, just from this one aspect that Blume chose to highlight and describe to readers. This same feeling exists when I read Andrew Clements's description of Mrs. Granger's dictionaries. *Zoom In* tells the reader to sit up and pay attention to something, and the writer's choice of what to zoom in on gives the reader clues about what the author thinks is important.

When Writers Make This Move

In informational text, *Zoom In* focuses more on highlighting a physical or personality trait of a person, an aspect of an object, or an experience. For fiction, this move is used most frequently to spotlight the physical traits of a character, spotlight a specific object of interest, or indicate what is most important to a character or to the story line. Imagine some of the more well-known fairy tales. If we were retelling Cinderella, we might want to zoom in on the glass slipper, or the clock, just as it is about to strike midnight. If we were retelling the story of Little Red Riding Hood, we might use the *Zoom In* move to focus on Grandma's big teeth, or the picnic basket filled with goodies. *Zoom In* is about stretching out a description to be much longer and more detailed and specific than the other details.

How I Introduce This Move

1. I explain that authors don't treat all description the same. In fact, if we described every aspect of a character equally, we would be writing for weeks!

2. As a class, we consider what kinds of things we may want to use *Zoom In* on in our writing, and we practice zooming in on objects in our classroom. I like to use a magnifying glass as I circulate around the room, zooming in and out and letting students use the glass as they describe objects.

3. Then, I ask students to describe me. They typically say things about the color I am wearing, my disposition, physical characteristics, or any personality traits that they know about me. After we have a wide variety of descriptions, I provide several different scenarios. ***What would you focus on if you were describing me when you had forgotten your homework or failed a test?*** Students commonly say that they would focus on my face growing unhappy. ***What if I was really sad?*** This often leads to a suggestion to describe tears falling or a sad frown. ***What if I was lost?*** Students tend to focus on the description of the path that I could consider. In each of these examples, it's the situation that helps students to decide where to zoom in.

4. I continue this discussion, prompting students to think about times when they intentionally focus on some details and leave others out. Next, I share some of the examples from the What Does This Move Look Like in Writing? section with students. We discuss each, naming what object, action, or trait the author zoomed in on, and we discuss *why* the authors might have chosen these subjects.

5. After a discussion, I read the first page of Louis Sachar's *Holes* out loud. This page briefly mentions a hammock. I point out that it is interesting that a comfortable hammock exists at Camp Green Lake while everywhere else in the camp is un-shaded, hot, and miserable. I tell students that I want to zoom in on the hammock.

6. On chart paper, or on the board, I write my own *Zoom In* description (Figure 2.12). I think out loud as I write, asking questions about word choice, pointing out sentence structure, or highlighting any other ideas I want my students to notice about my think-ing process. Afterward, we discuss my example.

7. Then, I name familiar characters, set-tings, superheroes, places in the school, or sporting events. I ask students to choose one and write their own *Zoom In* descriptions. Then, they share their descriptions in small groups and offer each other feedback.

> # ZOOM IN !
>
> The brown, mesh hammock slowly swayed from left to right. Somehow a breeze, which never reached any of the campers, always managed to help the hammock keep a steady rhythm—from left to right—over and over again. Covered by the shade of those two massive trees, the hammock almost seemed to mock the campers and their sweat-soaked bodies. Left to right — left to right.

Figure 2.12 My *Zoom In* description focuses on the movement of the hammock and builds a contrast between the heat that the campers endure and the shade and rhythm of the hammock.

5. For homework, I ask students to go home and select a place in their own homes—one aspect of one room only—to write about, considering what a description of that space will tell readers about their home, their family, and themselves. The next day, we share the descriptions in small groups and consider why the writers chose these places and what we have learned from their descriptions.

Guided Writing Practice Ideas

- When you introduce this move, project a Google Map or another online mapping view so that all of the students can see. Type in the name of your school. Zoom in and out using the plus (+) and minus (−) signs on the map screen. Ask students to explain which provides more detail, being very close or being far away. Emphasize that you can see a farther distance when you are far away, but that you lack any discernment between what really matters or is most important.

- Read the classroom! Encourage everyone to use their internal magnifying glasses to scan the room. When they find an object they like, they should stop next to the object and write a description using this strategy. Because they've chosen something they like, their description should help anyone who reads it to like the object, too.

- Select an image to show your whole class. Ask students to individually zoom in on one object in the picture. Individually, students can write a zoomed-in description, focusing on one object. Share the descriptions together.

- Ask students to describe an historical figure using this strategy. They can zoom in on a notable physical or personality trait. This can also work well with book characters, celebrities, or even authors.

- Rewrite a scene from a fairy tale. Ask students to include several descriptions, including *Zoom In*. Challenge students to defend why they zoomed in on specific areas.

- Show students a picture. Try to select an image that is busy or that includes multiple objects. Ask students to use *Zoom In* to write a description of part of the picture. Then ask students to write how they chose their focus and why it was most important. Group students together to read their descriptions and explain their reasoning. This can lead to lots of lively debates about writer's craft.

Repeaters

the *Repeaters* move replies on the repetition of a particular word or group of words. This repetition involves crafting multiple sentences that begin or end with the same words. Although any number of sentences can be used to do this, groups of three are most common.

What Does This Move Look Like in Writing?

First of all, I ended up having forty-two teeth. The typical human has thirty-two, right? But I had forty-two. Ten more than usual. Ten more than normal. Ten teeth past human.

> —Sherman Alexie, from The Absolutely True Diary of a Part-Time Indian

Welcome to the green house. Welcome to the hot house. Welcome to the land of the warm, wet days.

> —Jane Yolen, from Welcome to the Green House

I said I was being scrunched. I said I was being smushed. I said, if I don't get the seat by the window I am going to be carsick.

> —Judith Viorst, from Alexander and the Terrible, Horrible, No Good, Very Bad Day

His hat is borrowed, his suit is borrowed, his hands are borrowed, even his head is borrowed.

—Cynthia Rylant, from Scarecrow

Each of these excerpts uses this strategy with different effects. Yolen uses repeaters to offer readers with a clear description of the type of house they are being welcomed into. She wants readers to understand that physical setting before she moves forward with her story, so she has crafted a picture for readers that stands out as significant, rather than tucking the words into one sentence. Cynthia Rylant uses this strategy to communicate the speaker's specific point of view. She describes the scarecrow using virtually the same exact phrase repeatedly. Reading the same words over and over creates this sense that this "borrowed" scarecrow has nothing original or unique. The repetition drives that point home and offers readers not just a description, but a peek at how the author feels about the subject as well. Judith Viorst uses this same strategy to communicate the speaker's feelings: when you read Alexander repeating *I said* over and over, you understand that he is frustrated and has lots of negative feelings about his current situation. Without the repetition, his complaints might have been overlooked or read as less serious. Imagine if Viorst had written: "I told them that I was scrunched and might need the window seat." The intentionality of Alexander's words and the fierce intensity of how he felt would have been lost.

When Writers Make This Move

Writers use *Repeaters* to emphasize a particular description, character trait, or feeling. Using this strategy shows that the author is intentionally drawing the reader back to this pattern of words. This can show that something is important, or even communicate a specific emotion or mood. Note that three distinct sentences can be used, or, like Rylant's example, the repetition can be integrated into one sentence, separating each by a comma or dash. The *Repeaters* move also provides a distinct singsong type of rhythm to the text. This is a great way to interrupt the monotony of several sentences that follow similar sentence structures.

How I Introduce This Move

1. On the board, I write a few lines from a familiar picture book that uses the *Repeaters* move. Dr. Seuss picture books are a great fit for this. I typically use *Green Eggs and Ham*. The lines seem to be the most easily recognizable for most students.

2. After listing several lines on the board (without telling the class where these lines are from), I ask students to write the name of the book that they think these lines come from and then call on volunteers to share their ideas. Once someone names *Green Eggs and Ham*, I congratulate them and pull out my copy of this Dr. Seuss favorite.

3. I read a few pages from the book out loud. There are over 150 lines that rely on repeating words, sounds, or rhymes. Then, I ask students to consider why they remember these lines. **Why do we all remember that the main character will not eat green eggs and ham in a box, with a fox, here, there, or anywhere?**

4. We discuss how Dr. Seuss repeats some of the same words. I steer the conversation toward the question of why these lines stick with us. **Why do we remember lines from this book?** Then, I explain that we can steal this move and use it in our own writing to make it more powerful and more memorable.

5. At this point I write *Repeaters* on the board. I explain that there are three reasons that authors repeat words or phrases (Figure 2.13). This is to emphasize specific words, to communicate feelings or attitudes, or to provide rhythm to the author's words. As writers, we can also use this strategy for any of these three reasons. Then, I create an anchor chart that outlines the three reasons that authors turn to this strategy.

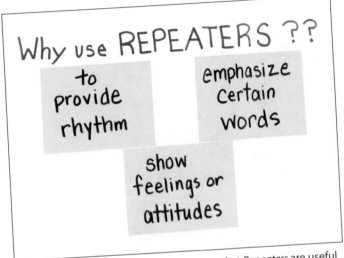

Figure 2.13 Our chart shows three reasons that *Repeaters* are useful in writing. Although one *Repeater* can do one or even all of these things, this chart helps students to think about why a move works for them and be intentional about their craft choices.

6. Next, I share mentor text examples with the class. We talk about how effective the sentences are, what stood out, what we liked or disliked about the writing.

Guided Writing Practice Ideas

- Stick with *Green Eggs and Ham* for a day or two. Have students work through the book, rewriting lines, changing the *Repeater* sentences to something new. Students can do this in small groups or with a partner. This is a fun way to both relive this classic and practice this move.

- Spend time helping your students use this strategy in one sentence. Rylant's earlier example is a great model. Show students how they can repeat words without creating three distinct sentences.

- Ask students to choose one of their favorite movie, book, or television characters. Ask students to bring in or print a photo of the character. In class, have students use the *Repeaters* strategy to write a description of that character. Post the character images on a bulletin board or wall of the class with the descriptions placed below as a caption.

- Students can also write descriptions of themselves or a family member. They can focus on physical or personality attributes. I avoid allowing students to describe anyone else in the class (that can be a recipe for disaster)! Ask them to use this strategy to craft a brief description. Ask for volunteers to share their descriptions with the class.

Pop Culture References

*t*his move—using references to pop culture—allows writers to insert a bit more of their understanding of the world and culture, challenges readers to make sense of the connection in a way that simple adjectives or adverbs would not, and gives readers a glimpse of the writer's or speaker's world.

What Does This Move Look Like in Writing?

He stretches his shoulders, hikes his Raider jersey sleeves up his black arms and points, Babe Ruth style, to the centerfield fence.

—Matt De La Pena, *from* Mexican Whiteboy

It was like the last scene in Star Wars IV: A New Hope when Luke Skywalker, Hans Solo, and Chewbacca are being applauded for destroying the Death Star. I could almost hear the Star Wars theme music playing in my head as I stood on the stage.

—R. J. Palacio, *from* Wonder

She was always in charge—even then, before you understood it, her beauty was hard to look away from: glossy dark hair and full red lips. Snow White with a tan and a strut.

Rebecca Strand, *from* Goodbye Stranger

These fun sentences make the writer seem more in touch with the culture of their time. They either offer a connection to readers or cause readers to draw a blank and become curious about the connection. What scene draws applause for the Star Wars heroes? What does this mean?

When Writers Make This Move

Writers make this move for a few reasons. One is to make their writing relevant and timely. The second reason is to connect with a specific audience. If authors are writing for a preteen audience, it makes sense to relate to name brands, celebrities, or sports heroes that the audience already identifies with. In novels, this strategy can backfire on authors. Nothing dates a book more than a reference to a celebrity who is no longer well known, or even worse, a brand that doesn't exist anymore.

For students, dated references are not as much of a problem, because students' writing will likely be read right away. The challenge for students is to consider their audience, not just their own preferences. For example, if their audience is often made up of both teachers and students (two very different demographics), they will need to consider their references to pop culture carefully. As a teacher, I may have no connection to the latest boy band or the hottest country stars.

How I Introduce This Move

1. I list several current popular culture names or events on the board—popular musical artists, comedians, or the celebrity of the moment— or I ask students to name people or things they identify with.

2. Next I ask students to share attributes that they think of when they read those names. We add as many attributes as possible (Figure 2.14).

3. After listing those attributes, I explain that we can compare the characters we write about to something or someone from our culture to help readers get a better understanding of who they are. Although I may discuss the difference between a simile and a metaphor briefly, I really want to focus on the writer's craft rather than just the terminology.

4. Finally, I start to add examples of ways that I can make a *Pop Culture Reference*.

Figure 2.14 For our list, I began by writing "Facebook." As you can see from the attributes listed, I asked the students to name people or things for this list.

What if I wanted to express that someone was a great athlete? I might explain that they were the next Lebron James or Kobe Bryant. I wouldn't have to even explain what that meant, the reference would do that for me.

5. After crafting several *Pop Culture References*, I put students into small groups. I ask for each group to come up with some of their own *Pop Culture References* to describe people. This can include fictional characters, historical figures, or anyone that students are studying across the curriculum.

6. This typically becomes a noisy session and students tend to get very excited about what they are creating. We share their sentences and post a few around the room as examples.

Guided Writing Practice Ideas

- Consider writing multiple examples on sentence strips and taping them to the front of your desk, a wall, or classroom door. Label this section as the *Pop Culture Reference* wall. Challenge students to add to the wall throughout the year. When you write, you will be surprised by how many students will rely on these examples to spark their own thinking and try out this writing move.

- Continue to add to the list of pop culture references. Encourage students to add attributes to the list throughout the year. This type of list is a helpful aid for struggling writers. They can grow this list, or turn to it when they want to make a *Pop Culture Reference*, but are unsure of where to begin.

- Invite students to reflect on their own personality, talents, or other attributes. Then, ask them to write *Pop Culture Reference* sentences to describe themselves (Figure 2.15). Share the sentences and discuss why that reference made sense.

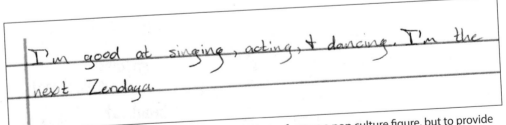

I'm good at singing, acting, + dancing. I'm the next Zendaya.

Figure 2.15 For this activity students tended to not just reference a pop culture figure, but to provide the attributes associated with that figure. Here Melissa compared her own singing and acting ability to the performer Zendaya. This name and many others sent me to the Internet to update my own pop culture knowledge!

- This is a fun opportunity to revise some of the serious, monotone sentences often found in some informational texts. Challenge students to take dry writing and make it more lively and kid-centric. I like to pull up articles online and tell students that we want to rewrite some of the sentences for a group of younger students. Time for Kids, online newspapers, textbooks, or websites like news.discovery.com are great places to start. Students typically have a ball with this and come up with wacky revisions that rely on *Pop Culture References* to help describe the topics in ways that their young audience will understand. It's okay to be very flexible here: trying out the strategy is what matters!

- Find pictures of people that reflect specific emotions or traits, such as pride, anger, solemnity, power, athleticism, serious-mindedness, or exhaustion. One by one, display the pictures and challenge students to write one or two sentences that describe the person pictured. The only rule is that they must use a *Popular Culture Reference*. Be prepared not only for high levels of engagement, but also to be schooled on all types of new names and information!

Personify It

Personify It is a reminder to students to use the powerful tool of personification in their descriptions.

What Does This Move Look Like in Writing?

Every moment more and more of the trees shook off their robes of snow.

> —C. S. Lewis, *from* The Lion, the Witch, and the Wardrobe

The next morning was a midsummer's morning as fair and as fresh as could be dreamed; blue sky and never a cloud, and the sun dancing on the water.

> —J. R. R. Tolkien, *from* The Hobbit

On the way up north to the cabin, the sunshine sits in my lap all morning.

> —Marsha Wilson Chall, *from* Up North at the Cabin

The woods became our savior, and each day I went a bit farther into its arms.

> —Suzanne Collins, *from* The Hunger Games

Personification gives humanity to nonhumans, enabling trees to shake themselves clean and sunshine to sit with someone as if it were a companion. This move not only helps writers to describe a scene, it also helps readers to consider the object the way they might consider a person—with a reaction such as pity, love, or sympathy.

When Writers Make This Move

Writers choose the characteristics they grant the objects—and, therefore, the mood, the scene, or the content—with connotations. Forcing a reader to react to an object the way that they would to a person can draw readers into descriptions that might otherwise leave them cold.

Like other strong descriptive moves, *Personify It* adds style and variation, serving to show, rather than tell. However, because it is such a unique tool, it's best used when it's balanced with other strategies: it feels forced when it appears in every paragraph.

How I Introduce This Move

1. I begin by bringing in a plate of my favorite cookies. I place them front and center and tell my students that these are treats for the class, but that I am working on cutting back on sweets, so I really should not have them. As I say this, I look at the plate lovingly and overexaggerate a desire to eat one.

2. I explain that personification means taking a nonhuman noun and pairing it with a verb. Then, I create a T-chart. On one side, we list as many nonhuman nouns as we can fit on the chart (making sure that *cookies* is added, too). On the other side, we list different verbs that we know. Typically, we add past-tense verbs. (See Figure 2.16.) This tends to work easier for forming sentences.

3. I ask students to watch me pair different nouns and verbs together to bring the nonliving objects alive. I tell them that I want to personify each one. I randomly match nouns with verbs. Once I pair them, I add an ending to form a full sentence.

4. After creating a few sentences, I ask for a volunteer to create a sentence that might express how I felt about those cookies. Students often suggest sentences like: The cookies called my name. The delicious aroma danced in the air. The cookies quietly whispered, "Take a bite!"

Figure 2.16 Our T-chart helped give students ideas for different actions that could be paired to nonliving objects.

5. Finally, I ask students to use our list to create and personify at least three objects. We share their sentences and I ask: **How can personification help you, as a reader, to understand a writer's feelings about an object? How can personification help you, as a writer, to communicate exactly what you mean?**

Guided Writing Practice Ideas

- In advance, type up a list of nouns and verbs. Print these and cut them into strips so that you have one collection of nouns and one of verbs. Walk around the room and let each student draw one from each collection. Invite students to use the *Personify It* move to craft a sentence that uses their noun and verb. When they finish, have them turn and talk with a neighbor about their sentence. Ask students to return the strips to the correct collection, then repeat several times. This is a fun activity to practice throughout the year!

- For more novice writers, consider doing more work providing examples of personification. I find that less skilled writers typically fall in love with one or two very specific examples of personification and overuse that in their own writing. The goal is to make sure that students see this move as a strategy and not just a line of text that they have committed to memory and force into text. I like to do this by reading picture books or poems that use personification. My standby favorite is Langston Hughes' short and simple poem, "April Rain Song." I ask students to raise their hands or stand up when they notice the *Personify It* move being used in the book. Fun picture books with lots of personification include *The Old Woman Who Named Things* by Cynthia Rylant, *Mike Mulligan and His Steam Shovel* by Virginia Lee Burton, and *Hurricane* by Jonathan London.

- Make a list of different descriptive sentences. Use personification in half of the sentences. For the other half, just describe the object, but avoid using personification. Read or display each sentence. Ask students to either classify the sentences or simply offer a thumbs up or thumbs down if they think that the *Personify It* move was used or not. Afterward, mark each sentence with an asterisk that did not use personification. Invite students to revise those sentences using the *Personify It* move.

- Ask students to select a descriptive sentence from their own writing, then use the *Personify It* move to revise the sentence. Share these revisions as a whole group if possible. The more that students hear and read examples of this move, the more likely they are to feel comfortable trying this out on their own.

Set It Up

*t*his move is about developing the setting before letting the story or an event unfold. For students, this is the moment when the author paints a picture of the scene. I often compare this to the opening sequence in a film when the title, directors, and actors names are displayed. Often, the camera pans the landscape or city. Viewers get to see where the story begins and who is present. The focus is on including descriptive and sensory language to paint a picture of what is present before the action begins. This move is never just about naming a location or date. This move is about sensory description and can be several sentences long. This move can be used in all types of writing, particularly when the physical location is important. Content-area writers can use this move to describe new and different places that the rest of the writing will teach about.

What Does This Move Look Like in Writing?

A shoebox-sized package is propped against the front door at an angle. Our front door has a tiny slot to shove mail through, but anything thicker than a bar of soap gets left outside. A hurried scribble on the wrapping addresses the package to Clay Jenson, so I pick it up and head inside.

—Jay Asher, *from* Thirteen Reasons Why

It feels like we've walked into a living fairy tale. Our heads are literally in the clouds. Though we're just a few degrees south of the Equator, we're bathed in a cool mist. We're 10,000 feet up in the mountains. Here the trees are cloaked in clouds. The ground is carpeted with thick green moss.

—Sy Montgomery, *from* Quest for the Tree Kangaroo: An Expedition to the Cloud Forest of New Guinea

When Mr. Arable returned to the house half an hour later, he carried a carton under his arm. Fern was upstairs changing her sneakers. The kitchen table was set for breakfast, and the room smelled of coffee, bacon, damp plaster, and wood smoke from the stove.

—E. B. White, *from* Charlotte's Web

Dorothy lived in the midst of the great Kansas prairies, with Uncle Henry, who was a farmer, and Aunt Em, who was a farmer's wife. Their house was small, for the lumber to build it has to be carried by wagon many miles. There were four walls, a floor, and a roof, which made one room; and this room contained a rusty-looking cooking stove, a cupboard for the dishes, a table, three or four chairs, and the beds. Uncle Henry and Aunt Em had a big bed in one corner and Dorothy a little bed in another corner.

—Frank Baum, *from* The Wizard of Oz

Each of these excerpts paints a picture for the reader. It might be of a house, of a room, or even just a front door, but it's enough to establish the setting and the character's place in it. Although the lengths of the excerpts vary, each includes enough information to let the reader see the scene—and sometimes hear it and smell it, too.

When Writers Make This Move

Writers make this move to establish a context for the writing that will follow. In stories, this move helps to provide a sense of where and when. This is most important to storytelling. In movies, this move is often in the opening sequence, panning in and out so that moviegoers get a sense of when and where the story takes place. Providing written context serves the same purpose as the opening sequence. This move is not reserved for the beginning of stories, but is most commonly found there. Professional writers use this to set the context when new information is about to be presented or a shift in events occurs. For students, I find that focusing on making this move at the beginning of a text is more manageable.

How I Introduce This Move

1. I pass out markers crayons, colored pencils, and drawing paper to my students.

2. Without telling students why, I ask them to draw the background scene from their favorite story. They can select a novel, movie, comic book, or any tale that appeals to them. The only rule is that they can only draw the background scene. There is no action allowed.

3. After about ten minutes, I ask students to partner up and describe their drawings to a peer.

4. Once everyone has shared, I lead a discussion about why these images matter: How do the settings help the stories? What information do they provide? What clues do they offer? Why do the scenes look different?

5. After our discussion, I point out that authors often want to paint a picture before they develop the action. Authors deliberately set up a scene to frame the action. Although descriptions are embedded throughout the story, it is usually key to develop the description of a setting at the beginning of a story or whenever a new setting is introduced.

Guided Writing Practice Ideas

- After students have created their illustrations, ask them to try out this move by writing several sentences about the setting they've drawn. Describing what they have illustrated will help them to connect this move with visual imagery and their senses.

- Display images from popular stories. Ask students to craft a description of the scene. Remind them that limited action is used in their description. Post the image and the students' descriptions around the image as a reminder of how this move works.

- Instead of asking students to write descriptions to match their own illustrations, have them swap pictures with a peer. Students can try out this move, by writing their own *Set It Up* descriptions for the new pictures that they receive.

- Make a fun game out of this! Write the names of different locations on strips of paper. Place the strips into a pencil holder or container and have students each draw a strip. Students then create brief descriptions of the scene. Share descriptions and continue until each student has practiced this move with a few different settings. Be certain to discuss how these descriptions helped readers to imagine the setting. I focus on the idea that this move paints a picture in our minds. What do we see? What sounds do we hear? What does the setting feel like? Help students to understand the power behind using this type of move.

- Ask each student to bring in a picture of a different setting. You can assign a specific setting to each student, or let students decide on their own. The next day, ask students to write their names on the back of their image and place it on their desk. Each person should write only one sentence that describes the setting. After a minute or so, ask students to switch papers and images with the person to their left. That person should look at the image and add an additional sentence to continue to set up the scene for readers. I typically switch four or five times. At the end, the pictures are returned to the owners. Call on volunteers to share the *Set It Up* descriptions and discuss each one. What worked? What fell flat? What senses did the students tend to rely on?

Move 10

Thought Bubbles

*i*n most narratives, the author tends to describe what the characters say and do. *Thought Bubbles* let characters or speakers share their private thoughts directly with readers. This move is a version of *Act & Think* in Chapter 3 and *Talking & Thinking* in Chapter 6. I deliberately include these moves to really emphasize the power of revealing a person's thinking, whether it is tied to action or dialogue or set apart on its own. This is a powerful move that students can make to add rich detail to their writing.

What Does This Move Look Like in Writing?

You're gonna be a flat-nosed baby if you don't shut up, I'm thinking.

> —Jerry Spinelli, *from* Crash

At first she did not see what had caused the noise. She thought that it was the wind echoing through one of the caves and was about to leave when she noticed silvery shapes on the floor.

> —Scott O'Dell, *from* Island of the Blue Dolphins

Why can't I hide it, too? Meg thought. Why do I always have to show everything?

> —Madeline L'Engle, *from* A Wrinkle in Time

Still, it would have been nice, he often thought, if he could have seen something of the world before he met Mrs. Popper and settled down.

—Richard and Florence Atwater, *from* Mr. Popper's Penguins

A nice book would have been a good idea, I thought. But a picture dictionary! That's for babies!

—Judy Blume, *from* Tales of a Fourth Grade Nothing

Instead of just being actors in a scene, the characters above seem to have their own voices and styles. Jerry Spinelli's character, for example, lets the reader see his aggressive personality through his thinking. If Spinelli had only described the character's outward actions, this aggressive streak would not have been apparent.

When Writers Make This Move

Shifting to the character's own thinking is a great way to share information with the reader that the other characters may not know, reveal the point of view of a character, or simply offer insight into shifts in mood as the story unfolds.

How I Introduce This Move

1. I begin by drawing a thought bubble on the board or on chart paper. Then, I ask students if they have ever had a conversation with someone and thought lots of things in their minds, but not said them out loud.

2. I encourage students to share reasons why they might keep their thoughts to themselves, rather than saying them out loud. Students typically share that the thoughts might be hurtful or embarrassing or might represent ideas that they had not fully formed or made sense of them for themselves yet.

3. After our discussion, I explain that readers often want to know what characters are thinking. When authors share a character's thoughts, the reader gets a quick peek into the character's mind—a glimpse of the character's raw thoughts, not the face they present to the world. I tell students that is a great way to help introduce a character to the readers.

4. Next, we make a list of different character traits that could be shown through the *Thought Bubble* move. I add these to a chart or ask students to record them in their notebooks. This becomes a handy reference later.

Guided Writing Practice Ideas

- This is a great time to show a few funny commercials, especially those that follow a narrative structure. I search online for past Super Bowl commercials. Take a moment to preview a few in advance. Select three or four of your favorites. Show students one commercial at a time. After the commercial, ask students to select a character that they like. Using the *Thought Bubble* move, ask students to write one sentence revealing what that character might have been thinking during the commercial. Encourage students to use language that matches that character's personality. Share and discuss the different sentences that they create.

- Read a fractured fairy tale or a picture book where the character has a distinct viewpoint. As you read, wonder out loud what the characters must be thinking. At different points, stop and ask students to "freeze" and tell what you think the character is thinking right at that moment. Record these thoughts on the board, sentence strips, sticky notes, or chart paper. David Shannon, Mo Willems, and Maurice Sendak are a few authors who craft picture books with very distinctive characters. For fractured fairy tale ideas, consider: *The True Story of the Three Little Pigs* and *The Stinky Cheese Man*, both by Jon Scieska.

- Select an opinion-based text, like an op-ed article for this activity. The *New York Times'* free online opinion articles for students are a great resource, and they provide a searchable archive on their website, http://learning.blogs .nytimes.com/. Read the article out loud. Ask students to write a *Thought Bubble* sentence that reflects their own reaction to the article. Continue this by asking students to try this move out, but for different fictional people. For example, what *Thought Bubble* sentence might be appropriate for someone quoted in the article, a police officer, a teacher, the school principal, their parents? This is most effective when you select a timely article that students have varied opinions about.

- Revisit familiar or well-known stories. These can be books or articles that have been previously read, or even well-known fables, fairy tales, or archetypal stories. Discuss the central characters. Ask students if they can pinpoint different places in the story when the character may have been thinking something significant or revealing and how the story might be different if the author had used the *Thought Bubble* move.

3

Details

THAT

Dance

Showing Action and Sequencing Events

*a*sk anyone to tell you about their favorite novel and watch what happens. They will probably gush and tell you all of the memorable or important *events* that happened in the story. The heart of any story is the unfolding of events—the action.

Storytelling's commitment to action is why cliff-hangers and season finales on television are so engaging. Everyone wants to see what will happen. What will the stars of the show do? If I miss my favorite television show one week, I avoid social media or warn friends not to spoil the episode for me. I don't read text messages out of fear that someone will type one sentence that tells me what the characters *did*. The action is king.

Before readers ever meet Charlotte in E. B. White's *Charlotte's Web*, they read about Fern furiously trying to spare Wilbur's young life, by trying to wrestle the ax away from her father.

> *Tears ran down her cheeks and she took hold of the ax and tried to pull it out of her father's hand. (2012, 3)*

When readers talk about Louis Sachar's *Holes*, they most certainly tell of the Camp Green Lake boys digging giant holes, or Mr. Sir falling victim to the warden's poisonous nail polish.

> *Suddenly, Mr. Sir screamed and clutched his face with both hands. He let himself fall over, rolling off the hearth and on the rug. (2000, 89)*

Actions like these work collectively to build an engaging story, to draw us in, and to move characters from the paper into our hearts. When a reader finishes a memoir or reads the final chapter of a novel, the action stays with them.

Although the action is always front and center, good storytellers don't just string together series of subjects and verbs to propel the action forward. Skilled writers weave plots and scenes together in a wide variety of ways. Readers, often oblivious to this conscious, intentional development of action, simply enjoy being immersed in the story. As readers, we remember the action in the stories we enjoy. As writers, students can make the action in their own memoirs, anecdotes, fictional stories, or accounts of events just as memorable by learning the behind-the-scenes moves of writing about action.

Details That Dance are the specific types of details that help writers to explain the action that takes place in a story. Many of the details focus on sentence structures and ways to organize and reveal action. *Details That Dance* are critical for writers who want the action to be front and center in their texts and want to invite readers along for the ride of unfolding their plots and storylines—they keep a story fresh and rich!

When Do Writers Make These Moves?

Authors use *Details That Dance* to show their characters' actions or to help move stories along from one event to the next. Typically, *Details That Dance* help to situate the way that characters or people move or take action. This could be as basic as one character waking up in the morning, or as complex as Cinderella running to beat the stroke of midnight, with pumpkins and mice transforming all around her. Questions that writers might ask themselves when thinking about this type of detail:

- How does this movement look, visually?
- What clues can I embed about this person or character as I show the action?
- Do I want this action to zoom by quickly or do I want it to be in slow motion?
- How do I want this action or movement to feel to readers?
- What senses do I want to rouse with this movement?
- Do I want to inform the reader of the action or just provide bread crumb clues?
- How can I connect one event to the next?

Modeling These Moves

The central requirement for effectively teaching any type of detail is to write with your students. As with each type of detail, always begin with your own writing so that students can have a peek into your own process. This helps to make the craft of writing more accessible and the skill more attainable for students.

To introduce *Details That Dance*, you will need to select two or three action movie trailers. Preview and select movies that are appropriate for your students. Use your knowledge of your class and the different personalities to choose something that will capture students' attention, while avoiding movies that your students are overly familiar with. You want them to watch what happens on the screen, not to reference the rest of the movie. For older students, I commonly show trailers for *Mission Impossible*, *Karate Kid*, or *Indiana Jones*. For younger students, I usually select trailers for older, classic, animated films.

I tell students that I need them to help me decide which movie I should watch tonight when I get home. Then, I show the class a set of movie trailers. I offer very little input as the trailers play, allowing students to react and respond to what they see. After each trailer has played, I invite students to tell me what they suggest for my movie night and why, asking them to name specific parts of the trailer that interested them. Students' responses typically reflect the action in the trailers.

After students have shared, I write the words action verbs in the center of a chart. I begin adding some of the different actions that students just shared (see Figure 3.1). I choose not to do this while they are sharing because I don't want to simply ask students to name actions—I want them to understand that most of the details they offered on their own were actions, even though I hadn't asked for actions specifically. I want students to see the power of action in their own perceptions of the trailers.

I explain that the action is the center of most stories, just like it is

Figure 3.1 Our chart was created after watching the original *Karate Kid* and *Indiana Jones* trailers.

on our chart. At this point, the students are typically demanding to know which movie I plan to watch. I choose one and tell students that this whole activity has made me think about a new type of detail that we can use to make our storytelling come alive, too. Then, I explain that we should work on writing about our characters and the things that they do in a way that will keep our readers engaged. ***Guys, I think that we can be on the lookout for ways to organize how we share action in our own stories to make it interesting. Let's try it out! What if a character ran down the street? I could write:***

He ran down the street.

Does that show action? It does, but man is it boring. Why is he running? Does he feel good about this running? What does it look like when he runs? What is he trying to do? What if I tried something different, something more engaging like in our movie trailers? I write:

> Embarrassed, he ran down the dark street. *(EDs Up Front)*

What does that make you think? Does that make the action come a bit more alive? I continue to revise the original sentence in different ways. Common revisions are:

> He ran down the street, wondering if they were gaining on him. (*Act & Think*)

> He ran down the street hoping to catch up to the others. (*But, Why?*)

Finally, I tell students that we are going to study ways to share action in our stories. These types of details are called *Details That Dance*. As you'll notice in this book, I introduce new concepts first and then introduce the terminology or the name of the skill. I like to let students see the value in the upcoming lessons first and then, after they are hooked and interested, point out that this just happens to be what we will be learning. This makes engagement painless and results in students' buy-in early on.

Details That Dance: The Writing Moves

Each of the *Details That Dance* moves in this chapter is listed in the table that follows. When you read students' writing and notice different things that you would like for them to elaborate on or revise, this chart provides direction to help move students to consider different possibilities.

Details That Dance

If you see this in the student's writing . . .		Try this . . .
No context for events	⟩	*Act & Think* (page 65) *But, Why?* (page 68) *Time Marker* (page 71)
Lifeless writing/no voice	⟩	*Adverb Comma* (page 79) *INGs Up Front* (page 83) *EDs Up Front* (page 88) *Explain That Sound* (page 92)
Flat/one-dimensional characters	⟩	*Act & Think* (page 65) *INGs Up Front* (page 83) *EDs Up Front* (page 88)
Abundance of simple sentences	⟩	*Adverb Comma* (page 79) *INGs Up Front* (page 83) *EDs Up Front* (page 88)
Listing or naming actions	⟩	*Act & Think* (page 65) *INGs Up Front* (page 83) *Explain That Sound* (page 92)
No transitions between events	⟩	*Time Marker* (page 71) *Location Marker* (page 75)

This chart is a tool to help *students* think about different ways to use *Details That Dance* effectively in their writing. Based on student goals, this chart can direct students to some possibilities. This is not all inclusive and moves can be used to meet lots of different writing goals. This chart just offers a beginning set of possibilities.

Details That Dance

If you want to . . .		Try this . . .
Help readers understand when or why an action is happening	❯	*Act & Think* *But, Why?* *Time Marker*
Add more of your personal voice and pizzazz to your writing	❯	*Adverb Comma* *INGs Up Front* *EDs Up Front* *Explain That Sound*
Create realistic characters	❯	*Act & Think* *INGs Up Front* *EDs Up Front*
Vary your type of sentences	❯	*Adverb Comma* *INGs Up Front* *EDs Up Front*
Make the events come alive and stand out for your readers	❯	*Act & Think* *INGs Up Front* *Explain That Sound*
Add transitions to sequence events	❯	*Time Marker* *Location Marker*

Act & *Think*

*t*his move shows a character moving through a scene while intentionally revealing his thoughts to the reader. This move is similar to both the *Details That Speak* move and the *Talking and Thinking* move. In both moves, writers share the thoughts of a character, but pair them with dialogue or action.

What Does This Move Look Like in Writing?

They met at the register. They walked past the man, cool, casual, not looking—("Don't look at him." Weasel had been firm about that)—though Mongoose mightily wanted to.

> —Jerry Spinelli, *from* The Library Card

Yep, *thought Flora,* that's me. *She bent her head and went back to reading about the amazing Incandesto.*

> —Kate DiCamillo, *from* Flora and Ulysses:
>   The Illuminated Adventures

It happens to everyone, *Tommy reminded himself as he kicked at a large brown stone.* At least in this century.

> —Blue Balliett, *from* Pieces and Players

Only ten million more to go, *he thought, then placed the shovel back in the crack and jumped on it again.*

> —Louis Sachar, *from* Holes

In this explicit type of thought revealing, the words *thinking* or *thought* are often present. It's also common for the ideas that are being thought to be isolated in quotations or italics. Each of these examples paints a picture of what the characters are doing, but also gives a peek into their personalities and attitudes toward their actions. Spinelli, for example, does this masterfully by creating a picture of Mongoose simply walking past a man. Yet, by revealing Mongoose's thinking, the reader is privy to possible intentions, prior conversations, and the character's own struggles not to look at the man.

When Writers Make This Move

Writers use this move to share the thoughts of a character without slowing down the action to speak directly to readers. The thoughts are embedded within the movement of the character. This move is also helpful when a character's actions don't show his or her true state of mind as well as for characters who are not likely to speak openly about their motives or who don't have another character to speak to. Narratives, memoirs, and accounts of events depend on this move to offer readers a more three-dimensional character.

How I Introduce This Move

1. I begin by pacing back and forth across the classroom.

2. After a few paces, I grab a marker and ask for volunteers to tell me what I was just doing. Then, I write one of their descriptions, such as:

   She walked back and forth.

3. I ask the students if this sentence is accurate and interesting. Immediately, most will agree that while it is accurate, it is not interesting.

4. I say to students, ***When an author wants to describe something that a character is doing that doesn't seem to be very exciting, the author can help us to see why the action is significant by pairing an action with the thoughts of the character(s). When you can see what a character is thinking, the action may become much more meaningful.*** Then, I revise my sentence to read:

   As she walked back and forth, she kept thinking to herself, *How bad could it be? She couldn't be in that much trouble.*

5. We talk about what we have learned about the character in this version, which pairs thinking and action. Students typically agree that this revision helps them to see *why* it matters to see a person pacing.

6. Then, I revise the sentence in a different way:

   She walked back and forth, thinking about how angry she was at him.

7. We discuss the differences between the two revisions. I point students to the idea that these sentences give clues about two very different types of thoughts and possible stories. Without the thoughts, the reader has nothing to go on, except for the actual movement.

8. I continue to revise the sentence, adding different thoughts and discussing the power of pairing action and thinking. Finally, I introduce the name of this writing move: *Act & Think*. We continue to talk about how this move can help build more well-rounded characters and make the actions more meaningful for the reader.

Guided Writing Practice Ideas

- Ask students to share a moment when they tried something for the first time. Encourage students to share their different events and how they felt. After a brief discussion, ask students to write about their moment, but to try out at least one *Act & Think* move in their accounts.

- Read an excerpt from a picture book where a character's emotions and feelings are obvious. Then, select a page and ask students to revise the text to include an *Act & Think* move to show the character's thinking. Great picture books for this include David Shannon's *A Bad Case of the Stripes* and Jacqueline Woodson's *The Other Side*. For more of a challenge, use a page from a novel. Gary Paulsen's *Hatchet* and Judy Blume's *Deenie* are great choices. Both main characters share their emotions quite openly and clearly, making it easy for students to consider what they may be thinking at different times in the novel.

- Write several directions on slips of paper: *jump*, *dance*, *slowly walk*, *cup your face*, and so on. Invite volunteers to pull a card and actually do what the card says. The rest of the class should only watch, not interact. Afterward, ask students to use the *Act & Think* move to make the actions come alive. Give them carte blanche to be creative and add thoughts that they think make sense. Share the sentences and point out how different they are.

- Show students a commercial or movie trailer that includes a lot of action. I usually go with the latest superhero or animated movie trailer that students are already familiar with. Then, ask students to tell what happened in the commercial or trailer, using the *Act & Think* move at least twice in their writing. Ask students to share their descriptions in small groups and discuss what this move helped them to accomplish. As a whole group, invite a volunteer from each group to share their writing with the class.

But, Why?

*i*n this move, a character takes an action while the author explains why the character takes that action. Although this might at first sound similar to *Act & Think*, there are a few important differences. First, the character is not acknowledging this as his own thinking, nor speaking to the reader. Second, the action in *But, Why?* is purposeful. Unlike *Act & Think*, where a character might be absently pacing the room and having a thought about something else entirely, *But, Why?* explains the reason why a character is doing something. The movement and reason unfold together. There's no set sentence structure for this move.

What Does This Move Look Like in Writing?

Stella inched forward, trying to get a better look.
   —Sharon Draper, from Stella by Starlight

Lily sank back on her heels to look around at the blue walls and ceiling, and the gold stars pasted on here and there.
   —Patricia Reilly Giff, from Lily's Crossing

I snatched my wallet and opened it to see if anything was missing.
   —Christopher Paul Curtis, from Bucking the Sarge

Each of these authors describes a specific physical move and the motive behind the move. Notice that this move focuses not on sentence structure—each author used a different style—but also on content and purpose. All three authors name the characters' motives directly.

When Writers Make This Move

Professional writers do this to explain why an action is or has occurred. This is used for physical movement and works in all types of writing. Students could use this move to retell about a special day just as effectively as a summary of a Civil War battle. As long as an action or sequence of events is included, this move works well.

Often students tend to write about lots of actions and events, but rarely tell why. When I notice students simply listing the sequence of events, I require them to make this move. When they try to and can't, I point out that maybe the description of this action or set of actions is not vital to the writing. This moves students from telling each step that they took to get on the bus on the way to school, or stretching out a car ride into seven steps with no real purpose, to describing actions that are essential to the text.

How I Introduce This Move

1. I write the Sharon Draper example from the What Does This Move Look Like in Writing? section on the board, but without the last part of the sentence that tells why Stella is inching forward. I write:

   Stella inched forward.

2. Then, I ask students why they think Stella is inching forward. I typically call on volunteers for suggestions.

3. Next, I add the end of the original sentence on and ask the question again. Why is Stella inching forward? Students will immediately answer that she wanted to get a better look. I ask why it was so easy to answer my question this time. Expect responses such as "Duh! You wrote it right there." "You told us." "We can read it."

4. Then, I remind students of the many different guesses they gave when I first asked why Stella was inching forward. I tell them, ***In our writing, we don't want our readers guessing all of the time. We want to help them understand the motives and actions of our characters. A simple way to do this is to add a bit more information to the different events and actions in our text to give our readers a clearer picture of what is happening.***

5. After that explanation, I introduce this as a *But, Why?* move. Then, I repeat this questioning process again with Patricia Reilly Giff's sentence, writing: "Lily sank back on her heels" on the board.

Guided Writing Practice Ideas

- I create a digital collage of holiday or vacation photographs that feature me, my kids, and husband. I project the images and ask students to write a *But, Why?* sentence for a few of the images. We share the different sentences and discuss how their sentences provided context for the action. My students, particularly my younger students, are usually very engaged with this activity. It may simply be the shock that I don't actually live at the school. Whatever draws them in, it keeps them focused and gives them multiple opportunities to test drive this move.

- Share a piece of your own writing with students. You can rely on an older piece of writing that you modeled before or create a new piece just for this purpose. Ask students to revise your writing to reveal why different actions take place. Let students share their changes and talk about how this makes the writing better. Finally, take a few of their suggestions and revise the piece with the students (see Figure 3.2).

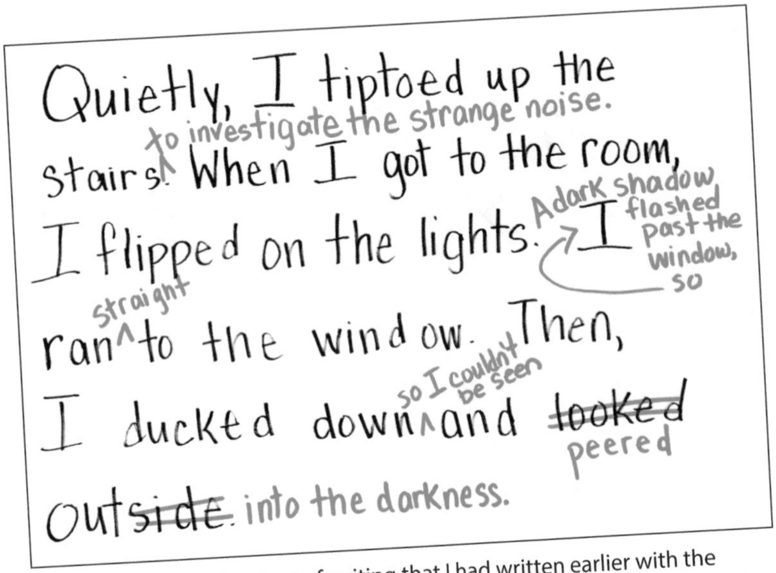

- Select a wordless picture book where the characters do something interesting or that invites curiosity. I like to share Aaron Becker's *Journey* or *Quest* for this. Each book is filled with wonder and will ignite curiosity in most students. Show the first page of the book and caption it, using this move. Because of the way these books are written, using this move to caption a page will necessitate a bit of a prediction, which will be confirmed (or disproven) on the next page. Then, flip to the next page and ask the students if your caption was accurate. I deliberately make my caption accurate so that the focus stays on the move, not my prediction. Challenge students to caption the next page using a

Figure 3.2 I revised a piece of writing that I had written earlier with the students. I thought aloud and showed students the messy process of revision by adding carets to show my additions.

But, Why? move. Call on volunteers to share their writing. Discuss the predictions imbedded in this move, to keep students curious and engaged, but continue to reinforce that their captions told what action was happening and why it could be happening. Continue through the book, crafting *But, Why?* sentences for several pages.

Time Marker

*a*uthors drop *Time Markers* to give a reference point for when specific actions take place. Typically, the *Time Marker* is named first, followed by a description of the action.

What Does This Move Look Like in Writing?

On November 14, 1960, a tiny six-year-old black child, surrounded by federal marshals, walked through a mob of screaming segregationists and into her school.

　　—Ruby Bridges, *from* Through My Eyes

Later that morning, just before nine, Tom and Frankie headed out the barn door and across the backyard.

　　—John Ritter, *from* The Boy Who Saved Baseball

Nearly 4 billion years ago in the earth's oceans, life began in the form of bacteria—single-celled organisms able to eat and reproduce.

　　—Joyce Sidman, *from* Ubiquitous: Celebrating
　　　Nature's Survivors

> *In the momentous year of 1776, on the twenty-second of*
> *September, my mother and I were rushing back to the city*
> *of New York.*
>
> —Avi, *from* Sophia's War: A Tale of the Revolution

> *Many years ago, in the winter of 1831, a boy was born*
> *to the family of Returns Again of the Hunkpapa band of*
> *Lakota Sioux.*
>
> —Joseph Bruchac, *from* A Boy Called Slow

Each of these examples names when the action occurs. Some of them are very specific *Time Markers*, like Ruby Bridges' sentence, where she provides the exact date and year, or Ritter's example, where he names the time. Other examples don't nail down the exact time or month, but offer a general context for the action. Sidman's writing is a good example of this. She lets the readers know that the action was billions of years ago. Naming a date would be virtually impossible in the context of her topic.

Both this move and the next move, *Location Marker,* use phrases at the beginning of sentences. In the examples above, authors use prepositional phrases and a few adverbial phrases. I've found that if students already know the *Time Marker* and *Location Marker* moves before we address phrases, telling them that these moves are phrases helps students to have some initial success with understanding what phrases are.

When Writers Make This Move

Writers use the *Time Marker* move to transition between events and actions or to provide context for a series of actions. This move is not just about naming a date, it is about situating the setting in which an action takes place. This could include the time of day or the year or could indicate elapsed time between two actions. Professional writers tend to rely on this move more frequently than simple transitions like *next, then, later,* or *finally.*

How I Introduce This Move

1. I write these actions on the board:

   I woke up late for school.

   I jumped in the shower.

   I got dressed.

   I ran downstairs and grabbed a piece of toast before I ran out the door.

   Mrs. Duncan, my teacher, frowned at me when I finally got to school.

2. Then, I ask read the sentences aloud and ask students what they think of my story. **Does it make sense? Do you understand what happened?**

3. Students typically agree that this is understandable, but kind of disconnected. I lead students to the idea that I showed different actions, but that I offered no transitions. Transitions help move the reader from one action to another. The transitions are bridges between different actions. Then, I revise the sentences by adding several *Time Markers*. I write:

> *Today,* I woke up late for school.
>
> *At five after seven,* I jumped in the shower.
>
> *Minutes later,* I got dressed.
>
> I ran downstairs and grabbed a piece of toast before I ran out the door.
>
> *Nearly thirty minutes late for class,* Mrs. Duncan, my teacher, frowned at me when I finally got to school.

4. We discuss each of the *Time Markers* that I added. I point out that I didn't add one to each sentence, but enough to create a series of bridges between actions. Although my short account needs more detail, it is now much easier to understand when the events occurred, and I have provided a context for each action.

5. Then, I ask the class to look at my sentences and revise them with different *Time Markers*. Students share their new sentences and we create an anchor chart of possible *Time Marker* sentence starters (Figure 3.3).

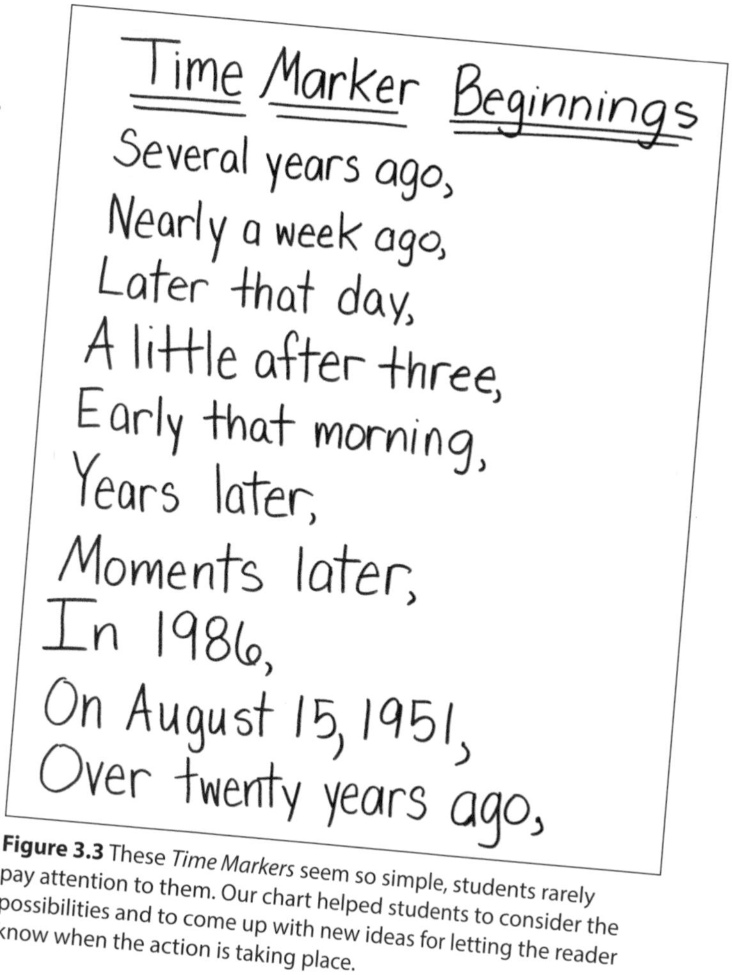

> **Time Marker Beginnings**
> Several years ago,
> Nearly a week ago,
> Later that day,
> A little after three,
> Early that morning,
> Years later,
> Moments later,
> In 1986,
> On August 15, 1951,
> Over twenty years ago,

Figure 3.3 These *Time Markers* seem so simple, students rarely pay attention to them. Our chart helped students to consider the possibilities and to come up with new ideas for letting the reader know when the action is taking place.

Guided Writing Practice Ideas

- Ask students to think about events that they participated in or observed in school. Call on students to share the different events with the class. After you hear a few, select one series of events to write on the board.

Deliberately omit any *Time Marker* moves from your list of events. After you have written sentences for the actions described, challenge students to take those sentences and add *Time Markers* to them. Share the different revisions and not only talk about how different they are, but focus on the power of the *Time Marker* move to situate and develop action in different ways.

- Ask students to revisit a piece of older writing. Challenge them to locate places where *Time Markers* could help to situate the action in the text. Note that students can use any type of text that includes action, not just narratives.

- Select a current or historical event. This is a great time to integrate social studies and writing. Discuss the event as a class. Then, ask each student to sequence the actions associated with the event. As students write, encourage them to use *Time Markers* as a bridge between events and to provide context.

- Ask students to write a short paragraph describing their best birthday, holiday, or special event. As students write, encourage them to not only include *Time Markers* in their writing, but to underline or highlight when they make this move. Invite students to share their writing with a peer for feedback and revision ideas. Post students' writing as exemplars on a board labeled *Time Markers in Action*.

Location *Marker*

a *Location Marker* is similar to a *Time Marker*. Rather than situate when an event or action occurs, a *Location Marker* situates where an action takes place. This move is typically structured in a similar pattern. Typically the author announces the setting through description or just by name at the beginning of the sentence, sets it off with a comma, then describes the action.

What Does This Move Look Like in Writing?

At the top floor, Friedrich pushed open a door and entered a cavernous room.
　—Pam Munoz Ryan, from Echo

Outside in the sunshine, thousands of bees droned happily, gathering honey from the clusters of acacia blossoms.
　—Kate Seredy, from The Singing Tree

On the sidewalk in front of their house, Joey-Mick finished tying his shoe with a double knot.
　—Linda Sue Park, from Keeping Score

In each of these examples, including a *Location Marker* helps to set the scene. As with *Time Markers,* the typical structure for *Location Markers* is to begin with a phrase. Each of these examples begins with a prepositional phrase. Typically students only get practice adding prepositional phrases to the end of their sentences. This move lets students explore a new way to structure a sentence.

When Writers Make This Move

Location Markers are great for storytelling because they help writers transition between events. This move provides context and situates actions quickly. This move helps students to avoid the overuse of words like *next* and *later,* which actually only transition through time.

How I Introduce This Move

1. I begin by asking if anyone can name transitional words. Typically, students will name transitional words that sequence time: *later, first, eventually.*

2. I agree that the examples are all transitions (or correct them if they name words that are not transitions). Then, I introduce the learning for that day. **Those are all great transitions. Today, I want to focus on a specific type of transition that we can add to the beginning of a sentence to help move the readers from one place or location to another. These transitions will help you to shift a scene quickly, without a lot of explanation about how the action moves from one place to another.**

3. I write the term *Location Markers* on the board and begin to ask students to consider my location: **Where am I?**

4. As students offer suggestions, I write them on the board.

5. After we have several examples, I point out that the students seem pretty good at naming *Location Markers.* Then, I tell them that a *Location Marker* is not just about stating the name of the place where the action takes place. Although writers can do that, they generally want to be as precise as possible.

6. Then, I model this example by writing these two sentences:

   In the cafeteria, I picked up my lunch.

   At the front of the line, I picked up my lunch.

7. I point out that both of these *Location Marker* sentences are correct, but one names a place, while the other one is more precise and specific. I explain to students, **If you want a reader to truly be able to picture the scene, aim to be as specific as possible to paint a clear picture of your location for the reader.**

8. Next, I tell students what I did after I picked up my lunch: I ate at my desk while I read over some student papers. Then, I welcomed students back to class from the doorway as the next period started.

9. I ask students to use the *Location Marker* move to describe what I did, and then I take a few of their examples to write a short, three-sentence paragraph. After we read it together, I explain, **The** Location Marker *move lets you take your reader from one action in one place to another action in another place quickly.*

Guided Writing Practice Ideas

- Take a walking field trip throughout the school. When you enter a location tell students to freeze and write a *Location Marker* sentence to capture an action in that location. Invite volunteers to share their sentences. Encourage students to avoid just naming the location, but to think outside of the box in how they describe the location.

- Share each of the examples from the What Does This Move Look Like in Writing? section. Invite students to revise each one to change the scene to a new location. Challenge students to use specific and precise locations.

- In advance, select two locations in the city where you live. For example, I might select our school and the local library. Use Google Maps (www.maps.google.com) to map directions between your two locations. When students arrive, project the map and route on the screen. Have students create a set of directions, using *Location Markers* to explain how to travel from one location to the other. Challenge students not to use the same word more than once. This fun activity will help students think of different ways to write *Location Markers* and stretch their own working vocabulary.

- Create an anchor chart of different *Location Markers* (see Figure 3.4).

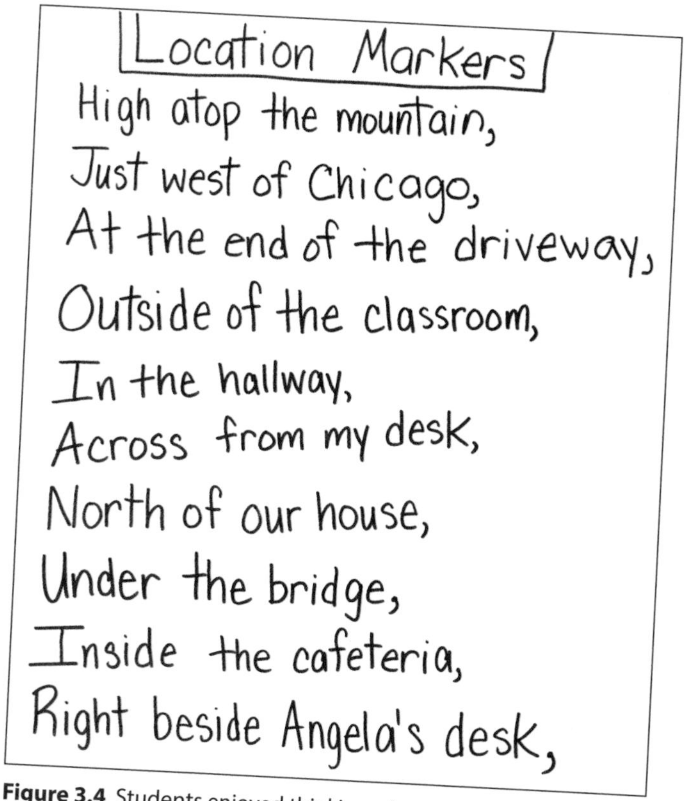

Location Markers

High atop the mountain,
Just west of Chicago,
At the end of the driveway,
Outside of the classroom,
In the hallway,
Across from my desk,
North of our house,
Under the bridge,
Inside the cafeteria,
Right beside Angela's desk,

Figure 3.4 Students enjoyed thinking of creative and varied locations to add to our chart.

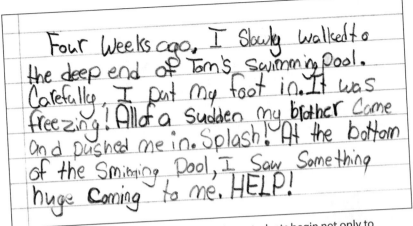

Four weeks ago, I slowly walked to the deep end of Tom's swimming pool. Carefully, I put my foot in. It was freezing! All of a sudden my brother came and pushed me in. Splash! At the bottom of the swimming pool, I saw something huge coming to me. HELP!

Figure 3.5 Abby's revised paragraph shows how students begin not only to practice specific moves during guided practice, but also begin to test-drive other moves. Abby added a *Time Marker* at the beginning to situate when she first dived in the deep end of the pool along with a *Location Marker* to show where she was when she noticed something huge coming toward her. Notice that she used an *Adverb Comma* as well.

- Ask students to revise some of their own writing by adding *Location Markers* to clarify where the action is taking place (see Figure 3.5). Invite volunteers to share their revisions. Then, challenge each student to come up with at least one *Location Marker* sentence starter to grow the class list. As students share ideas, confirm with the class if it is indeed a *Location Marker*, then add it to the list.

Move 5

Adverb *Comma*

*t*his move is simply about adding an adverb to a sentence. What makes this move different for most students is that the adverb is placed in the beginning of the sentence. Most students believe that you begin a sentence by writing the subject first. Consequently, students seem to avoid sentence structures that don't conform to this belief. This causes many unique writing moves and sentence structures to be left behind.

What Does This Move Look Like in Writing?

Slowly, one by one, they left.

> —Patricia MacLachlan, *from* Sarah, Plain and Tall

Desperately, the people tried to save the potatoes.

> —Susan Campbell Bartoletti, *from* Black Potatoes: The Story of the Great Irish Famine, 1845–1850

Nervously, he rubbed the notebook one last time, then cautiously lowered his hand around the windup toy he wanted.

> —Brian Selznick, *from* The Invention of Hugo Cabret

Stupidly, I stayed. I watched.

> —Markus Zusak, *from* The Book Thief

Professional writers twist and move words around in a wide variety of ways. These examples show the same *Adverb Comma* move, but they do not have identical structures. Even in the very simple sentences above from MacLachlan, Bartoletti, and Zusak, the *Adverb Comma* move adds depth and varied sentence structure.

When Writers Make This Move

Writers use this often to help readers grasp the mood and the feel of the action, before letting readers have a peek at what the action is. Students can easily use this move to show how a character does something in a narrative, but the *Adverb Comma* move can be used with any genre of writing—just as any adverb can and would.

How I Introduce This Move

1. On the board, I write several sentences with an adverb written next to the verb.

   > Jessica hungrily devoured her lunch.

   > I energetically danced to the soundtrack.

   > He crept slowly across the room, moving like a snail.

2. Then, I ask students to help me find the subject, verb, and adverb. I label each of these for all of the sentences.

3. Then I ask students what they notice about the order of these sentences. Eventually I lead them to the idea that the adverbs are adjacent to the verbs.

4. Then I write *Adverb Comma* on the board. I explain that this move involves two things: an adverb and a comma.

5. Then, I revise each of the sentences using this move.

   > Hungrily, Jessica devoured her lunch.

   > Energetically, I danced to the soundtrack.

   > Slowly, he crept across the room, moving like a snail.

6. I point out that moving the adverb to the beginning of the sentence gives readers a preview of the mood of the action. It also helps to vary the sentence structure, which keeps writing flowing well. We would not want all of our sentences to be *Adverb Comma* sentences—then, we would still have writing that sounded repetitive.

Guided Writing Practice Ideas

- Visit the Instructables website (www.instructables.com). This fun website has instructions for multiple crafts, recipes, and just about anything you can think of to make. Select something to learn about. Read the instructions aloud (typically just a few steps). Then, create a numbered list and rewrite the instructions using the *Adverb Comma* move. As you write, think out loud, asking which adverb makes sense or would help readers. When you have your final list, point out that it seems kind of silly to have every single sentence begin with this move. Point out that this move should only be used sparingly. Too many sentences like this become repetitive and overwhelming. Erase a few and point out how that works much better. Then, let students try this out with a different set of instructions. Have students share their steps and discuss why they chose different words.

- Show students a clip (preview in advance) from *America's Funniest Home Videos* or any kind of blooper show that is appropriate for your students. An Internet search will lead you to lots of possibilities. After each clip, invite students to use this move to write about what happened. Share their sentences and repeat with a new clip.

- Ask students to help you generate a list of adverbs. Record these adverbs on the board or chart. Next, ask students to name as many past-tense action verbs as they can; draw a second circle and fill it with a list of these verbs (Figure 3.6). Then, randomly select one verb and one or two adverbs. Turn those words into *Adverb Comma* sentences. Invite students to select words from each circle to use in their own sentences. Share these sentences and discuss how this move helps to show movement and reveal more about the character.

Figure 3.6 Our chart was created as a resource and as a model for how to make this move in writing.

- Show the students pictures of people or animals in action. Try to include a wide variety of images. Consider action images (Olympics, sports stills, and superheroes), heartwarming images (puppies, babies) or humorous images (clown cars, people with silly expressions), and so on. Ask students to use this move to caption each picture. Share the captions and discuss how well they captured the action from the image (see Figure 3.7).

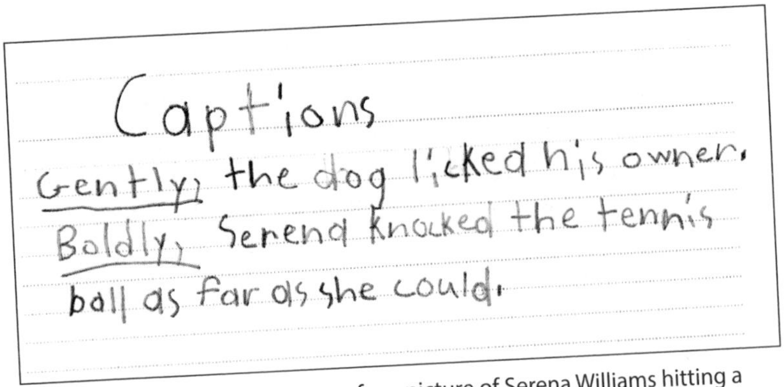

Captions
Gently, the dog licked his owner.
Boldly, Serena knocked the tennis ball as far as she could.

Figure 3.7 Brooke wrote captions for a picture of Serena Williams hitting a tennis ball and a golden retriever licking a woman's face.

INGs *Up Front*

the *INGs Up Front* move is a way to describe characters by showing two actions that are happening at the same time. For example, the character may be breathing deeply and running. Instead of writing multiple actions after the subject is named, this move places one of the actions at the front of the sentence, allowing that action to work as an adjective. Technically, *INGs Up Front* sentences are really just sentences that begin with present participles (*-ing* verbs) in participle phrases. These phrases function as adjectives for the characters.

What Does This Move Look Like in Writing?

Cupping his hand very steady, Mario walked back to the newsstand.

> —*George Selden, from* The Cricket in Times Square

Chewing on her lip, Hazel unlocked the front door and went back into the house.

> —*Anne Ursu, from* Breadcrumbs

Taking a deep breath, he pulled hard on the iron rod.

> —*Deron Hicks, from* Secrets of Shakespeare's Grave

Inhaling and exhaling into her mouth organ, Ramona closed her eyes and tried to pedal around the coffee table without looking.

—Beverly Cleary, from Beezus and Ramona

Treading very carefully, Mr. Lemoncello walked to the podium.

—Chris Grabenstein, from Escape from Mr. Lemoncello's Library

Rounding a bend, Billy came to a pair of massive wrought-iron gates set between twin columns of stacked stone.

—Chris Grabenstein, from The Island of Dr. Libris

Scrambling up the bank, he plunged through a clump of bushes, skirted a barnyard and picked up a path through the meadows.

—James Ramsey Ullman, from Banner in the Sky

These examples are structured similarly. Each has the first phrase set off with a comma. Most of these examples added only one participle at the beginning of the sentence. Cleary's sentence pairs two participles at the beginning of her phrase. I like to show students how to do both.

When Writers Make This Move

This move helps writers to situate the action (as in the examples from Grabenstein and Ramsey Ullman, above) or to include a minor action that helps the reader to understand the character, situation, or action better (as in the other examples above). The *INGs Up Front* move is also an easy way to vary sentence structures in a text.

How I Introduce This Move

1. I begin by asking students: ***In real life, do we really ever do just one thing? Have you guys only done one thing before? Think about it.***

2. We discuss times when it might have seemed like there was only one thing going on, but in reality lots of actions were happening. ***When you play a sport, what are some of the things you might be doing at the same time? Running? Sweating? Dodging? Scrambling?***

3. I ask about other activities and encourage students to tell me some of the actions that might be happening at the same time, recording these verbs on chart paper (Figure 3.8).

4. I ask students, **So if we don't do only one thing at a time in real life, why do we write about characters that only do one thing at a time? Rich writing captures more than just singular, flat movements. If we want our writing to come alive, we have to think about how real things happen.**

5. Then, I follow with, **What am I doing?** I call on different students for their ideas and write them on the board: talking, explaining, walking, pacing, looking, writing, and so on. As I read over the list, I tell the class, **I have a lot of action going on for someone who is just talking to you guys.**

Figure 3.8 Our chart served as a resource to help students think of the multiple verbs that can occur simultaneously.

6. Then, I explain that I want to share an easy way to write about some of the different things that I am doing, without just listing a bunch of verbs separated by commas. I really build this up as a move that can take their writing and make it more sophisticated and richer.

7. I write several sentences using some of the verbs that the students just named:

> Pacing back and forth, Dr. Linder explained a new writing move.
>
> Talking quite loudly, Dr. Linder wrote on the chart.
>
> Writing on the board, Dr. Linder modeled a new strategy.
>
> Looking at her students, Dr. Linder talked about the day's lesson.

8. **Do you notice a pattern? Can you see what I am doing? Can anyone tell me what these sentences all have in common?** I call on students for ideas and add more sentences if I need to. I keep prompting until someone mentions

the *-ing* words being added at the beginning. I stop and immediately tell them that they guessed it. ***I am adding -ing words to describe my actions, followed by a comma.***

9. I end by restating the power of this move. ***In your writing, think about your verbs and actions. Then, consider what else this character is actually doing. In real life, what else would really be going on? This helps you sequence your events in a more multidimensional way.***

Guided Writing Practice Ideas

- Pass out slips of paper with different activities written on them: ballet, choir practice, bike riding, wrestling, eating, and so on. Have students craft an *INGs Up Front* sentence about a character doing that activity. Prompt students to think about real life. ***What would a real person be doing? Capture that in your sentence.*** Share the sentences, talk about how they came up with the ideas, then have students swap slips and try again with a different activity. Repeat as many times as possible (see Figure 3.9).

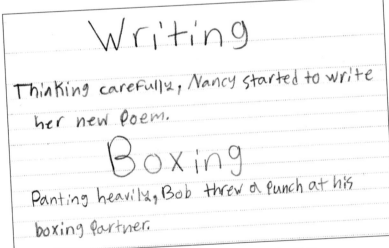

Figure 3.9 Sydney tried out this move with boxing and writing.

- I share the examples from the What Does This Move Look Like in Writing? section. We name the past and present verb in each one and talk about how this move helps us imagine the scene better. Then, I have the students revise each of the mentor examples to create a different scene. This is powerful because students get to explore the different patterns that these examples follow and play around a bit with the sentence structure, while still thinking about how to change it.

- Label different parts of your room with signs that have the names of different fictitious characters on them or even pictures of different characters. Consider superheroes, book and television characters, even yourself (if you are feeling brave). When students come in, assign or let them choose a name to sit near. This becomes their group. I like to keep my group sizes to four or five. Ask each group to write *INGs Up Front* sentences to tell about the character's day. Instruct students to work with their group to come up with the most creative sentence that they can. Tell students that they only have two minutes to do this. Set a timer and walk around listening to their discussions. Working as a group is a great way to get students to verbalize how to structure and use this move. This lets them verbalize the same thinking process that later they will have to do on their own. It also lets you hear any misunderstandings. When the timer goes off, listen to each sentence and discuss if it is structured correctly. Then, have students switch areas and try again with a different character.

- Pair students with a partner. Ask students to select a piece of their own writing that they feel could be improved. Then, have students swap papers. Challenge the students to revise at least two of their partner's sentences using the *INGs Up Front* move. Students should write their revisions on sticky notes, not directly on the other student's work. Have students talk about the two revised sentences and decide if the revision helps the writing or not. Invite volunteers to share some of the revisions with the whole group.

Move 7

EDs *Up Front*

*e*Ds Up Front are similar to *INGs Up Front*. Technically, the *EDs Up Front* move is simply the addition of a past participle that describes the subject at the beginning of a sentence. For students to use this in their writing, I explain that the *EDs Up Front* move is a simple way to share the feelings of the character before telling what sequence of events or actions that the character takes.

What Does This Move Look Like in Writing?

Humiliated, Ida shrank down.

—Avi, *from* The Secret School

Embarrassed, I slide my drawings underneath my blank writing assignment.

—Lynda Mullaly Hunt, *from* Fish in a Tree

Startled, he looked and saw a man climb up the bleachers and sit beside him.

—Matt Christopher, *from* The Kid Who Only Hit Homers

Refreshed, he ran without stopping to the large front entryway.

—Wendy Mass, *from* The Candymakers

Inspired by his fun, I poked my head into my tree and whistled.

—Jean Craighead George, *from* My Side of the Mountain

Each author uses a word that ends with -ed to show how a character feels before showing their action. Notice that the structures are very simple. The author begins with an emotion stated with an -ed verb, inserts a comma, then adds the sentence that shows the action. Craighead George goes a step further. Although the move is still *EDs Up Front*, she specifies what caused the emotion. Instead of simply being inspired, the character was "inspired by his fun." Each of these authors could have extended their words as well, but it is not necessary to do so. The beauty of this move is that it is short and sweet. Students get to reveal information about a character and vary their sentence structure simply by adding a single word. Many students equate more words with better writing. This move helps students to see that is simply not true: a well-chosen word can be more powerful than a clunky, forced, or redundant statement.

When Writers Make This Move

This subtle placement of the feeling up front lets the readers grab onto the emotion and anticipate the next event. It gives the reader a feeling of wonder. When you read the first word and learn that a character is embarrassed, you wonder how he or she will handle it. When you see that someone is startled, you want to know why; what happened? This offers a much higher level of engagement than placing the emotion at the end, where readers have already read about the action. No anticipation there. Imagine if Jean Craighead George has written "I poked my head into my tree and whistled because I was inspired by the fun." It doesn't have the same ring to it, does it? Something about the feeling being first keeps the sentence fresh and interesting.

How I Introduce This Move

1. I write several past-tense emotions, followed by a comma on the board.

2. Then, I ask students if they know why someone would feel that way. I call on students for suggestions. Then, I point out that the word all by itself makes us kind of curious. I explain, **Writers want readers to be interested and curious about what is going to happen next. Writers want readers engaged with their text. They don't want bored readers. One of the ways that they engage readers is to put the emotions up front. Instead of structuring a sentence where the emotion is at the end, they move it right up front. They take an emotion, write it in past tense, with an -ed on the end, and just set it right in the front. This gives the reader that emotion, but they have to read on to find out what happens next.**

3. Then, I model this strategy by writing a sentence with the emotion at the end, then revise it by moving the past-tense emotion to the front of the sentence (Figure 3.10).

4. We discuss each of my sentences and how they make us feel. Then, I name this move as *EDs Up Front*.

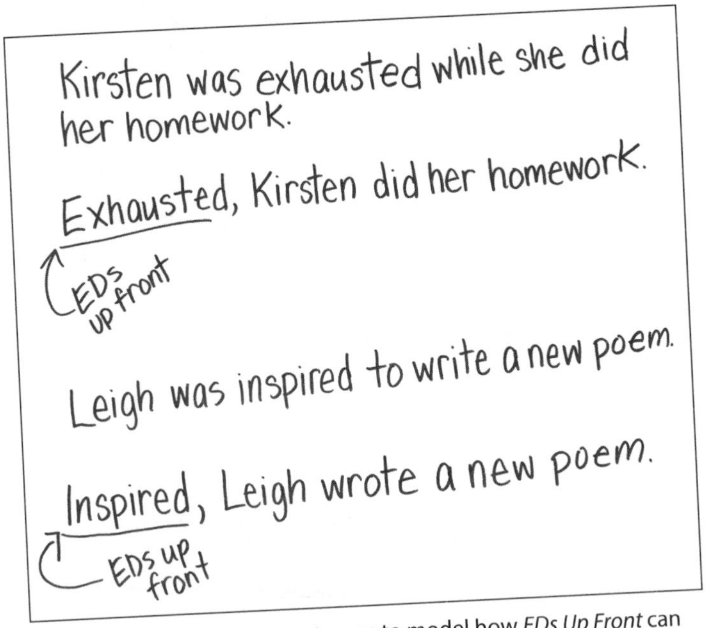

Kirsten was exhausted while she did her homework.

Exhausted, Kirsten did her homework.
EDs up front

Leigh was inspired to write a new poem.

Inspired, Leigh wrote a new poem.
EDs up front

Figure 3.10 I revised two sentences to model how *EDs Up Front* can help sentences to flow better.

Guided Writing Practice Ideas

- Generate an anchor chart of different *EDs Up Front* words. This is invaluable for students and will give them a word bank to refer to and help them to generate other ideas. After the list is created, invite students to revisit earlier writing and find a couple of sentences where they can make this move and put the emotion up front for readers. Keep the list visible throughout the year. I like to encourage students to share examples from books that they read throughout the year. I am always surprised how many times a student will find this move in books that they are reading and ask to add it to the chart (Figure 3.11).

- Photocopy four comic strips onto one piece of paper and pass out one to each student. I visit www.gocomics.com to access a wide variety of free comic strips. Challenge students to recaption each box of the comic using this move. Although the move is not necessary for each box, it not only gives students practice making this move, but requires them to think deeply about different emotions and which words to use. This practice will help make the process of attaching emotions to actions much easier when they work independently on their own writing. Afterward, read one comic strip at a time and call on volunteers to share their different versions.

- This move works well with spooky or mysterious writing where characters are unsure of something or have to explore unknown terrain. Write mysterious locations on one side of the board and a list of different characters on

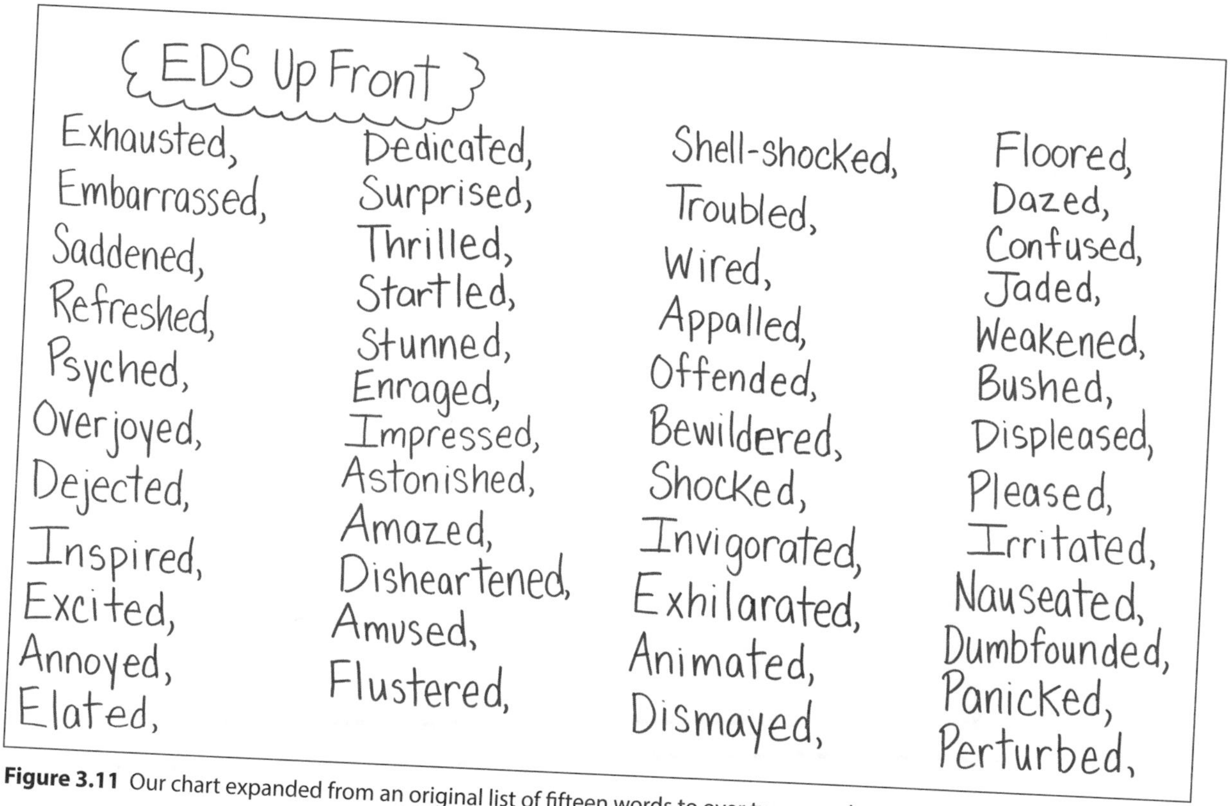

Figure 3.11 Our chart expanded from an original list of fifteen words to over two complete charts.

the other side of the board. Ask students to choose one from each side and write a short paragraph telling about what happened when that character went to the location that they selected. Ask students to write asterisks next to any *EDs Up Front* sentences that they use. Share the stories and discuss how this move worked in their stories.

- Write one of the mentor examples from the What Does This Move Look Like in Writing? section on the board. When you write the sentence, leave off the beginning, the words before the comma. Ask students to read each sentence and share what they know about the character. Ask, ***Why do you think they are doing these things? How do you think they feel?*** Invite students to revise the sentence by adding an emotion up front. Call on volunteers to share how they revised the sentence. Then, reveal the author's original beginning to the sentence. Discuss how differently everyone positioned the character. Lead students to the idea that this one tiny move can control how the writer thinks about what it happening. You want students to see that this move, although simple, can color their writing in very different ways. Repeat this activity with one or two more examples. You may want to have these physical books on hand in your classroom. I find that these single sentences tend to pique students' curiosity and they will ask to read the book that the sentences came from.

Explain THAT Sound

*t*his is when an author describes the sound words to let the readers hear the movement, but also goes ahead and explicitly names the movement for the readers. This move came from teaching my students how to use onomatopoeia. After a great lesson, I started seeing it in their writing, in place of telling me what sound I was hearing. This resulted in a lot of *BOOM!* and *BAM!* throughout their papers, but at times I wasn't sure what had happened. So, of course, I started digging through real novels. Just as I suspected, real writers rarely just show a sound. When they use onomatopoeia, they almost always skillfully explain what caused the sound. This caused me to go back and teach my students that we don't just show a sound, we have to explain the sound as well.

What Does This Move Look Like in Writing?

Ba-room, ba-room, ba-room, baripity, baripity, baripity, baripity—*Good. His dad had the pickup going.*
    —Katherine Paterson, *from* Bridge to Terabithia

My serve is what is called an epic fail, and some of the girls start doing the slow clap.
Clap.
Pause.
Clap.
Pause.
Clap.
It's sarcastic clapping.
    —Rebecca Stead, *from* Liar & Spy

His other leg was a scratched-up chunk of wood from the knee down and it made a solid thunk *with each step.* Thunk. Creak. Thunk. Creak. Thunk.

—*Liesl Shurtliff, from* Jack: The True Story of Jack and the Beanstalk

Vroom vroom. Bang! Crash! *The sports car hit the sedan and rolled over off the highway stripe.* Pb-pb-b-b-b. *The motorcycle came roaring to the scene of the crash.*

—*Beverly Cleary, from* The Mouse and the Motorcycle

Cleary and Paterson both use onomatopoeia to show readers the sound. Then, they add a second sentence to explain what the sound was. Stead and Shurtliff make this move, but reverse the order. For example, Shurtliff explains, in detail what caused the sound—the wooden leg, taking steps. Then, she used onomatopoeia to show the readers what the action sounded like. Either method works for this move. I encourage students to try both for the sake of variety.

When Writers Make This Move

This move is associated with action and sequence, because typically the noise is caused by an action or precedes an action. The idea is that the action is easier to picture in the reader's mind and it seems more real. It can be overused and should never replace the act of describing or telling about an action. This move is used in narratives, memoirs, and even some informational texts—any type of writing where an author describes an event.

How I Introduce This Move

1. I ask students to close their eyes and imagine that they are at a concert, football game, or a school assembly. I call on a few students to share the location that they are imagining.

2. Next, I ask students to think about the sounds that are around them. Do they hear applause? Are people talking? What other sounds are around?

3. We open our eyes and discuss the types of sounds that they name. As we discuss, I write the sounds on the board or on chart paper. Typical things like *Swish! Slosh! Whoosh! Pow! Bam!* are listed.

4. After we have several sounds listed, I point out that these sounds alone don't tell the reader what caused the sound. Although we have done a great job naming the sound, we have not told the reader what the sound is. We have shown something, but not told about it.

5. I explain that a common move that writers make is to *Explain That Sound*. I tell them, ***You show the sound, like we have done here, but then you tell the reader what that sound is.***

6. Next, I ask students to select one of the sounds that we wrote down and tell what action could have caused the sound. I record their ideas on the chart and we talk about each one. I focus on how showing and telling helped to paint a picture in my mind, but that the power of telling helped to clarify that picture.

Guided Writing Practice Ideas

- Gather students and brainstorm different sounds that they have heard. Generate an anchor chart list of the different sound words. This is also a good time to introduce the term *onomatopoeia*. After creating the chart, challenge students to select three words and use the *Explain That Sound* move to explain what that sound word could be. Have students share their sentences in small groups.

- Ask students to revisit their own writing. Ask students to find sections that might benefit from the addition of this move. When students find an area that could use an *Explain That Sound* move, ask them to add it and share why they think the move works (Figure 3.12).

- Tell students that you are going to play a song and you want them to write what they imagine is happening when the song is played. What do they visualize? Typically, I play a clip of the song "The Sorcerer's Apprentice" from *Fantasia*. A quick online search will result in a video clip from the movie. I only let students hear the music, not see the images associated with the song. While they listen, ask them to create several *Explain That Sound* sentences to explain what they imagined. Share and discuss the ideas. You will be amazed by the creative responses that students will come up with. After your discussion, replay the same music clip, but this time let students see the actions that match the sounds. Point out how different these actions are from some of the things that they wrote. I like to do this to help students see that a sound is not always interpreted in the same way by listeners. This is the same with using sound words on paper. The sound, without the explanation, can be confusing or communicate a different meaning. Pairing the explanation with the sound makes the writing clearer.

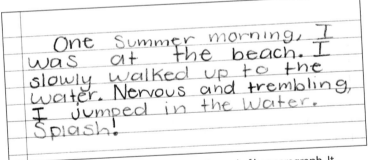

One summer morning, I was at the beach. I slowly walked up to the water. Nervous and trembling, I jumped in the water. Splash!

Figure 3.12 Jessica added this move to the end of her paragraph. It worked to paint a picture of her jumping into the water as opposed to just explaining the action.

- Ask students to search through novels in the classroom. Ask them to locate different sentences where the authors name a sound or action. Then, have students revise the sentences using the *Explain That Sound* move.

- Show students a few minutes of a silent movie. Good choices are Rupert Julian's *The Phantom of the Opera* (somewhat scary) or Charlie Chaplin slapstick classics like *The Kid*, *The Circus*, or *City Lights*. Then, ask students to retell the scene using the *Explain That Sound* move. Invite students to share their sentences and explain the choices they made. Point out how they brought the sounds alive by combining both showing and telling.

4

Details
THAT
Convince

Opinions, Persuasion, and Arguments

*t*o begin a chapter on opinion, persuasion, and arguments, let's start with one of the richest sources for models of this kind of writing: presidential speeches.

> *Ask not what your country can do for you.*
> *I am not a crook.*
> *The only thing we have to fear is fear itself.*
> *Read my lips: no new taxes.*

These are all lines spoken by former presidents: Kennedy, Nixon, Roosevelt, and G. H. Bush, respectively. Each spoke these words in an attempt to convince the world of their own stances and beliefs. They all crafted words that either shouted their opinions loudly or quietly whispered about the possibility of an idea or new direction.

When someone wants to convince readers of a viewpoint, regardless of the merit of the ideas, they rely on *Details That Convince*. Speeches, political slogans, advertisements, and op-eds are filled with these types of details. Convincing details are the building blocks of argumentative writing.

When Do Writers Make These Moves?

Writers rely on *Details That Convince* not only to communicate their own ideas, beliefs, or opinions but also to try to sway readers to their way of thinking. This type of detail shows up most often in informational text, argument essays, and persuasive writing. Authentic formats for this type of writing include newspaper and magazine articles, white papers, and online news sources. In English classes, the argument essay is often a familiar requirement.

This move also shows up in some stories, especially those with untrustworthy narrators. A few fun picture book examples include *Believe Me, Goldilocks Rocks!*; *The True Story of the Three Little Pigs*; and *Seriously, Cinderella Is So Annoying*. Each of these books features narrators who are telling a familiar story, but from a different viewpoint. They rely on using details that try to convince readers to trust them. As students think about how and when to use this type of detail in their writing, they may consider the following questions:

- What do I want to convince my reader of?
- Might my reader have any reservations about adopting my point of view? If so, how can I eliminate or overcome their reservations?
- If I can prove that my ideas are popular or supported by lots of others, would that help to convince my reader?
- Would it help my argument to present (and disprove) counterarguments?
- Would it help to convince my reader if I evoke emotion?
- Am I more likely to convince *this* reader of *this* viewpoint by shouting or by whispering?

Modeling These Moves

I introduce *Details That Convince* by writing several topics on large sticky notes and placing them around the room or on the board, depending on how much space I have (Figure 4.1). Some of the topics I include are extended curfew, mandatory summer school, shorter school hours, lowering the voting age, and English course requirements. For younger students, topics can be expanded to include cafeteria rules, shorter recess, or playground renovation, and so on. I ask students to stand by the topic that they have a strong opinion about or actually take the sticky note down that they are interested in. Typically, I like for only two students to share a topic. If there are an odd number of students, I join in and partner with a student.

Figure 4.1 Our wall of topics included a wide variety of both serious and lighthearted topics.

After students are paired up, they remove their topics from the wall and choose a space to sit together in the class. After everyone is settled, I explain that students will work together to write one sentence in support of the topic and one sentence that is against the topic. Then, once students have written their sentences, I invite them to share their writing. This sharing time often offers a great opportunity to ask students what it was like for them to write sentences that they disagreed with. Discuss how the moves for argument, persuasion, and opinion are tools that can be applied whether or not the viewpoint is merited, and even whether or not the writer agrees with the viewpoint.

Finally, I start a discussion asking students which of their sentences they actually agree with. As I call on students to read the sentences that match their own viewpoints, I encourage students to begin justifying their thinking by asking questions like: **Why? What makes you think that? That's interesting; how did you decide that?**

I continue this type of questioning, often shifting into responses that are more oppositional: **I don't know about that. Are you sure you agree with that statement? How would that possibly work?** Students immediately began to defend their stances and often chime in to support or disprove one another. Without explaining why, I encourage the discussion among the students. After we have heard from most students, I call the class back together and ask students how they would describe our activity. **What did we really do just now?**

As students respond, I write their responses on the board. Common responses: "We argued." "We disagreed." "We explained." "We told you a lot of different facts and reasons." Finally, I write on the board *Details That Convince*. I explain that students all shared different details to support the opinions and arguments that they wrote down. **Watch how I do the same thing with some of your opinion sentences.** I ask for a student to volunteer one of their sentences. I copy it onto the board and underline it. Then, I think out loud by overexaggerating my thinking, saying things like: **I wonder if I could convince someone if I had important facts about this? What about pointing out mistakes in the other side of this argument—the counterclaim? Maybe I could evoke the reader's emotion here.** After naming general possibilities, I write a sentence after the underlined sentence—one that applies one or more of the moves in this chapter—and ask students if the sentence's effect on them, the readers, had changed.

Finally, I explain that we will be spending some time studying *Details That Convince*. I frame these types of details as the support for different ideas and beliefs. These are ways that writers can argue for a stance or even try to win over a reader. These details build up an idea in the same way that bricks build up a home. Afterward, I go ahead and name several of the details that we will learn over the next few days or weeks and post these on a chart (Figure 4.2). Later, as we move on to introduce each type of detail, we refer back to this original anchor chart.

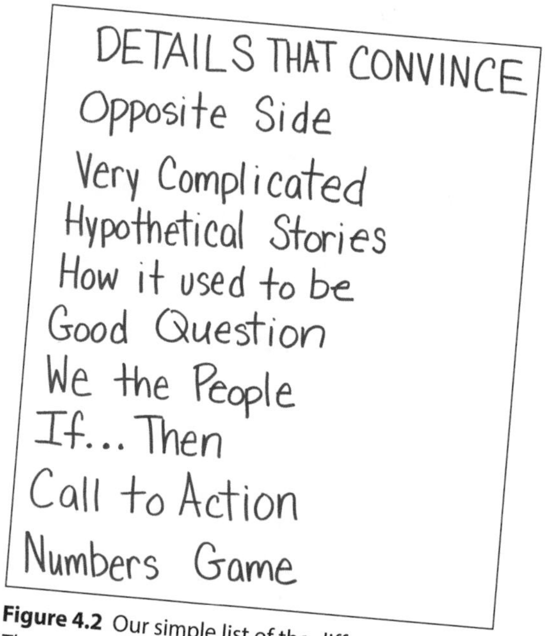

DETAILS THAT CONVINCE
Opposite Side
Very Complicated
Hypothetical Stories
How it used to be
Good Question
We the People
If... Then
Call to Action
Numbers Game

Figure 4.2 Our simple list of the different *Details That Convince* moves piqued the curiosity of the students and many wanted to learn more about the different moves in advance.

Details That Convince: The Writing Moves

Each of the *Details That Convince* moves in this chapter is listed here. When you read students' writing and notice different things that you would like for them to elaborate on or revise, this chart provides direction to help move students to consider different possibilities.

Details That Convince

If you see this in the student's writing . . .	Try this . . .
Limited context or background	*Opposite Side* (page 107) *Imagine This* (page 116) *Very Complicated* (page 120) *Now and Then* (page 126)
Counterarguments ignored	*Opposite Side* (page 107)
Hard to identify topic/ focus	*Good Question* (page 112) *Very Complicated* (page 120)
Dry or bland writing that feels like a list	*If . . . Then* (page 102) *Good Question* (page 112) *Imagine This* (page 116) *We the People* (page 129) *Call to Action* (page 133)
Weak conclusion	*If . . . Then* (page 102) *Good Question* (page 112) *Call to Action* (page 133)
Weak or limited support for ideas or points	*Opposite Side* (page 107) *Numbers Game* (page 123) *Now and Then* (page 126)
Formulaic writing with typical claim, followed by three supporting details	*If . . . Then* (page 102) *Opposite Side* (page 107) *Good Question* (page 112) *Imagine This* (page 116)

This chart is a tool to help students think about different ways to add more *Details That Convince* to their writing. Based on student goals, this chart can direct students to some possibilities. This list is not all-inclusive, and moves can be used to meet lots of different writing goals. This chart just offers a beginning set of possibilities.

Details That Convince

If you want to . . .		Try this . . .
Provide some background to get your reader ready for your opinion or argument	⟩	*Opposite Side* *Very Complicated* *Imagine This* *Now and Then*
My writing just lists and tells. I want to describe more.	⟩	*Opposite Side*
Show what the other side of the argument/opinion is	⟩	*Good Question* *Very Complicated*
Show your voice and connect with readers	⟩	*If . . . Then* *Good Question* *We the People* *Call to Action* *Imagine This*
Wrap up your ending	⟩	*Call to Action* *If . . . Then* *Good Question*
Help readers really understand what you mean after you write your main points	⟩	*Numbers Game* *Opposite Side* *Now and Then*
Show your voice and make the text feel more interesting	⟩	*If . . . Then* *Opposite Side* *Good Question* *Imagine This*

Move 1

If...Then

*i*f...*Then* sentences suggest a relationship between two events, ideas, or concepts. Although using the if–then structure implies that there is a cause-and-effect relationship, the *If...Then* move may be a little slipperier than that, as the examples below show.

What Does This Move Look Like in Writing?

> *I am here to say that if you like to do artistic things, or anything that's "different," then you should do what makes you feel good.*
>
> > —Michelle Roehm and Marianne Monson-Burton, from Boys Know It All: Wise Thoughts and Wacky Ideas from Guys Just Like You

> *If you love chocolate, then you should celebrate every September 13.*
>
> > —James Buckley, from Who Was Milton Hershey?

> *If you're like most guys, you actually do like to write, even if you don't advertise this fact.*
>
> > —Ralph Fletcher, from Guy-Write: What Every Guy Writer Needs to Know

In each example above, the author has used the *If...Then* move to make it seem as though anyone who agrees with or identifies with the first statement must then, logically, agree with the assertion that follows. In the examples above, the *if* part of the move reaches out to readers who see themselves as "artistic" or "different," who enjoy chocolate, or who consider themselves to be "like most guys." These descriptions are broad: a large number of readers are likely to see themselves in these descriptions. Next, the authors use the *then* part of the move to link their assertion to the readers' views of themselves. For example, Fletcher seems to be saying that if you really are "like most guys," you like to write (even though he doesn't use the word *then* in his sentence). A skeptical reader might counter each of these statements, replying to Roehm and Monson-Burton that being artistic or different shouldn't affect whether people should do what makes them feel good; shaking a head a Buckley's comment that chocolate lovers are obligated to celebrate the birthday of Milton Hershey; and questioning Fletcher's assertion that "most guys" like to write. However, the *If… Then* move is only about logic on the surface—it does not require an airtight argument.

When Writers Make This Move

Although this move can be used in narrative writing, it's most common in arguments and informational texts. Writers use this move to help lead readers from an idea they can likely get onboard with to an assertion that may be new to them or that they may not already believe or agree with.

How I Introduce This Move

1. I write two sentences on the board.

   > Vote for me for student government president.

   > I will make sure that vending machines are installed in the cafeteria.

2. Then, I ask students if these sentences are connected. Do they have a relationship?

3. We have a brief discussion about this apparent campaign promise.

4. I explain that the author of these two sentences is attempting to convince readers by making an *If… Then* move. The author wants readers to see a connection between voting for her and getting vending machines.

5. Next, I revise the sentences to read:

   > *If* you vote for me for student government president, *then* I will make sure that vending machines are installed in the cafeteria.

6. I draw attention to the comma in front of the word *then* and discuss how I have connected the two ideas for readers into one sentence. I make sure to mention that there is no proof that *If… Then* sentences are true. The person crafting the sentence wants to get into the reader's head and have him

start to think that these two things go together, whether they really do or not, is not the author's aim. I want students to see that this is about convincing the reader that these things are related.

7. I continue with a new sentence, revising it in the same manner.

8. Next, I ask students to help me create new *If . . . Then* sentences. Sometimes I use chart paper to record the students' *If . . . Then* sentences. Other times, I like to use an interactive whiteboard to type these up as students share them (Figure 4.3). This allows me to save them, print them, and easily pull them up later for a reference.

If _____, then

- If kids keep getting long homework assignments, then they will start to feel overwhelmed.
- If global warming continues, then our planet could be destroyed.
- If you never study, then you will definitely get bad grades.
- If we work together, then we could get done much faster.
- If you visit our classroom, then you will see how awesome Mr. Brown really is.
- If you understand multiplication, then learning division is so much easier.

Figure 4.3 We recorded our different *If . . . Then* ideas on the whiteboard screen and printed out some of our sentences as exemplars.

Guided Writing Practice Ideas

- Write the name of two familiar or recently read books on the board or chart. Lead a conversation about each book by inviting students to share memorable scenes, favorite parts, or even criticisms of each book. Then, ask students to consider who else would enjoy these books. Then, craft an *If . . . Then* sentence for each book (Figure 4.4). Point out the similar structure to students, then ask students to write down the names of their favorite television shows, sports team, and book or author and repeat your process. Call on volunteers to share their sentences and tell about which type of audience they are trying to convince.

- Send students to the media center or your classroom library. Encourage them to look for books that they have read before and loved. When they find a favorite, ask them to think about what type of audience they think the book would be great for. Have students use the *If . . . Then* move to craft a sentence that convinces the audience to read the book. Turn the *If . . .*

Then sentences into a book recommendation wall by adding the sticky notes to a door, wall, or cabinet surrounded by a label that says "Our Book Recommendations." (See Figure 4.5.)

- Select debate topics and ask students to choose sides. Group students with their respective sides and have students try to convince you to agree with their side. The only caveat? Their entire argument can only be made up of *If… Then* sentences. When they finish sharing their ideas, talk about how this move is convincing, but obviously cannot be your only type or detail. Lead students to the notion that using this move *too* much starts to feel disingenuous and empty. This will help students to avoid heavy-handed use of this move when they craft their own arguments.

Figure 4.4 After briefly discussing the last two class novels, *Inside Out and Back Again* and *The Crossover*, a sixth-grade class crafted three *If… Then* sentences for each novel.

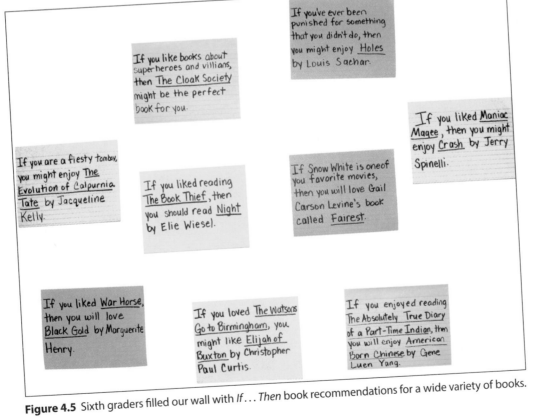

Figure 4.5 Sixth graders filled our wall with *If… Then* book recommendations for a wide variety of books.

REAL LIFE   IF... THEN MOVES

If you don't pay attention to where you are going, then you will eventually crash into something.

If you drink too fast, then you may start to cough or even spit out the water.

If you overfill sandwich bags with too much stuff, then they will most like break.

If you rush through your writing, then it will be sloppy and difficult to read.

If you always talk loudly on your cell phone, then you will annoy the people around you!

Figure 4.6 Our chart captured the student examples and generated lots of discussion about the power of *If... Then* sentences, but it also reinforced the idea that these sentences aren't based on fact, they are simply predictions and inferences, but they seem to lead the reader to the notion that they should accept the relationships as valid and factual.

- Walk around the room pretending to talk on your cell phone and accidently bump into chairs, tables, file cabinets, and so on. Invite students to craft sentences, using the *If... Then* move to explain what they saw. Share the sentences in small groups or with the whole class. Repeat by acting out multiple scenarios. Fun scenes to act out: take a big sip of water and immediately start to cough uncontrollably and tap your neck or chest; fill a snack-size plastic bag with lots of objects, until it breaks and the objects fall out; or write a very sloppy, almost illegible sentence on the board very quickly. After each scene, invite students to suggest *If... Then* sentences to explain what they saw. Record these on a large anchor chart to reference later (Figure 4.6).

Opposite *Side*

*t*he *Opposite Side* move is when the author acknowledges or states a counterclaim. This could be a broad opposing argument or lots of small, individual counterarguments throughout a larger piece. The move is not focused on developing the counterclaim; it simply recognizes that there is another point of view. Authors often immediately refute the claim in the same sentence or in the subsequent sentences.

What Does This Move Look Like in Writing?

Some people think that recycling is the answer and devote all their energy to that. Of course recycling is important, but there are better ways.

—John Coad, from Reducing Pollution

They say I'm too young. I'm not too young. I'm actually very mature for my age.

—Judith Viorst, from Earrings!

Some evidence suggests that BMI testing in school is not useful.

—Toney Allman, from Food in Schools

Notice that each of these examples uses very general terms for the counterclaim. "They say . . ." "Some say . . ." "Some evidence . . ." This is a common way of acknowledging other views without naming a direct name, organization, or group that advocates for the viewpoint. Even when Allman names a group (math experts), it's broad, and he still avoids specificity. This move allows the opposite side to remain faceless. It focuses the attention on the content and the sides, not the validity or strength of who is saying it. Coad and Viorst both state the opposite side and immediately refute it without much discussion. When making this move, students can consider both options. They can state the counterclaim and immediately respond with their own claims, or they can simply state the counterclaim and build up to their own claim later in the piece. They don't have to pair the two together as subsequent sentences.

When Writers Make This Move

Writers make this move in argument writing. Often this comes early in the piece and serves as a way to acknowledge that there are multiple viewpoints. Some writers go further and develop the counterargument, debunking each counterpoint, one by one.

How I Introduce This Move

1. I begin by asking students to make a judgment about a trivial but high-interest topic, something like, "Which is better: 3-D or 2-D movies?" Of course, you can use any two ideas, people, places, or activities that you want.

2. Then, I ask the students who claim that 3-D movies are better to stand on one side of the room, while 2-D stands on the other, making sure they take their pens and pencils with them.

3. Next, I ask students to write down their opinion (in one sentence) on a piece of paper. Students are simply writing that they prefer one type of movie over the other. Some may get into specific reasons or start to support their opinion, but they don't have to for this activity. Stating a basic opinion works fine.

4. Then, in rapid-fire succession, I call on students to read their sentences. After I hear from one side, I call on students on the other side.

5. Then, I stand in the middle and explain that these sides are opposites. *What do opposites have to do with writing?* I invite students to share their responses.

6. At this point, I explain that when we write *Details That Convince*, we often acknowledge the opposite side. *Your two sides are opposites. To make an Opposite Side move, all you have to do is say what the other side thinks. What would they say?*

7. Then I ask students to leave their papers with their sentences on their side of the room and switch sides. When they get to the other side, pick up one of the claims that the opposite side wrote down. Be patient here, it will get a little busy and noisy—but it's worth the student engagement.

8. When students pick up a new paper, ask them to read it silently first. Then, tell students to turn those sentences into *Opposite Side* sentences by adding one of these beginnings. Remember that these are guiding suggestions. You or your students may have additional ideas and variations that work well here. Grow this list as long and as varied as you choose.

Some people think . . .   Some argue . . . .

There are those   Many people suggest . . .
who believe . . .

It is often believed . . . .   Granted, others may think . . .

9. Quickly, I call on students to come to the front and read the new *Opposite Side* sentences. I write several of these on the board or on chart paper in one color. Then, underneath each one, in a different color, I add the other side (Figure 4.7). I like students to see how they can state opposite sides and pair them together.

10. After everyone is seated, we talk about the sentence starters that I suggested and the students help me add more to the list. We record these as *Opposite Side* sentence starters (Figure 4.8).

Guided Writing Practice Ideas

- Pair students in teams. One team member turns around while the other writes down her opinion about a topic on a small whiteboard, minichalkboard, or simply a sheet of paper. When the opinion has been written, ask the team member to turn around and read the opinion. Then, the other team member

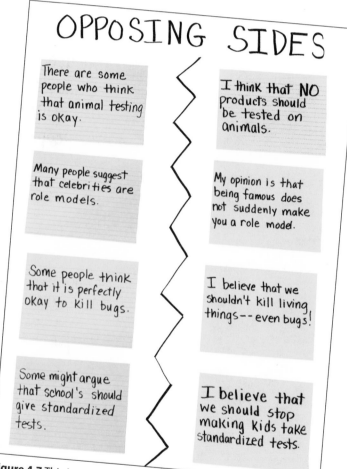

Figure 4.7 Third graders worked to craft sentences that identified two opposite views on a topic. This helped students to see how the sentences are crafted differently and can be paired together in writing, to begin opinion or argument writing.

> **Opposite Side Sentence Starters**
>
> Some people think...
> There are those who claim...
> Many people suggest...
> It is often believed...
> Some argue that...
> A common belief is...
> Some might say...
> One viewpoint is...
> It could be argued that...
> It is often suggested...
> Granted, one argument is...
> There may be some support for the idea...
> On one hand...
> Some people may claim that...

Figure 4.8 Our Opposite Side sentence starter list grew pretty long and was regularly used by students to craft counterarguments in their writing.

turns around and the second student writes an *Opposite Side* sentence to counter the first student's opinion. When students have both sentences, they raise their hand so that you can quickly confer with them about their work. Have pairs repeat, slowly removing the requirement to call you over. Let students check each other and other groups. This practice is critical for younger students who will rarely see counterclaims in their daily lives. This rapid-fire practice helps to build up a set of experiences recognizing and crafting these types of sentences so that they can independently use them with ease.

- Have students revisit arguments that they have written before. Encourage students to read through and mark with a highlighter areas that could benefit from the *Opposite Side* move. Encourage students to share their ideas with a partner, then revise that section or paragraph to include this move.

- Write a debatable topic on the board that might interest your students. Ask students to write a sentence with their own claim or opinion about the topic. Ask students to write an *Opposite Side* sentence first, followed by their opinion. Then, ask students to take the same two sentences and reverse them, putting their own claim or opinion before the *Opposite Side* sentence. Talk about which way flows better. Most will find that it sounds better to have the *Opposite Side* sentence first, followed by the author's own claim or opinion. This flow allows students to focus on developing their argument immediately after the claim and sounds more like a qualified response to the opposite side. Let students experiment with the order to see what works best for them.

- Invite students to write short paragraphs to convince you of something (Figure 4.9). Encourage students to try out this move in their writing. I like to allow students to select a topic that matters to them. When students need more guidance, I provide several suggested topics as possibilities, but ultimately leave the choice of topic to the students. Ask volunteers to share their writing. Invite volunteers to share their paragraphs. Discuss if and how this move was used in the paragraphs. If you find a particularly persuasive argument, consider making a change based on what your students have written! Beware: this has led to conducting class outside, homework-free nights, and me learning new dance moves and even wearing a boy band shirt for the day. Wacky but fun and meaningful for students, who get to see their writing translated into action and change.

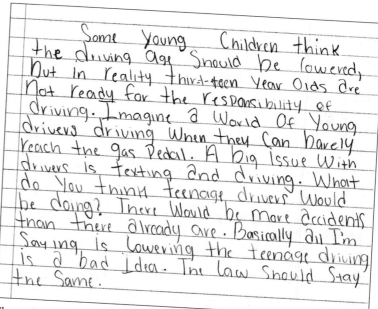

Some young Children think the driving Age Should be lowered, but In reality thirt-teen Year Olds are Not ready for the responsibility of driving. Imagine a World of Young drivers driving When they can barely reach the gas Pedal. A big issue With drivers is texting and driving. What do You think teenage drivers Would be doing? There Would be More accidents than there already are. Basically all I'm Saying is Lowering the teenage driving is a bad Idea. The law Should Stay the Same.

Figure 4.9 Sixth grader Emma wrote her brief paragraph about the driving age being lowered to thirteen. In an earlier discussion, most of her classmates felt that thirteen was a better new driver age. Emma acknowledged this opposing viewpoint with her own sentence starter. She also included other *Details That Convince* in her writing. Notice an *Imagine This* move (see page 116 for this move) and *Good Question* move (see page 112) embedded into her brief paragraph.

Move 3

Good Question

*t*his move is about asking the reader a question. This can mean a series of questions, one lone rhetorical question, or posing a question and answering it as well. Students are often taught to use questions as a hook or beginning to engage readers, but this move is actually a great way to engage readers or add voice *throughout* a text.

What Does This Move Look Like in Writing?

What's the point of studying history? Who cares what happened so long ago? After all, aren't the people in history books dead?

—Joy Hakim, from A History of US

And what is interesting, anyway, about a slim few acres of trees?

—Natalie Babbit, from Tuck Everlasting

What forces drive the ocean currents? What boundaries, if any, guide their path through the ocean? Can understanding ocean currents help us to preserve the marine environment and the creatures that live in it? These are just a few of the questions that occupy the minds of modern-day oceanographers.

—Loree Griffin Burns, from Tracking Trash: Flotsam, Jetsam, and the Science of Ocean Motion

Maybe you've heard the phrase, "Necessity is the mother of invention?" It's true.

—*Catherine Thimmesh, from* Girls Think of Everything: Stories of Ingenious Inventions by Women

When Writers Make This Move

This move can serve many different purposes. One reason that authors make this move is to establish context by introducing questions that may drive the development of the writing. This move is also used to connect with readers by asking a common or universal concern that may connect with the audience. Another purpose is to help authors inject their own style, voice, or point of view. Authors do this by raising a variety of questions that may provoke emotion, interrogate accepted norms, showcase the author's stance, or examine different viewpoints.

How I Introduce This Move

1. I write a list of basic facts about America on the board. I read them out loud.

    The United States is a country of fifty states.

    Sometimes America is called a melting pot.

    America is often considered the land of opportunity.

    English is the most commonly spoken language in America, followed by Spanish.

2. Then, I ask students if they think my writing is interesting. We discuss their opinions and I lead them to the idea that argument and explanatory writing can risk sounding boring or impersonal. It is easy to get stuck in the trap of sounding like a robot or a dictionary.

3. Then, I introduce the *Good Question* move to students by adding a question to my original set of sentences.

4. We discuss how the question changed how the sentences felt. Students often say that they can picture the person or their ideas better or that they already have a clue as to the direction that the rest of the writing is going in. Others will say that they feel like the author is talking directly to them.

5. I continue to revise by changing the question and in some cases answering it. Each time, I change the sentences, we discuss how it changed the feel of the sentences and whether or not we think that the question helps the overall set of sentences (Figure 4.10).

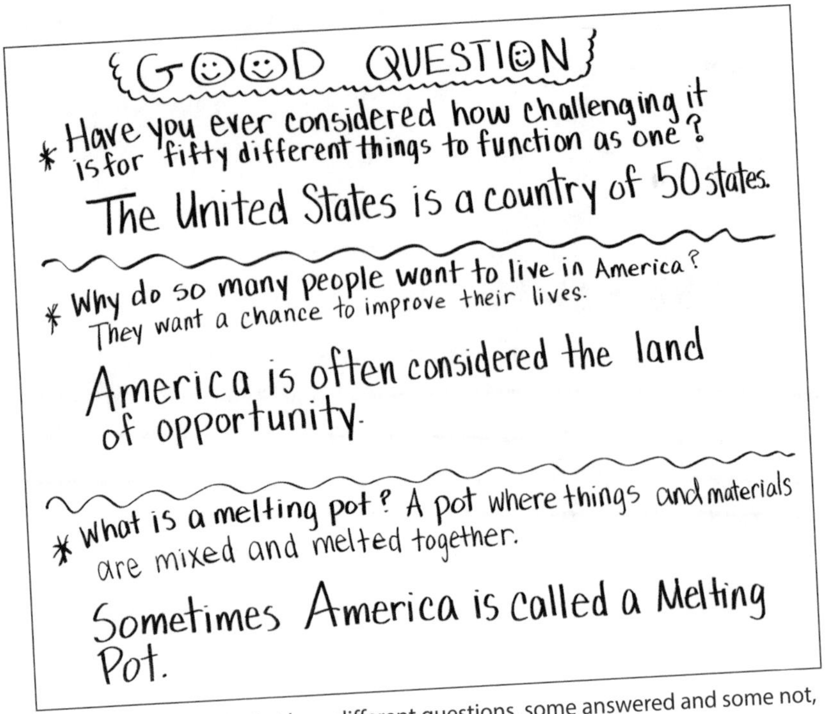

Figure 4.10 We looked at how different questions, some answered and some not, had a different impact on the writing. Students started to notice that this move had the power to shape the tone of the writing.

Guided Writing Practice Ideas

- I ask students to think about how this move can impact readers. Then I ask students to write a question that would make a reader curious about our school. I call on three or four students to share what they wrote and explain why it would make a reader curious. We continue this for a few more rounds, focusing on eliciting other emotions from the reader, such as anger about a decision, gratitude to be a citizen, surprise at the number of people that live on the Earth. Each time, we stop to discuss why students wrote the questions that they did and how effective the questions were in drawing out the emotions the students were aiming for.

- Ask students to select one of their older pieces of writing (drafts or free-writes are fine for this) to revise. Then, challenge them to find places in their own writing that could benefit from *The Good Question* move. Invite students to try two different types of questions. Then, let students share with partners or in a small group to discuss which type of question works best and why.

- Share examples of writing—informational, narrative, or argument—that feels boring or dry. Ask students to independently revise sections of the text using this move. Share the revisions as a whole group to highlight how different this move can look. Discuss the differences and how this move changed the text. This discussion goes a long way to get students talking and thinking about the purpose and intentionality in their writing. We want students to not just memorize a move, but know how and why a move can impact their own writing.

- Ask students to write an opinion paragraph appealing to a specific audience (parents, peers, teachers, school administration, and so on). Typically, I encourage students to choose something that they genuinely want to ask, rather than assigning a topic like uniforms or cell phones in school. Students are much more committed to practicing this move when it is a genuine topic that matters to them. The paragraph needs to include this move and students need to be able to tell you how they used the move. Was it to show their point of view? Was it to question the status quo? Was it to establish the point of the writing? Encourage students to offer feedback and constructive criticism to their peers. (See Figure 4.11.)

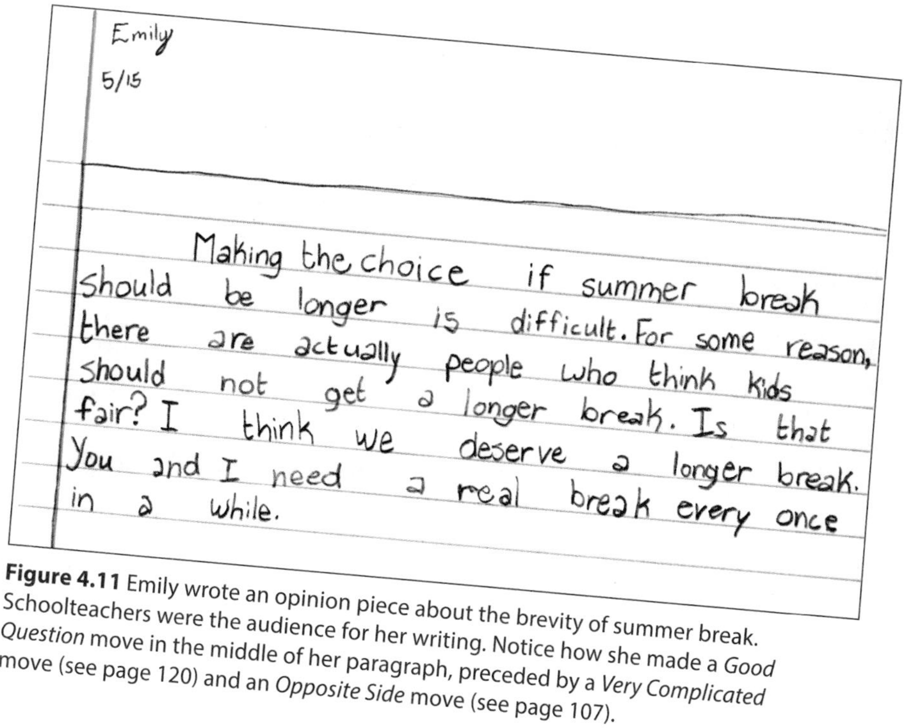

Emily

5/15

Making the choice if summer break should be longer is difficult. For some reason, there are actually people who think kids should not get a longer break. Is that fair? I think we deserve a longer break. You and I need a real break every once in a while.

Figure 4.11 Emily wrote an opinion piece about the brevity of summer break. Schoolteachers were the audience for her writing. Notice how she made a *Good Question* move in the middle of her paragraph, preceded by a *Very Complicated* move (see page 120) and an *Opposite Side* move (see page 107).

Move 4

Imagine *This*

*t*he *Imagine This* move bypasses a formal argument and places the reader directly into a situation that they can nearly feel, playing on readers' emotions more than on their logical thoughts. It is the description of a hypothetical situation to complement an argument, to show the ridiculousness of a counterargument, or simply to get readers to envision an unfamiliar or unlikely situation.

What Does This Move Look Like in Writing?

Picture this: It's late at night. You're asleep in bed, with lots of blankets covering you. Suddenly, you wake up all hot and sweaty, so you kick off the covers.

—Laurie David and Cambria Gordon, from The Down-to-Earth Guide to Global Warming

Imagine yourself slurping a soup full of tadpoles or finding a stuffed frog nestled in your rice.

—James Solheim, from It's Disgusting and We Ate It! True Food Facts from Around the World and Throughout History

It is 2025. A catastrophic accident occurred when some toxic waste in India exploded. It was one of the worst environmental disasters in history, with consequences that no one can predict. Thousands of people have been

killed or seriously injured, and the death toll is likely to rise dramatically over the next few years. The accident polluted many of the country's rivers, and drinking water is now running low.

—Christiane Dorion, *from* Earth's Garbage Crisis

Imagine you're living in Percy's world: Does that donut store on the corner make a shiver run down your spine? Does the popularity of a certain coffee chain have anything to do with the mermaid on the logo? And what about the homeless man under the bridge near your apartment: Does no one think it strange that he wears a muffler and trench coat all year-round? Or maybe you live in the country, and suddenly a lot of cattle are mysteriously disappearing.

—Rosemary Clement-Moore, *from* Demigods and Monsters: Your Favorite Authors on Rick Riordan's Percy Jackson and the Olympians Series

Imagine. You are a paratrooper suiting up for a jump. Guys on either side of you are doing the same. One jokes about having a dream that the chutes didn't open. Another one says he's glad everyone paid their insurance.

—Tanya Lee Stone, *from* Courage Has No Color, The True Story of the Triple Nickles: America's First Black Paratroopers

Each of these examples shows how authors use the *Imagine This* move to help readers quickly feel that they are *in* a new place or situation. David and Gordon, Solheim, and Stone all rely on strong sensory details. Dorion and Clement-Moore give rapid-fire, emotionally charged descriptions of very specific details in the new worlds they're creating. Although *Imagine That* details support arguments rather than explain them fully, it's easy to tell from these brief examples that Dorion believes that we need to take steps to avert a global garbage crisis and that Solheim does not find tadpoles or frogs to be foods.

When Writers Make This Move

This move helps writers to manipulate a reader's emotions rather than appeal to a reader's sense of reason. It is most frequently used in argument writing. Although appreciated in elementary and middle school argument papers, this move is used on a much more limited basis in high school and collegiate writing where facts and numbers tend to dominate the text. Ironically, in real-world arguments (editorials, news commentary, and debates) this move appears quite frequently.

How I Introduce This Move

1. I ask students to close their eyes. Then I share a writing excerpt that includes a hypothetical story. The examples in the What Does This Move Look Like in Writing? section work well for this. After I share the example, I ask students to open their eyes and draw what they pictured while I read.

2. We discuss the similarities and differences among the illustrations. I deliberately make sure that I repeat phrases like *you imagined*, *visualized*, *painted a picture*, and *in your mind's eye you saw*. I want to cement the idea that this move is all about creating a world or a scene in the reader's head to stimulate and play off of the reader's senses and emotions.

3. We repeat this activity with at least two other excerpts.

4. Afterward, I name this move and tell students that this helps readers to imagine something. This move works to connect readers to the argument emotionally. At times, this could be something horrible, unexpected, shocking, or just really good. The purpose is to get readers to be able to draw our words in their minds, just like we did in class.

Guided Writing Practice Ideas

- Share a set of hypothetical global, local, or schoolwide changes, such as an end to school rules, the institution of a three-day school week, an end to world hunger, or world peace. Invite students to illustrate what one of the changes would look like (Figure 4.12). Then, ask students to caption their images by writing *Imagine This* sentences. I like to write the *Imagine This* move on sticky notes and post these captioned drawings around the room as exemplars.

- Select a text that makes an argument. Ask students to read the text, then use the *Imagine This* move to craft a rebuttal statement. Invite volunteers to share and explain their responses.

- Select a topic and craft a hypothetical situation for both sides of the topic. Share your sentences and discuss. Ask students to use this move to write a hypothetical situation for two sides of a topic. I like to let them choose their own topics, something that they are familiar with (Figure 4.13).

- Go on an online scavenger hunt for articles that use this move. When students find examples, challenge them to revise the example to paint a better picture. Ask volunteers to share both the original and their revision. Discuss the differences and what the other students pictured while they listened to each one.

- As with most writing moves, it always makes sense to have students revise earlier drafts that can benefit from a newly introduced move. Students are often happy to rescue pieces of writing that they may have given up on. Invite students to revisit their writing and find places where the *Imagine This* move can help bring the piece alive.

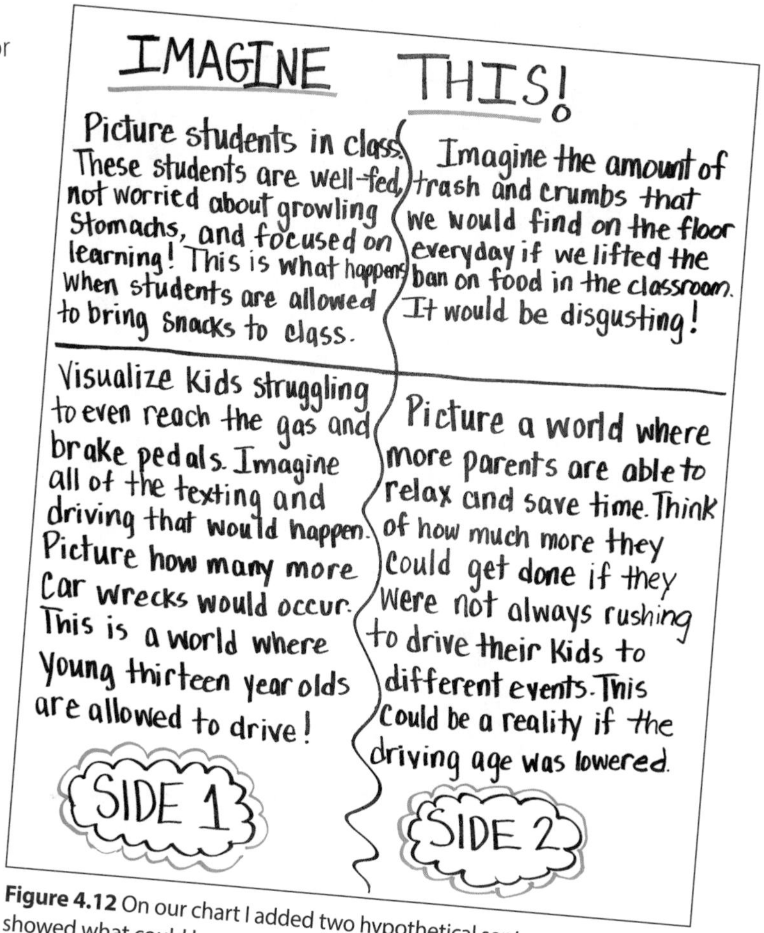

IMAGINE THIS!

Picture students in class. These students are well-fed, not worried about growling stomachs, and focused on learning! This is what happens when students are allowed to bring snacks to class.

Imagine the amount of trash and crumbs that we would find on the floor everyday if we lifted the ban on food in the classroom. It would be disgusting!

Visualize kids struggling to even reach the gas and brake pedals. Imagine all of the texting and driving that would happen. Picture how many more car wrecks would occur. This is a world where young thirteen year olds are allowed to drive!

Picture a world where more parents are able to relax and save time. Think of how much more they could get done if they were not always rushing to drive their kids to different events. This could be a reality if the driving age was lowered.

SIDE 1   SIDE 2

Figure 4.12 On our chart I added two hypothetical sentences that showed what could happen if students were allowed to eat in class. On the other side, I showed what could happen if students were banned from eating in class. Then, students helped to extend the chart by sharing *Imagine This* sentences for lowering the driving age.

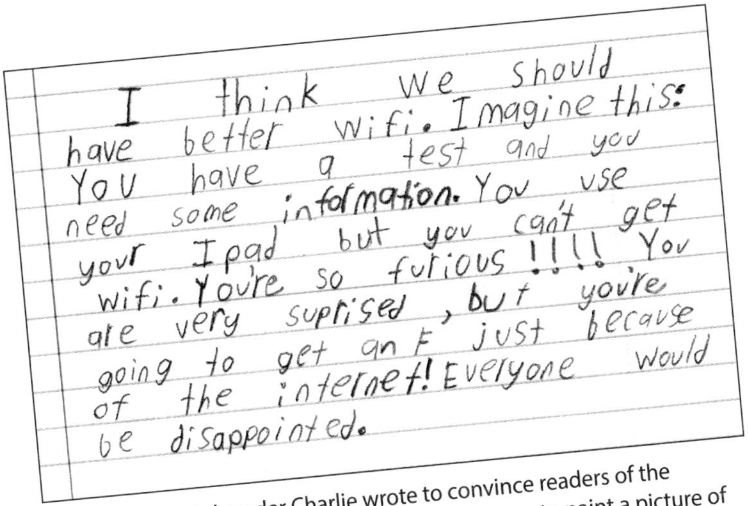

I think we should have better wifi. Imagine this: You have a test and you need some information. You use your Ipad but you can't get wifi. You're so futious!!!! You are very suprised, but you're going to get an F just because of the internet! Everyone would be disappointed.

Figure 4.13 Third grader Charlie wrote to convince readers of the horrors of a world without Wi-Fi. He used this move to paint a picture of an unfortunate world, devoid of Internet access. This small move helped Charlie to show his own voice and style instead of just stating that the Internet is a necessity.

Move 5

Very *Complicated*

*t*his move does not provide reasons, support, or explanation. The *Very Complicated* move simply announces that a topic is hard. Writers use this move to announce a topic, but to save the elaboration and points for subsequent sentences.

What Does This Move Look Like in Writing?

The recycling debate is complex.

—Carla Mooney, from Recycling

Cheating is a difficult issue to discuss.

—Bonnie Szumski, from Cheating

Your brain is very complex.

—David Kessler, from Your Food Is Fooling You:
How Your Brain Is Hijacked by Sugar, Salt, and Fat

At first glance, these sentences may seem overly simplistic and almost insignificant. Although they are short, they serve as a way to situate the author's topic as nuanced, complicated, and multifaceted. Each author is very simply saying that this can be a hard topic to discuss. Each of these examples let the reader know right away what the text is about, without indicating the author's viewpoint. We know that we are about to read about the brain, cheating, and recycling.

When Writers Make This Move

Authors begin arguments in this way to lay out that their topic is complicated and can be challenging. This move is a great way for students to announce the subject of their writing without giving away their own viewpoint right away. This move helps to establish context and set the stage for the rest of the writing.

How I Introduce This Move

1. I ask students if they have ever written about a topic that is confusing or has lots of moving parts that might confuse readers.

2. We discuss our experiences and the challenges when introducing a big topic. Then, I tell students that there is a really quick secret to introduce a big topic without trying to cram all of the information into a weighty topic sentence. I say, ***Don't say anything! That's right. Instead of telling any big details, just announce that your topic is pretty big. Right up front tell your reader that this is complicated.***

3. Then, I write *This is complicated* on an anchor chart. Underneath it, I list a series of synonyms and ideas that students can consider when announcing to the world that their topic is complicated. (See Figure 4.14.)

4. Using the chart, I create *Very Complicated* sentences as examples. Then, I ask students to help me develop more examples and we post those sentences around the chart as well.

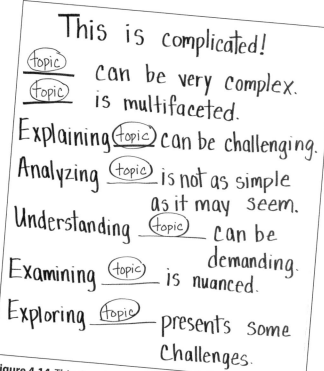

Figure 4.14 This chart helped students to consider different ways to share that their topic is complex. Students frequently referred to and added to this chart throughout the year.

Guided Writing Practice Ideas

- Ask students to review an earlier draft of an argument that they have written. Invite them to find a location where this move would help to situate the topic or subtopic more effectively. This is a good time to talk about how this move can be used in the beginning of a piece or at the beginning of a section. Discuss and share the revisions.

- Write two sides of an argument on different notecards. Mix it up with both serious and silly topics (rock/rap, summer/winter, freedom of speech/limited free speech, and so on). Pass one folded notecard out to each student. Count to three and have students open their cards. Give them a short amount of time to craft a *Very Complicated* sentence for their faux arguments. When time is up, call on students to share. Collect the cards and redistribute. Repeat the same process several times to help students see how simple yet effective this move is at situating a topic while not giving away any other information.

- Visit a website that publishes online arguments. Ask students to craft a new topic sentence for each article using this move. One of my favorite sites for arguments is the *New York Times*'s Learning Network at http://learning .blogs.nytimes.com. Always preview the site before using it because they cover current events and change weekly. Scan for appropriate content for your students.

Numbers
Game

*n*umbers Game is probably the most frequently suggested type of detail for students. This move is simply about providing some type of numerical data to support arguments and claims. These facts, statistics, and dates quantify the ideas and information in the argument.

What Does This Move Look Like in Writing?

From 1930 to 1940 the number of farmers and agricultural workers in the Dust Bowl states declined by approximately 400,000; by 1937 the unemployment rate in Oklahoma, Arkansas, and Texas had soared to 30 percent.

> —*Jerry Stanley, from* Children of the Dust Bowl: The True Story of the School at Weedpatch Camp

Up to 66 percent of a human's body weight is made up of water.

> —*Richard Spilsbury, from* Managing Water

Forty-two percent of all game players are women. In fact, 37 percent of all gamers are women over the age of 18. Boys the age of 17 or younger make up only 13 percent of gamers.

> —*Hayley Mitchell Haugen, from* Video Games

This move can be used to share a multitude of dates, facts, and percentages like Stanley does in *Children of the Dust Bowl* and Mitchell Haugen does in *Video Games*. Authors can also make this move by writing a simple sentence that offers a statistic about the topic as Spilsbury does in *Managing Water*. Either way, the goal is to provide some type of statistic that helps to support or develop the author's claim.

When Writers Make This Move

Writers make this move when they want to add a stronger sense of validity to their claims or points. Readers, whether consciously or subconsciously, tend to view numerical data as factual and accurate. The inclusion of numbers and figures gives an argument a weightier feeling and indicates that possible research has been done. Although numbers can always be manipulated in real life, in writing it is harder to argue with numerical data, making the argument feel stronger.

How I Introduce This Move

1. I write a paragraph aimed at convincing my students that smoking is bad for their health. You can use any topic that you have readily available data and statistics for. When I write my first paragraph, I deliberately include no numbers or data.

2. I ask students to read my writing and to discuss how I could make it stronger and more factual. If no one suggests it, I point out that I have not a single number to support my claims.

3. Then, I share some of the facts on smoking with the class and ask if these help to support or refute my claims. Then, I add these into the paragraph and we talk about how this move helped me to craft a better argument.

4. I name this move and share the exemplars from the What Does This Move Look Like in Writing? section.

Guided Writing Practice Ideas

- Visit Time for Kids' News Archive of various student polls at http://www .timeforkids.com/news-archive/polls. This archive has several short (4–7 paragraphs) opinion articles. Underneath each article is a poll. Students can view the results of the poll as well. Ask students to read one article, view the poll results, then craft a *Numbers Game* sentence for the article that includes the poll results. Share the sentences, and discuss how the numbers help to support or discredit the arguments.

- Project a website with facts about a topic. An Internet search for facts and the topic of your choice (global warming, oil spills, Civil War, and so on) will yield hundreds of possible websites. Then, challenge students to craft a convincing paragraph built solely from *Numbers Game* sentences. The goal of this is for students to mine for facts and practice forming these types of sentences. Warning: These paragraphs will read like lists and will lack voice. Bring this to the forefront by asking students how these paragraphs sound to them and whether the paragraphs would help to convince them to change their mind on a topic. Then, revise these paragraphs with other moves, such as *Good Question* or *Imagine This*. This work can be a powerful example of how different moves have different effects on readers and how the moves can work well in conjunction.

- Visit the computer lab or get a laptop cart so that students have access to the Internet. Pair students with a partner and challenge each group to create five *Numbers Game* sentences to convince you that homework is obsolete or that homework is valuable (or any topic you approve that works for your students). Allow the students time to search for facts. Then, provide a time for students to share their sentences. Discuss which ones resonate more or seem more important. The goal is to not only practice crafting these sentences, but to encourage students to think about the type of numbers that help to convince a specific audience—in this case, you. Ask students about the kind of data they might have used if they were writing for a very different audience, such as their peers.

- Invite students to develop longer opinion or argument-based papers (Figure 4.15). Encourage students to find specific numbers and facts that support their opinions. When students share their writing with the class, discuss how the numbers either supported or negated the author's opinion.

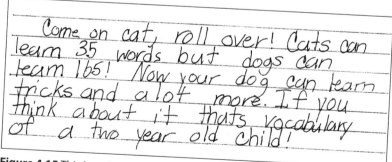

Come on cat, roll over! Cats can learn 35 words but dogs can learn 165! Now your dog can learn tricks and a lot more. If you think about it thats vocabulary of a two year old child!

Figure 4.15 Third grader Chloe wrote an essay explaining why dogs make better pets than cats. In this paragraph she not only relies on the *Numbers Game* move to draw comparisons between the number of words that the two types of animals can recognize, but also adds a sentence to reinforce how significant those numbers are.

Move 7

Now AND Then

*t*his move is used in explanatory and argument writing. *Now and Then* moves point out how beliefs, ideas, or practices that used to be universally accepted are now perceived differently. This move can also help to show how specific situations and experiences, often anchored by geographical locations, are different.

What Does This Move Look Like in Writing?

For many years, pollution was considered a local problem. But a series of major environmental accidents began to change people's thinking.

—Clive Gifford, from Pollution

Well, you might find this hard to believe, but there was once a time when girls weren't allowed to become doctors.

—Tanya Lee Stone, from Who Says Women Can't Be Doctors? The Story of Elizabeth Blackwell

Once upon a time in America, long before stores the size of cities and pockets full of plastic credit cards, people traded goods.

—Coleen Paratore, from Recycle This Book: 100 Top Children's Book Authors Tell You How to Go Green

In each of these examples, the author's opinion of either the previous practice or the new practice is clear. Although Gifford and Stone advocate for more recent thinking, Paratore seems to be longing for a time before "stores the size of cities and pockets full of plastic."

When Writers Make This Move

Writers often use this move at the beginning of their writing to establish a context and show how things have changed. Often, the goal is to convince readers that an older way of thinking or living is out of date, even ridiculous or dangerous, and to show the idea or mind-set that the author holds is superior. However, writers can also use this move to criticize a current belief or practice and to make an argument for a return to a past way of thinking or living.

How I Introduce This Move

1. I display an image that depicts something from the past that is very different now. I like to show a picture of Thomas Hart Benton's painting *First Crop*. An Internet search will yield an image of a group of people, a horse, and a dog. The image shows how people used to get food each year. I ask students to silently observe the details in the image.

2. After a few seconds, I display an image that shows how modern families get their food (search for the term *modern supermarket* or the name of a local chain for lots of different images).

3. Then, I ask students to jot down ways that these two images are different. We share our ideas and marvel at the differences between now and then.

4. I explain that sometimes writers want to show different pictures of how things are now and how they used to be. This move is the *Now and Then* move.

5. Then, we create a web listing the reasons that a writer would want to compare the past to the present. We discuss each reason and brainstorm possible writing tasks that might benefit from this move (Figure 4.16).

To show shifts in attitudes and beliefs

To provide context or background for an idea

Reasons to make the NOW & THEN move

To emphasize how long-standing a relationship, place, or idea is or has been

To contrast extreme differences

Figure 4.16 We identified four key reasons to include this move in writing. Students felt that this move could be used when writing in multiple genres, not just opinion or argument.

Guided Writing Practice Ideas

- Continue using images to practice this move. Collect a series of photographs that show contrasts between life in the past and present. Invite students to craft *Now and Then* sentences about the images. This can be done in small groups or as a class. After students read their sentences, they can reveal their images to the class.

- Ask students to reflect on their lives when they were in a younger grade. I almost always pick kindergarten or first grade. Then, ask students to brainstorm how they were then, compared to now. After students have discussed this, create a larger *Now and Then* chart and record some of their ideas. (See Figure 4.17.)

- Make a list of landmark events from American history. Consider events that students in your grade level are already familiar with (Independence Day, drafting of the Constitution, the Civil War, the Civil Rights Movement, the fight for Women's Rights, among others). Ask students to select one that they feel is important. Ask students to argue the importance of the event in a short paragraph, using this move at least once in the paragraph. Share and discuss whether the move worked to make readers feel connected to the event, cause, or outcome.

Figure 4.17 Students enjoyed comparing their present lives to the memories of the past. It made this move seem more accessible and not just reserved for seminal or historical events.

Move 8

We THE People

*W*e the People is about deliberately using the first-person pronouns *we, us,* and *our* and the second-person pronoun *you* in argument writing. Because of the simplicity and flexibility of this move, it is often integrated into other moves. Moves that frequently include these types of pronouns are *Call to Action* and *Good Question.*

What Does This Move Look Like in Writing?

We look at the clock and know that we have five more minutes to sleep, or catch the bus. We know that things called events happen as those minutes tick by.

—Bruce Koscielniak, *from* About Time:
A First Look at Time and Clocks

You are one of more than 2.2 billion (2,200,000,000) children in the world.

—David Smith, *from* This Child, Every Child:
A Book About the World's Children

Two main ways to tackle our energy problems are to use less energy and to find energy sources that do not harm the environment.

—Andrew Solway, *from* Designing Greener
Vehicles and Buildings

Although all three of these examples use the *We the People* move, they all use it differently. Koscielniak doesn't present new information in his sentences, but he describes a few pretty universal encounters with time that *we* (not "people in general") are likely to identify with. Smith combines two moves. He is really offering a fact or statistic (the *Numbers Game* move) to his readers, but he brings the reader into the sentence by using *you*, softening the figures and building the idea that the reader is a part of this topic. Solway's use of this move is subtle. He refers to the energy problems as *our* energy problems. This automatically positions the topic as a shared one that we all, collectively, have to bear the burden of.

When Writers Make This Move

This move makes the reader feel as though both the reader and writer are together in their experiences and thinking. In argument writing, authors use this to help readers feel as though the problem is a shared one, or that a viewpoint belongs to both parties. In explanatory writing, the authors typically do this to shift the tone from one of telling to one of recounting and explaining shared situations or experiences. This is a subtle way of inviting the reader into the text.

Personally, I've seen the power of this move in real-world writing by my students, as well. You may remember that, in Chapter 1, I shared a story about being called down to the principal's office. My students had witnessed an altercation, and the principal had asked them to write their own accounts of what they saw. However, when he read their work, he became suspicious that students had not written it on their own because the texts were so well written. Of course, they had written it on their own, and they had done something very clever with *We the People*: they had intentionally done the *opposite* of this move. Although writers often want to show the reader how connected they are to the reader or to the subject of the writing, many of my students wanted no part in the incident. They distanced themselves from it by writing in third person. Students' understanding of *We the People* allowed them to make intentional decisions in their writing for a very specific purpose.

How I Introduce This Move

1. I begin by writing three rules.

    Clean up all messes.

    Be kind.

    Speak with respect.

2. Then, I ask students if these rules seem like my rules or our shared rules. I call on students to share their ideas and explain why they feel that way.

3. Next, I revise the list of rules by adding in *we*, *our*, *you*, and *us*.

> Let's keep our room clean.
>
> We will practice kindness.
>
> Show respect for yourself and others in our class.

4. Then, we talk about how this list feels different. I lead students to the idea that the second list feels like we are in this together.

5. I explain that writers often want readers to feel that they have a shared viewpoint, problem, or situation—it helps readers to be more receptive to the author's viewpoint. Subtly using first-person plural pronouns *we, us* or the second-person pronoun *you* helps writers to create a personal connection with readers. I also point out that, as my students once showed my principal, authors can do the opposite and appear to be detached from a topic and uninvolved by *not* using first-person pronouns or *you*. Speaking only in the third person is the antithesis of this move.

Guided Writing Practice Ideas

- Select a paragraph of informational text or of an argument written in third person or written with first-person singular (*I*). Invite students to revise the paragraph to include the *We the People* move. Share and discuss the revisions. If you use passages from your science or social studies books, consider photocopying the original paragraph and displaying it next to some of the student revisions.

- Invite students to revise an earlier draft of an argument using *We the People*. Consider using paragraphs that students drafted when practicing moves like *Numbers Game* or *Opposite Side*.

- Consider linking this to your yearlong language arts instruction. This is a great time to have a discussion about first-, second-, and third-person pronouns. Ask students to circle any of the targeted first-person pronouns whenever they write. This is a good way to get students consciously thinking about how they use pronouns and why.

- Ask students to select a strong opinion that they believe in. Call on students to share their ideas to verify that they are in fact opinions and to offer students who struggle to select a stance some suggestions and ideas. Ask students to craft two different paragraphs supporting their claims. One should be entirely in third person, while the other uses the first-person pronouns form of the *We the People* move. Invite students to share their writing and solicit feedback from their peers about how each paragraph felt. Discuss how writers are intentional when they select words, even down to the types of pronouns that they use.

- This move relies on *some* first-person pronouns, but typically does not use *I*. Spend time exploring why this move focuses on *plural* first-person pronouns and the word *you,* not the single first-person pronoun *I*. Write three or four sentences on sentence strips using the word *I*. Sentence possibilities: *I believe recycling is helpful*; *I support equal pay for men and women*. Ask students if they feel as though these sentences are about the author or about us, collectively. Students will easily see that using *I* doesn't have the same effect as *we, you*, or *us*. Ask students to revise each of your sentences from *I* sentences to *We the People* sentences.

Call TO Action

*t*his move is about directly asking or telling readers to take action. Sometimes authors do this at the end of their writing as a final word of advice to the readers. This move can be simple and include just a directive or also restate or explain the rationale and benefit of taking action.

What Does This Move Look Like in Writing?

Make a promise to yourself that you'll stand up when you need to.

> —Patti Kelley Criswell, *from* Stand Up for Yourself and Your Friends: Dealing with Bullies and Bossiness and Finding a Better Way

Carry a reusable bag and you won't need to accept yet another plastic bag.

> —David Rothschild, *from* Earth Matters: An Encyclopedia of Ecology

So the next time you buy a new laptop, don't just dump the old one into a bin—give it to someone who needs it! You can even contact the company you bought it from. It may take the laptop back and reuse the parts.

> —Aanchal Broca Kumar, *from* Why Should I Recycle?

You need to talk to your parents and discuss how to conserve gas, save energy, and reduce waste.

—Dan Gutman, *from* Recycle This Book: 100 Top
Children's Book Authors Tell You How to Go Green

All of these examples use the pronoun *you* to speak directly to the reader. They don't offer reasons or try to explain background information—the writer would have addressed all of that *before* using the *Call to Action* move. These statements just tell the reader, very directly, what to do to take action.

When Writers Make This Move

Writers make this move to ~~urge readers to move beyond passive agreement and to take action~~. Often found in the writing of authors who feel passionately about a cause or movement, this move is most readily visible in editorial pieces. Taking action is often implied in argument writing, but with this move the author speaks to the reader directly.

How I Introduce This Move

1. I begin by sharing a few articles from Dan Gutman's *Recycle This Book: 100 Top Children's Authors Tell You How to Go Green* or Anne Jankeliowitch's *Kids Who Are Changing the World.* You can use any collection of writing that includes a *Call to Action.* I read an excerpt from one of the short sections.

2. Then, I stop and lead a discussion with students. I ask students what they think the author wants us to do. I record their ideas on the board. I repeat this process, with several additional passages.

3. Finally, I read what we wrote. I point out that the authors don't want us to just read their books, they want us to do something! I explain: ***This idea of wanting us to do something is called a* Call to Action. *This is when the author tells you to go out and act or think in a certain way.***

4. I ask students to name beliefs or actions that they would want to tell others to consider or do. I call on multiple students to share (Figure 4.18).

5. Finally, I tell them that in their arguments, they can use the *Call to Action* move to suggest that readers do something.

Guided Writing Practice Ideas

- Invite students to research causes that are important to them. In groups, have them craft *Call to Action* sentences as mini–picket signs and banners. This activity is fun, and it also focuses on students experimenting with different sentence structures, ways to arrange their words, and organize their thinking. You can even extend this and have students present their banners and signs to the class or school—as part of larger arguments that use a variety of *Details That Convince*.

- Ask students to revise their own past argument or opinion writing, considering two different places where they could add a *Call to Action* sentence. Encourage them to share with a partner why they picked those potential places in their writing, then to revise to include this move in the best place.

- Send students on a *Call to Action* search. Invite students to read online news articles and look for examples where authors have made this move. When students find an example, they record the *Call to Action* sentence(s), the title of the article, and the author. Share these findings in small groups or with the class. Discuss what the authors ask readers to do and whether or not the students think the move has been used effectively.

Figure 4.18 Capturing the beliefs and actions that students name in this lesson will give you and your students a handy list of ideas to refer to when they are considering topics for their independent writing.

- Talk to students about subtle *Call to Action* moves and more aggressive, explicit ones. Then, name a topic that students are already familiar with or have talked about before and ask them to write an aggressive *Call to Action* and a more subtle version. Invite students to share their ideas with the class. Then, discuss how they feel about the two versions. Ask, ***What audience would these work with? Do the two types make you feel differently when you hear or read them? How would you choose which type to use?*** Call on other students to share and continue the same discussion.

5

Details that Inform

Defining, Comparing, and Clarifying

"**a**dd more details!" "Elaborate!" "Tell your readers more about your topic." These three directives are heard in virtually every writing class on a weekly, if not daily, basis. Teachers seem to be on a mission to get students to add more details to their writing, but students often struggle with this mandate. It seems that although students have heard that they need to elaborate, they need moves that show them *how* to elaborate. *Details That Inform* are the tools that help students to do this more effectively.

When Do Writers Make These Moves?

Details *That Inform* are primarily spotted in informational text. In a sense, they are the bones of explanatory writing in the same way that *Details That Describe* are the foundation of narratives and other types of storytelling. Of course, elaboration is also used in narratives, and description is also used in informational text, but you'll find more examples of elaboration in informational texts and more examples of description in narratives.

Writers rely on this type of detail to extend their main ideas and topics, expanding, enriching, and extending their central ideas. These details are carefully included to provide clarity for readers. Questions that writers should consider when thinking about adding *Details That Inform*:

- Did I define all of the big ideas and terms?

- Is there a different way that I can explain this?

- What other information could I share to help readers understand?

- Is there any background information that my readers need to know?

- Do my readers have enough information?

- Is my writing clear and easy to understand?

- Do any of the details in my writing confuse or distract the reader?

1. I begin by telling the class that we will play a guessing game today. I will give clues about a person or place. Students can use the clues to guess the answer.

2. I explain the rules of the game: I will not give any verbal clues, only written clues. When students are ready to guess, they raise their hand. I will call on two students to guess after each clue. To keep this game going long enough to illustrate the importance of details that elaborate, I choose a person or place that students will be able to guess but that might not be the first name or location they think of. For reference, students' initial guesses usually include teachers and students in the school, celebrities, and characters from books that we have recently read.

3. Next, I write the first clue on the board:

   This person is a man.

4. I call on students to guess. When they don't guess correctly, I remind them that it's unlikely that they'll be able to figure out who or what I'm thinking of with just that one vague clue to guide them. Then, I add another sentence:

   This person is a man.

   He is well known.

5. I call on students to guess again. I continue this same pattern of adding sentences and calling on students until I have completed this series of sentences:

   This person is a man.

   He is well known.

   He is an American.

   He is no longer living.

   His influence impacts our lives, even today.

   This man had strong opinions.

I use this set of sentences because multiple correct answers could fit here. Martin Luther King, Abraham Lincoln, John F. Kennedy, and Steve Jobs could all fit here, to name a few.

6. Finally, I add a final sentence that helps to give away the identity of the man I have described. For example, I might add that he was president, name his birthplace, identify a landmark named after him, or mention a famous speech he wrote.

7. When a student finally guesses, I ask students to consider why they didn't guess the person correctly after my first clue: *He is a man.* Invite students to share and to also explain where in the list of sentences they started to get closer to the correct name (they will all swear that they were just about to guess who it was). The goal of this discussion is for students to come to the realization that the early sentences did not offer enough information. Readers simply did not have enough information to determine who I was writing about. My limited elaboration made it difficult to really make sense of who I was describing.

8. I point out that just as my writing was unclear and they were lost, readers can feel lost when writers don't elaborate, clarify, or define their ideas.

9. Then, I introduce the types of detail that we will explore: *Details That Inform.* I point out that not only will we learn writing moves that help us to elaborate, but we will explore different ways to structure the details we include. Because I may want to reference the clues I use in this introductory lesson throughout other lessons, I don't try to revise them now with the class. For now, my goal is simply to model *why* this is important and to create a sense of usefulness for these types of details.

Details That Inform: The Writing Moves

Each of the *Details That Inform* moves in this chapter is listed here. When you read students' writing and notice different things that you would like for them to elaborate on or revise, this chart provides direction to help move students to consider different possibilities.

Details That Inform

If you see this in the student's writing . . .	⟩	Try this . . .
Unclear purpose for writing; hard to tell what the writer's focus is	⟩	*What's Next?* (page 146) *Big Deals and Famous Firsts* (page 154) *In Other Words* (page 169) *So Important* (page 172)
Repeating same adjectives and descriptive words throughout writing	⟩	*Polar Opposites* (page 142) *Sweet and Sour* (page 150) *In Other Words* (page 169)
Vague descriptions	⟩	*Polar Opposites* (page 142) *What's Next?* (page 146) *Define It* (page 158) *In Other Words* (page 169)
Ideas not connected	⟩	*Name an Example* (page 161) *So Important* (page 172)
Listing, rather than explaining	⟩	*Name an Example* (page 161) *In Other Words* (page 169) *So Important* (page 172)
Cold and detached; impersonal	⟩	*Sweet and Sour* (page 150) *Name an Example* (page 161) *Also Known As (AKA)* (page 165) *Share the Love* (page 175)
Limited details, not enough explanation	⟩	*Polar Opposites* (page 142) *Name an Example* (page 161) *Also Known As (AKA)* (page 165) *So Important* (page 172)

This chart is a tool to help *students* think about different ways to use *Details That Inform* effectively in their writing. Based on student goals, this chart can direct students to some possibilities. This is not all inclusive and moves can be used to meet lots of different writing goals. This chart just offers a beginning set of possibilities.

Details That Inform

If you want to . . .		Try this . . .
Make sure the purpose of your writing is really clear for readers.	〉	*What's Next?* *Big Deals and Famous Firsts* *In Other Words* *So Important*
Stop using the same words to explain your information.	〉	*Polar Opposites* *Sweet and Sour* *In Other Words*
Clarify what you meant so that readers are really clear about your ideas.	〉	*Polar Opposites* *What's Next?* *Define It* *In Other Words*
Help connect your sentences better so that readers see how they explain and support each other.	〉	*Name an Example* *So Important*
Elaborate, not just write a sentence that tells one or two things.	〉	*Name an Example* *In Other Words* *So Important*
Sound more conversational and make your topic (especially about a person) come alive.	〉	*Sweet and Sour* *Name an Example* *Also Known As (AKA)* *Share the Love*

Polar *Opposites*

*t*he *Polar Opposites* move helps to elaborate about a concept, idea, or person, but doesn't just list the information. In fact, it does the opposite. It helps to clarify information by creating a juxtaposition between the thing the writer is describing and something that it is not what the author is describing. The difference does the heavy lifting of explaining.

What Does This Move Look Like in Writing?

Unlike football bowls, there had been no season tallies for the academic teams.

—E. L. Konigsburg, *from* The View from Saturday

Few people are entirely honest. Many people lie once in a while. Heinrich Schliemann lied more often than that.

—Laura Amy Schlitz, *from* The Hero Schliemann:
The Dreamer Who Dug for Troy

But most babies didn't have nineteen older brothers and sisters to watch over them. Most babies didn't have a mother who knew home remedies and a father who worked several jobs.
Most babies weren't Wilma Rudolph.

—Kathleen Krull, *from* Wilma Unlimited: How Wilma
Rudolph Became the World's Fastest Woman

E. L. Konigsburg uses this move to compare the perks that football bowls have over the academic bowls. This is a common way to use this move, establishing a difference between two ideas or things that will be discussed throughout a text. Notice the way that Krull makes this move to explain how unique Wilma Rudolph was. Rather than just tell the readers this directly, she told about how most babies were, then simply stated that Wilma was obviously not like most babies. This provides detail about Wilma, but it also highlights how very different Wilma's infancy was in comparison to other babies. Schlitz not only points out that Heinrich Schliemann was dishonest, she makes a point of explaining that Schliemann's dishonesty goes beyond what many people might consider typical. This helps to show that a person has a trait that is the polar opposite of the general population.

When Writers Make This Move

Writers use this move most often in informational text. In biographies, for example, authors use this move to establish characteristics of a person, place, or situation. This lets the reader see how far the topic or idea leans in one direction by comparing it to a baseline. Science texts also feature this move when they are attempting to explain two ideas or concepts. The writers may immediately contrast some of the qualities of each concept to point out extreme differences.

How I Introduce This Move

1. Before the lesson, I select a set of pictures that represent opposites. Height, gender, size, and age differences are basic opposites that are noticed quickly.

2. I project the first pair of images and ask students how these images are different. Most frequently, I display a picture of the state of California and another picture of Tennessee—both drawn to scale. Students are usually immediately drawn to the size differences. I write:

   > California is a huge state. Tennessee is
   > not California.

3. Then, I revise the sentence to read:

   > Unlike California, Tennessee is small and
   > has a small population.

4. We continue looking at pairs of pictures and recording a sentence to explain the differences. I try to write at least two different versions of the same sentence so that students will start to think about possibilities and multiple ways of structuring their own sentences.

5. As I continue, I invite students to help me craft and revise sentences about the different sentences.

6. Finally, I name the move that we have been making: *Polar Opposites*. This is a way to provide more detail about a person, place, or idea by pointing out how unlike it is to something else. I explain that authors use comparisons to highlight a particular difference. Rather than randomly choosing something to compare their subject to, they consider what the difference will tell their readers. I share some examples of ways in which authors have used *Polar Opposites* in their writing (the previous examples are a good start).

Guided Writing Practice Ideas

- Pair students together and invite each pair to think about two books, places, or people that are polar opposites in some way. Then, set a timer (to encourage urgency) and ask students to try the *Polar Opposites* move to point out that difference. When students share their writing, ask about what difference or trait their sentence(s) explained. Discuss times when they think they might make this move in their independent writing.

- Draw a T-chart and write opposites on either side. Plain/spectacular, outgoing/shy, and so on. Invite students to continue the list by developing their own *Polar Opposites* charts. Then, ask students to craft as many *Polar Opposites* sentences as possible, using their charts for ideas. Some teachers assign topics or general subjects that students have to write about. This is just a time for free practice, so be as flexible or rigid as you choose here.

- Have students revisit an earlier draft of an informational text. Invite students to circle the subjects of at least three sentences. Then, challenge students to reread the sentences and consider how they could revise each one using this move. For more reluctant writers, consider pairing students up to do this together.

- I like to share that students don't have to compare two things. They can take their topic, place, person, or idea and simply compare it to *all* other topics, places, people, or ideas. A good example to share is the excerpt from *Wilma Unlimited: How Wilma Rudolph Became the World's Fastest Woman*, by Kathleen Krull. You can also model this by drawing from a location. I do this by telling students that my mom is from the most boring town in the world. Then, I share this sentence:

  > When you visit most places, there is always at least one interesting thing to do. I guess my mom's hometown is nothing like most places.

  This is usually a good model to get students thinking about polar opposites that compare to an imaginary or understood baseline group—all others or most. Let students try this move with partners and share their favorites with the class.

- Project a short news article on your whiteboard or overhead. For older students theweek.com and www.nytimes.com/roomfordebate both have higher-level news articles about current political, technology, and international news. For younger students, www.timeforkids.com offers a variety of articles about numerous topics. As you read the article aloud, stop to notice sentences where the author is just listing or naming details. Highlight these sentences and share that the information is just named but does not have much style or variety. After reading the article, revise one of the sentences together as a group. Then, invite students to choose which sentences they think could benefit from revision. It is important not only to let them choose their own sentences, but to share why they made that choice. This helps them to understand and think about being intentional when they develop sentences on their own. When students have revised their sentences, call on volunteers to read the original sentence, followed by their new versions.

- Ask students to freewrite about a person who has impacted their lives (Figure 5.1). This type of freewriting may look different for each student. Some students may jump right in and start composing paragraphs; others may create a web, use bullets, or create a list of sentences. I rarely demand one format over another. As students describe this person, invite them to craft a *Polar Opposites* sentence to help readers understand more about that person's personality or why they are special. Invite students to share some of their *Polar Opposites* sentences and consider extending them into longer, more polished pieces.

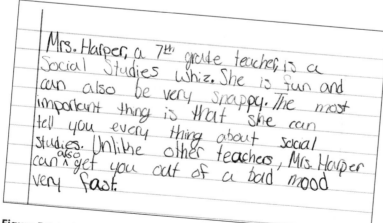

Figure 5.1 Ansley explains Mrs. Harper's ability to get students in a good mood. What she writes must indeed be true! Although I have never met Mrs Harper, I worked with students at the school where she teaches. Whenever I have asked students to write about a special teacher, they almost always write about her. As a result, I have dozens of papers where students have expressed these same sentiments, two of which are featured in this book. So a big shout-out to Mrs. Harper!

Move
2

What's Next?

What's Next is a quick statement from the author that offers a high-interest explanation of what is coming up next in the text. This move sets the context for the text that follows and provides a road map for not only the content, but the tone of the writing.

What Does This Move Look Like in Writing?

This book investigates different mummies discovered around the world.

> —Harriet Griffey, from DK Readers:
>   Secrets of the Mummies

The point of this book is to take that strong impulse we all feel—our hunger for sweet, salty, fatty fast foods—and make you think about it.

> —Charles Wilson and Eric Schlosser, from Chew on This:
>   Everything You Don't Want to Know About Fast Food

In this book, three of the issues will be covered in more detail: Should people have the right to smoke? Should smoking be banned? Are tobacco companies responsible for smoking-related health problems?

> —Peggy Parks, from Matters of Opinion: Smoking

This is the story of a community of animals that live in one tree in the rain forest.

> —Lynne Cherry, *from* The Great Kapok Tree: A Tale of the Amazon Rain Forest

This book explores the debate over where to draw the line between church and state.

> —Geoffrey C. Harrison and Thomas F. Scott, *from* Great Debates: Church and State

So get ready to step back in time and discover men and women who were the explorers of the New World and the kings and queens who sent them on their journey!

> —Carla Mooney, *from* Explorers of the New World: Discover the Golden Age of Exploration with 22 Projects

In each of these examples, the author tells the reader what the text is about. All of the examples are direct and straight to the point, but none of them are dull: the authors have used vibrant words and have targeted the most interesting pieces of their subjects. Griffley's book is not a list of facts about mummies but an *investigation*. Wilson and Schlosser aren't just writing about food, they're writing about sweet, salty, fatty foods—words that make us start craving as soon as we hear them. Parks targets some of the most controversial questions surrounding smoking, a topic that always elicits high emotion. Cherry frames her book—an informational text—as a "story." Harrison and Scott introduce us not to a rehashing of old ideas but to a "debate." Mooney's book invites us not just to read but to "step back in time."

When Writers Make This Move

Writers make this move in the introductory sections of essays, explanatory text, and even in argument pieces. The move also works well at transitional points in longer, more detailed writing. For example, after an anecdote or lengthy explanation, this move serves as a way to clarify the purpose of the text or the objective of a particular section.

How I Introduce This Move

1. I play the theme song from *The Brady Bunch* for the class.

2. I ask them to tell me what the first line was. I write this on the board and ask why they think the song writer chose to begin with this line.

3. I lead students to the idea that this line provides context for what is coming. If a viewer has never seen the show before, they learn right away what the point of the show is and learn a bit about what to expect.

4. In writing, we do the same. Unfortunately, we don't have the benefit of fun music and cool pictures flashing across the screen. As a result, we have to make sure that we craft an interesting sentence. We can't say, "This essay is all about . . ." That would be boring. Because we don't have music and images, we want to make sure that our sentences get readers excited.

5. Then, I share a few of the examples listed in the What Does This Move Look Like in Writing? section. We read each one and talk about how the language of each one draws the reader in.

Guided Writing Practice Ideas

- Create a list of sentences that announce a topic. Share one sentence at a time with the class and challenge students to revise the sentence to be more interesting, but communicate the same message. Talk about the different revisions and what worked well and what didn't (Figure 5.2). Be frank about sentences that felt robotic or lackluster. This practice time is an opportunity for students to see how potential readers might respond.

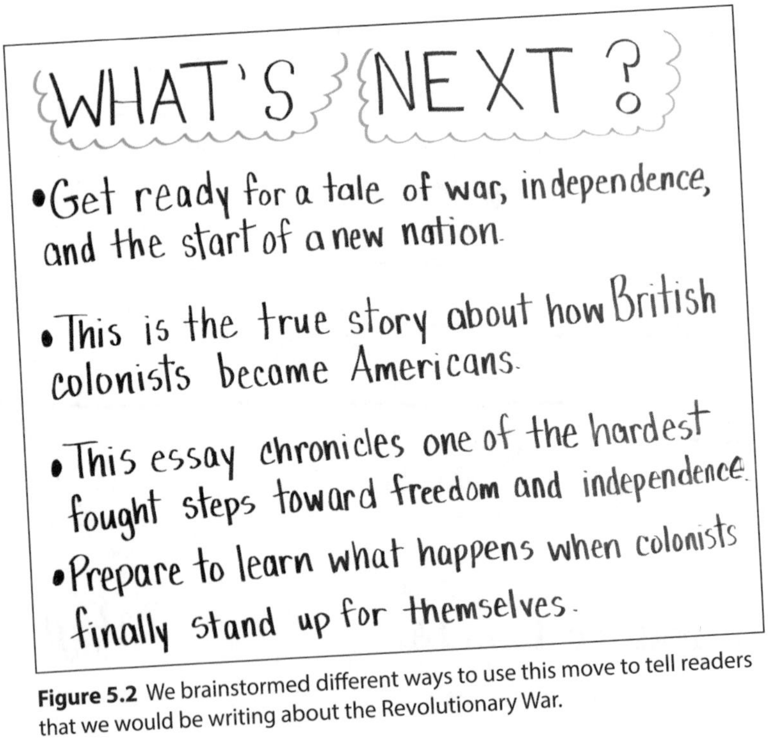

WHAT'S NEXT?

- Get ready for a tale of war, independence, and the start of a new nation.

- This is the true story about how British colonists became Americans.

- This essay chronicles one of the hardest fought steps toward freedom and independence.

- Prepare to learn what happens when colonists finally stand up for themselves.

Figure 5.2 We brainstormed different ways to use this move to tell readers that we would be writing about the Revolutionary War.

- Select a group of songs that are appropriate, yet interesting to your students. I like to grab older songs that they are unfamiliar with. Disco, country, ballads, go to town! Worried about lyrics? Just use the instrumental version of each song. Play a snippet of a song, then pause it. Ask students to use this move to craft a sentence to introduce this song. The trick? No titles, no authors, just what this song is about, what it does. Then, call on students to read their introductions and play the song. This fun activity will result in lots of entertaining sentences and students will begin to connect that the *What's Next?* sentence is not just about naming, but about providing context for the feelings, mood, or events about to come.

- Send students to look for examples of this move in informational books. Science books tend to use this move often. When students find examples, add them to an anchor chart or write them on sentence strips. As a class, discuss what the author did and how it helped readers. Encourage students to critique how the author used the move and even consider if it was useful or could have been omitted.

- Read an explanatory paragraph to your class. Consider content-area textbooks, biography.com, or Time for Kids. Ask your students to craft a *What's Next?* sentence to introduce the passage. The challenge? Use words and descriptions that are true to the subject, but compelling for readers. This is a great opportunity to consider a brief lesson on audience awareness: How would the *What's Next?* sentence be different for fellow classmates, the principal, a historian, or a parent?

Move
3

Sweet
AND
Sour

weet and Sour details combine both sweet (or positive) information about a subject with sour (or negative) information about the same subject.

What Does This Move Look Like in Writing?

But our successes have not come without consequences.
   —John Johnson, Jr., *from* Living Green

In every century, black discoverers and inventors have made their marks on history. Yet their inventiveness and ingenuity are known to only a few.
   —Otha Richard Sullivan, *from* Black Stars:
       African American Inventors

In the early 1930s, Jews made huge contributions to the industrial, social, and artistic life in Germany. But Adolf Hitler, who became chancellor in 1933, blamed them for Germany's defeat in the First World War and its economic crisis.
   —Ruth Thomson, *from* Terezin: Voices *from*
       the Holocaust

Did you know that Albert was a peace-loving person who hated war? Well, he was. Yet, his work led to the creation of the most destructive bomb ever.

> —Jess Brallier, *from* Who Was Albert Einstein?

The UCLA football team was not expected to be very good that year. They did, however, have two outstanding players.

> —Barry Denenberg, *from* Stealing Home: The Story of Jackie Robinson

Each of these examples gives the reader something sweet and something sour about the same person or topic even though the structures differ—some stretch across a few sentences, some are contained in a single sentence, some ask questions, some offer the author's viewpoint, some just report the facts.

When Writers Make This Move

Writers make this move for two very different reasons. One is to remove emotion; the other is to add emotion! The first approach is when authors want to show the readers that a topic is nuanced and has both positive and negative attributes, as in the example from Denenberg. This is common in reporting or when authors attempt to stay neutral, but inclusive of all information. Writers can also use *Sweet and Sour* to build an emotional investment from readers, as in the other examples above. For example, laying out all of the positive attributes may set the reader up for a positive outcome, but when that last negative event is introduced it can take the reader on a bit of an emotional roller coaster, building engagement.

How I Introduce This Move

1. I gather lots of sour candy and place it in a bowl. In a second bowl, I add lots of sweet candies.

2. I walk around the classroom and (using a gloved hand) give each student one piece of candy from each bowl. After each student has one, I ask them to taste both.

3. Then, I ask students to describe the tastes. We discuss this briefly until they come to the idea that one bowl was sweet and one was sour.

4. I write *Sweet and Sour* on the board and announce that this is the name of our new writing move. *Sweet and Sour* sentences have a little bit of something that is bitter, sour, and sometimes bad, and pairs it with something that is positive, sweet, and generally considered good.

5. Next, I read two or three examples from the What Does This Move Look Like in Writing? section. Invite students to share which parts were sweet and which ones were sour.

6. We talk about each one and how the excerpts felt to us as readers. I make sure to say: ***When explaining or elaborating on an idea, writers sometimes pair the good and bad together. To do this, you give the reader a bit of the good and then switch it up and give the bad. When you're using this move to show both sides of an issue equally, it makes the writing feel balanced, and it shows the reader that you're not taking sides. However, when you use this move with more emotionally charged examples, it catches your reader by surprise, just as those examples caught you by surprise.***

Guided Writing Practice Ideas

- I like to draw a T-chart and label one side *sweet* and the other *sour*. Then, I invite students to share several rules that they have to follow at home or at school. One by one, we discuss the rule and how we feel about it, and we add to the chart the sweet benefits of the rule and the sour consequences of the rule. After we finish the chart, I invite students to craft their own *Sweet and Sour* sentences about several different rules with the aim of making an emotional impact on the reader. We share the sentences and discuss how they worked. I ask, ***How do we feel about this rule after hearing this sentence? Did this evoke any emotions? How could we use this move but write this sentence differently if we wanted readers to feel that we were not taking a side? When might you want to try this out in your writing?***

- Give each student a large sticky note. I like the huge 6 × 8-inch ones. Ask students to write two *Sweet and Sour* sentences to introduce themselves. Place these on a wall around the room. Encourage students to rotate around the room, reading the sentences. As they read, they are to write their own thoughts, connections, or reactions to the sentences. They can write these on the large sticky notes, or one smaller, 3 × 3-inch sticky notes and stick them below the original, larger notes. Afterward, have students collect their original sentences and the responses. Discuss the responses and let students spend time clarifying and asking each other questions about some of the sentences and getting and giving feedback. This feedback helps students to think about how this move impacts readers, which encourages them to be intentional about their use of this move.

- Read book reviews of popular books that students look forward to reading. Ask students to take a moment or two to think about how they feel about the book. Then, invite students to tell if they would want to talk about the book with the class to build an emotional reaction or stand back and have an unbiased, neutral reaction to the book. After they choose one, ask students to craft their own *Sweet and Sour* sentences about the book. Share and discuss as a class.

- As with many of the other moves, encourage students to revisit their previous writing. I revisit writing so often with students because I want them to recognize that writing is never really done. We can always go back with new moves and make our writing clearer or more engaging. This also lets students think about how and why a move is used. When they reread earlier pieces, they have to consciously think if this move is a compliment to what they already have and evaluate where and how to revise their work. (See Figure 5.3.)

- Ask students to name pivotal events or moments in history. These can be very specific or broad. To get students started I usually begin by naming possible moments: civil rights movement, Independence Day, the civil war, space exploration, and so on. Invite students to think about the sweet and sour elements of these moments. Discuss some of their ideas and experiences. After talking as a whole group, invite students to select one of the moments (or select an entirely different one) and craft as many *Sweet and Sour* sentences about the event that they can. This is usually a good way to practice this move because students don't have to uncover or read any information—*they* are the information. Bring students together to share and discuss their writing.

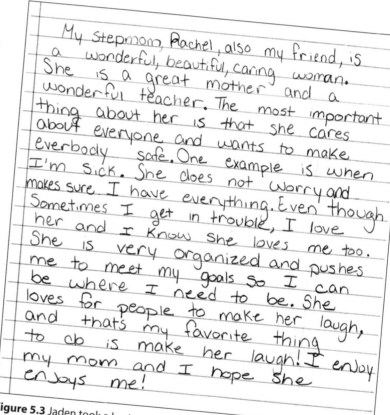

My Stepmom, Rachel, also my friend, is a wonderful, beautiful, caring woman. She is a great mother and a wonderful teacher. The most important thing about her is that she cares about everyone and wants to make everbody safe. One example is when I'm sick. She does not worry and makes sure I have everything. Even though Sometimes I get in trouble, I love her and I know she loves me too. She is very organized and pushes me to meet my goals so I can be where I need to be. She loves for people to make her laugh, and thats my favorite thing to do is make her laugh! I enjoy my mom and I hope she enjoys me!

Figure 5.3 Jaden took a basic piece about her stepmother and added a *Sweet and Sour* sentence to contrast the idea that even though she gets in trouble, she is also very loved. During this same revision time, she also added a *Name an Example* sentence (see page 161) and a *Right in the Middle* move (see page 31). She was able to draw from several different intentional moves to revise her writing and make it stronger and clearer.

Big Deals
AND
Famous Firsts

*t*he *Big Deal and Famous Firsts* move is about establishing not that a subject is important (see the *So Important* move for more on that), but about laying out what makes the subject important. This move often involves dates and figures that establish an event or action that is noteworthy. Although the move is about doing something first, it can also be used for other notable contributions that make a subject stand apart and seem worthy of further investigation.

What Does This Move Look Like in Writing?

The summer after the hearings, on June 16, 1963, Valentina Tereshkova became the first woman to fly in space.

—*Tanya Lee Stone, from* Almost Astronauts: 13 Women Who Dared to Dream

At forty-two, he became the youngest president in the history of the country.

—*Michael Burgan, from* Who Was Theodore Roosevelt?

Amelia set many records. She was the first woman to fly solo across the United States. She was the first person to fly alone from Hawaii to California.

—*Cynthia Chin-Lee, from* Amelia to Zora: Twenty-Six Women Who Changed the World

When Writers Make This Move

Writers primarily make this move in informational and explanatory writing. They use this move to establish a context for the rest of the text or at the beginning of sections to help point out what the section will reveal or explain about a specific accomplishment or event.

How I Introduce This Move

1. I write the name of a well-known person on the board—someone like George Washington—and ask students, ***What did this person do that was notable or well known? What was the big deal about this person?***

2. I invite students to share their thinking, and I offer background about the person, if needed.

3. When students share what the person did that was well known or represents a seminal moment, I record that next to the name. I give a few more examples and repeat this process.

4. Next, I ask students to think about people who have done something that was well known because they broke a record or were the first to do something. Although students brainstorm for ideas, I walk around and ask questions about the accomplishments of their person. Be prepared for lots of popular culture and school-related references!

5. After five minutes or so, I ask for volunteers to share. We discuss as many as possible.

6. Then, I write *Big Deals and Famous Firsts* on the board. I explain that writers may want to tell readers what makes a person so special directly, before they start explaining the details of *how* the person gained their fame. They use the *Big Deals and Famous Firsts* move to do this.

7. I revisit my earlier examples and write a complete sentence about the people on my original list. I make a point of drawing attention to how this sentence helps readers to understand why the subject or person matters; readers may be more interested in the details of someone's childhood if they know that the child will grow up to be, say, the first president of the United States.

8. Then, I invite students to write *Big Deals and Famous Firsts* about the people on their lists, then share and discuss in small groups.

Guided Writing Practice Ideas

- Select an informational text to read together—a short biography or a description of an important historical event are good for this lesson. Ask students, *Could this information be something that we need our readers to remember? Why? Why not? How did you make your decision?* Then, ask students to craft a *Big Deals and Famous Firsts* sentence for the information that the class decides is a big deal. This process is about students practicing and exploring the thinking *behind* determining what type of information is significant. This will help students when they work independently on different writing tasks to think carefully and intentionally about *how* to make this move.

- Ask students to craft their own short *Big Deals and Famous Firsts* paragraphs about their future selves. This is always a fun activity that brings out the imaginative nature of students. It's also a lot easier for students to explain how they chose their *Big Deals and Famous Firsts* sentences when they are experts on the topic! The paragraphs students write are also fun choices to display in your classroom—both as introductions to other students and as text for later revision when you introduce new writing moves.

- Select an author's bio to share with the class. After reading the bio, ask students to craft *Big Deals and Famous Firsts* sentences to share some of the things that make the author notable. Share their sentences and talk about how they decided what was most important. Ask, *Were there key words that helped you figure out what to include? Why did you select some information over others?* To find author bios, it's quick and easy to look up a favorite on Amazon.com, find a favorite book, then click the author's name to read their author profile and enlarge it for students to see clearly. Every author doesn't have one, but most children's and young adult authors do. Authors I have selected include Seymour Simon, Suzanne Collins, and Judy Blume. If you have basal readers, this is also a good time to make use of them. Most feature long stories, but normally include a one page or less About the Author section at the beginning or end of the story.

- For more advanced writers, consider asking them to craft three or four *Big Deals and Famous Firsts* sentences about a person. You can integrate this with learning goals from another content area or research authors that you have been reading. Consider providing students with one text, or provide links or access to multiple sources. Students can save these *Big Deals and Famous Firsts* sentences for later use. They could evolve into section headers for a larger research project or be expanded into longer, essay-style paragraphs where students incorporate multiple *Details That Inform* later in the year.

- Challenge students to write about a person (historical or from their own lives) who has done something that no one else has done or that they were the first to do. Then, ask students to craft a *Big Deals and Famous Firsts* sentence about that person. Then, ask students to add additional sentences or details about that person. These short paragraphs can later be developed into longer papers, or used for later revision as students learn additional moves. (See Figures 5.4 and 5.5.)

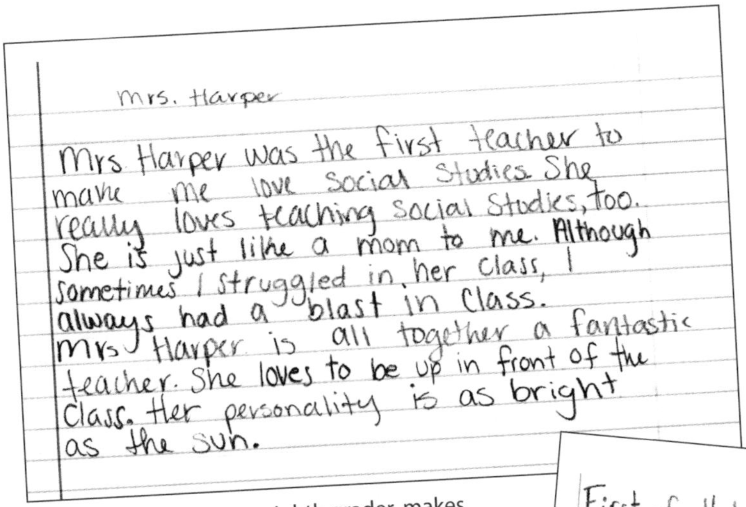

> mrs. Harper
>
> Mrs Harper was the first teacher to make me love social Studies. She really loves teaching social Studies, too. She is just like a mom to me. Although sometimes I struggled in her class, I always had a blast in class. Mrs Harper is all together a fantastic teacher. She loves to be up in front of the class. Her personality is as bright as the sun.

Figure 5.4 Makenzie, an eighth grader, makes this move in a very personal way. She describes one of the most popular teachers at her school by explaining that she was the first teacher to make her fall in love with social studies. Although this is not about a historical or unknown figure, it still situates Mrs. Harper as being the first to accomplish something.

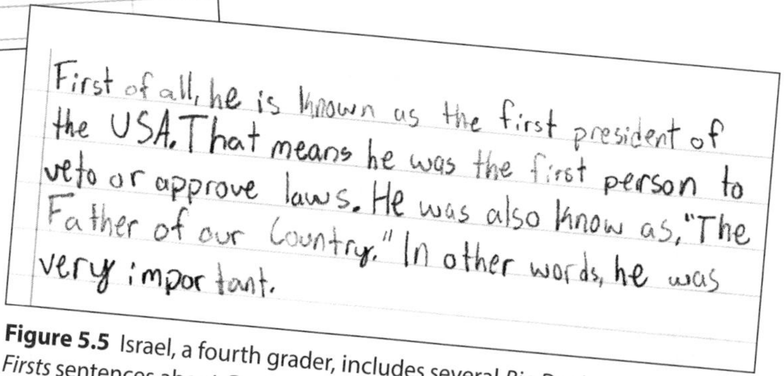

> First of all, he is known as the first president of the USA. That means he was the first person to veto or approve laws. He was also know as, "The Father of our Country." In other words, he was very important.

Figure 5.5 Israel, a fourth grader, includes several *Big Deals and Famous Firsts* sentences about George Washington. He explains that he was the first president and the first to veto laws. As students progress throughout the year, notice that they make multiple moves, as Israel does here—he concludes his brief paragraph by making an *Also Known As (AKA)* move (see page 165) and an *In Other Words* move (see page 169).

Define It

*t*his move is an important one that students will need to do often when crafting explanatory/informational text. When writing about content that involves academic language or domain-specific content, students need to recognize a few ways to structure definitions so that they don't sound like robots.

What Does This Move Look Like in Writing?

In many places in the United States during the 1950s, black and white people were forced to stay separated. This separation was called segregation.

> —Belinda Rochelle, *from* Witnesses to Freedom: Young People Who Fought for Civil Rights

It took years of struggle for women in the United States to be granted suffrage, a new term coined during the Civil War meaning the right to vote.

> —Frieda Wishinsky, *from* Profiles #4: Freedom Heroines

Forensics is the science of finding that evidence and analyzing it for clues.

> —Carla Mooney, *from* Forensics: Uncover the Science and Technology of Crime Scene Investigation

In 1921, Congress passed the Emergency Quota Act. A quota means a limit was placed on how many immigrants could enter the United States each year.

—Patricia Brennan Demuth, *from* What Was Ellis Island?

Each of these authors simply defined a term or word for the readers, but they all structured their sentences differently. Mooney named the term and defined it. The others provided the content and meaning first, then revealed the term. These variations are simple, but often unnoticed by most students.

When Writers Make This Move

Writers use this move to clarify the meaning of a term or concept that readers may commonly be unfamiliar with. This move is most common in science and social studies reports, content-area essays, and informative articles. The writing that students encounter in textbooks or materials that teach or explain often features this move.

How I Introduce This Move

1. I write a complex word on the board that most students will not have heard of. I like to use fun or silly words. My favorites are *funambulist* (tightrope walker) and *pigsney* (darling). Use any word what makes you smile!

2. Then, I explain that students will be reading about this topic. Typically, students have puzzled expressions and eventually someone will say that they don't know what that is.

3. We discuss the important role that definitions have for readers. If they don't know what a word means, a definition is like gold! It helps lay the groundwork for any other details.

4. We discuss if a writer should define every term in their text. Of course students will agree that doing that would be impractical. I lead students to the idea that the terms that need definition are the ones that might be confusing. This is a great moment to talk a bit about audience awareness and how different audiences might need more definitions than others.

5. Finally, I define the word for students and ask if that helps them to think about the term. Then, I let them know that we won't actually be reading about tightrope walkers or darlings. You'd be surprised how many will moan about that! Instead, I share the examples of real writers making this move and discuss them with students, helping students to spot how authors can use different structures with the *Define It* move.

Guided Writing Practice Ideas

- This is a great time for media clips. Show students movie trailers. Ask them to craft a *Define It* sentence about the movie. Students have to think about the core of the movie, defining it based on the trailer alone.

- Read a short informational text aloud to students. I have grown fond of reading from the Environment news section of Time for Kids (www.timeforkids.com). These often have heartwarming articles that share about an event or idea. Make sure that students can follow along and see the text. After reading, ask students to craft a *Define It* sentence about the event, person, or subject of the text. Share and discuss the wildly different sentences that students create.

- Gather a set of passages or books about inventions (you can use any topic, of course, but I find this topic works well and there are lots of books to choose from). Don Wulffson has two compilations of short informational texts about inventions called, *Toys! Amazing Stories Behind Some Great Inventions* and *The Kid Who Invented the Popsicle*. Pair students in teams of two or three. Ask each team to select an invention to read about. After reading, ask students to craft a *Define It* sentence to tell what their invention is or who their inventor is. To extend this, consider having students prepare a short definition based on what they read and a longer definition that gives information from multiple sources. You can also consider having groups swap inventions and repeat the activity.

- Divide the class into groups of four. Show students the examples from the What Does This Move Look Like in Writing? section and assign one to each group. Ask each group to study the example for organization and structure. Ask, ***How is it organized? In what order did the author place the definition and the term? What other information is used? How is punctuation used?*** Ask each group to attempt to deconstruct the example and explain it. Have each group share and combine the explanation onto a chart as a reference. Then, let students pick a word or event that they would like to define. Ask students to write the definition in different ways. Let students share what they wrote with their group and discuss what worked and didn't. Throughout the year, add other ideas for sentence structures to the chart.

Move 6

Name AN Example

*t*his type of detail is quite common in informational/explanatory and argument writing. This move can be written in a simple, straightforward way with the author providing an example. This same move can also be stretched to span over a full paragraph, identifying multiple types of examples. At times, the word *example* is included in the sentence(s). Other times, it is omitted entirely and examples are couched between commas or given sentences of their own.

What Does This Move Look Like in Writing?

The ramp is an example of an inclined plane.

—David Macaulay, *from* The New Way Things Work

There are a great many scary stories to tell. There are ghost stories. There are tales of witches, devils, bogeyman, zombies, and vampires. There are tales of monstrous creatures and other dangers. There are even stories that make us laugh at all of this scariness.

—Alvin Schwartz, *from* Scary Stories to Tell in the Dark

Barbara talked about Moton's inadequacies and Farmville High's superior facilities. Farmville High, the school for white students, had modern heating, an industrial-arts shop, locker rooms, an infirmary, a cafeteria, and a real auditorium complete with sound equipment.

—Teri Kanefield, *from* The Girl from the Tar Paper School: Barbara Rose Johns and the Advent of the Civil Rights Movement

161

> *Most cowboys were not sharpshooters, yet their work*
> *demanded exceptional skills. A cowboy had to be an expert*
> *roper and rider, an artist at busting broncs and whacking*
> *bulls. He had to know how to doctor an ailing cow or find*
> *a lost calf, how to calm a restless herd in the middle of the*
> *night, how to head off a thousand stampeding longhorns.*
>
> —Russell Freedman, *from* Cowboys of the Wild West

Each of these excerpts provides examples. Macaulay's sentence follows a lengthy paragraph defining what an incline plane is. His sentence is direct: it states outright that this is an example. Swartz states that there are lots of different types of scary stories. Then, in a series of sentences, he explains multiple examples of scary stories. Kanefield mentions a school with superior facilities, then goes on to give specific examples of what facilities that school has. Freedman states that cowboys need exceptional skills. In the very next sentence, he names examples of those skills.

When Writers Make This Move

This move shows up in any type of text where authors are teaching about a topic. The purpose of this move is to provide additional clarity for readers. *Name an Example* moves are commonly made in conjunction with the *Define It* and *Also Known As (AKA)* moves, which serve to set up the term that the author is interested in discussing. Following up with a *Name an Example* move helps readers make sense of the idea or term by offering substantive examples.

How I Introduce This Move

1. I begin by telling students that I want to rent a funny movie that a visiting family member (that is in the same grade as my students) would like. I ask, ***Can you guys name any examples of funny movies that might be good choices?***

2. As students offer suggestions, I write them down. When I have about six or seven, I draw a circle or box around the entire group.

3. Then, I pretend as if I just thought of another question. ***Wait—what if we want to go out to eat? What are the names of places that are fun to eat and hang out at?*** Once I have several suggestions, I circle or box in that group of words as well.

4. I repeat this process with a wide variety of other questions. Possible subjects:
   * video games
   * musical artists
   * city or state landmarks
   * stores to get "cool" clothes

5. Finally, I step back and ask the students what all of the boxes have in common. I lead them to the idea that all are sets of examples. Some are examples of funny movies, fun restaurants, songs, and so on. (See Figure 5.6.)

6. I ask, **Do you guys think that I have a better idea of what to do? Do I have something that I can picture or even learn more about?**

7. I thank students for their suggestions and explain that in their own writing, readers can get a better idea of different topics if there are examples. I tell them, **To help readers, an author uses clear, tangible examples of what they are talking about. When you read your writing and it seems fuzzy or is really short, an example or two is a great move to help your readers understand you better.**

Figure 5.6 Students guided me through examples of restaurants, video games, and movies that I might enjoy.

Guided Writing Practice Ideas

- Using the ideas from the introduction, have students work in small groups to turn the lists of examples into complete *Name an Example* sentences. Add the sentences to sentence strips or sticky notes and stick above or below the board as exemplars.

- Ask students to think of a person who has made a difference in the world and to write about how that person has impacted our world or their own lives. Encourage students to not only name an example of how they impacted others, but to explain that example and what it means. (See Figure 5.7.)

- Write a simple sentence on the board with no examples. I usually write something like: *In school, there are lots of rules.* Read it to students and invite them to craft their own *Name an Example* sentences that could be added to make the writing more clear. Call on students

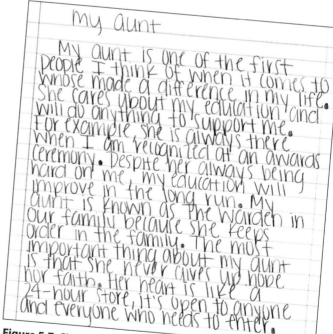

Figure 5.7 Chandrea uses the *Name an Example* move in her writing to show how her aunt supports her education. She also intentionally makes two other moves in her writing: an *Also Known As (AKA)* move (see page 165) to explain that her aunt is often referred to as "The Warden" and a *Just Like That* move (see page 23) to share how she is there for anyone and everyone.

to read their sentences and discuss how they are clearer than the original sentence. Repeat with different sentences.

- Read a brief, informational text or content-area passage aloud with your students. Ask students to name places where the author could have added an example. Discuss whether including an example would help them, as readers, to understand the ideas in the text better. Then, share a second piece and ask students to find places where a *Name an Example* move could improve the writing. Then, ask students to brainstorm different types of *Name an Example* sentences that would improve the piece. Discuss how and why their different *Name an Example* sentences help to clarify the ideas in the passage.

- Ask students to select a reading genre that they enjoy. Then, ask students to craft a paragraph about that genre made up entirely of this move. Students can organize their examples and sentences as they choose, but they must give lots of examples of texts in that genre. When students finish, discuss when they think writers should only give a few examples compared to many. Consider posting their writing on a genre chart or poster in the class. When it's time to talk about genre, it will be much more interesting to see a paragraph full of well-loved book titles than a bland definition of a genre.

Move 7

Also Known As (AKA)

*t*he *Also Known As (AKA)* move offers readers a different name, a nickname, or a notable alias that belongs to a person, place, or event. It might not be surprising that a move that gives different names has been called a wide variety of different names throughout my teaching career. *By Any Other Name* and *The Nickname* were favorites for a while. I ended up settling on *Also Known As (AKA)* simply because it has a clear acronym that students seem to enjoy. Choose what works for you and your students. This move can be structured in many ways—exploring the exemplars here is a good starting point to show students some of the many possibilities for how they can try out this move.

What Does This Move Look Like in Writing?

This war is called the "American Revolution." Some call it the "War of Independence" or the "Revolutionary War."

—Kay Moore, *from* If You Lived at the Time of the American Revolution

The Northern states (the Union) had developed an industrial economy, while the Southern states (the Confederacy) remained largely agricultural.

—Laurie Halse Anderson, *from* Thank You, Sarah: The Woman Who Saved Thanksgiving

My real name is John. John Coogan. But everybody calls me Crash, even my parents.

—Jerry Spinelli, *from* Crash

165

Because she led so many to freedom, she was called "Moses."
Like Moses in the Bible, Harriet Tubman believed that her
people should be free.

—Yona Zeldis McDonough, from Who Was Harriet Tubman?

In these examples, the authors revealed alternate names for their characters or topics. As you can see, this move can use a variety of structures. Although a common fixture in introducing readers to people, places, or ideas in informational writing, this move is also used to tell stories. In narrative writing, this happens often when a character is also the narrator. Spinelli makes this move in *Crash* when readers meet the main character.

When Writers Make This Move

This is a useful move for topics that themselves seem larger than life or challenging to understand. Topics that introduce notable figures or events with far-reaching consequences often benefit from this type of move.

This move has a humanizing effect that triggers a bit of curiosity in the reader. Why do people call him or her that? How did this name come about? Authors can even respond to this curiosity by not only naming the other name, but by explaining the name, in the way that McDonough did in *Who Was Harriet Tubman?* This move can also help readers of informational texts to make connections to their prior knowledge, as the example from Moore does.

How I Introduce This Move

1. I give each student an index card and ask students to write down a nickname that they tend to go by. If they don't have one, I suggest that they make one up. Then, I collect all of the cards and put them in a container.

2. I draw out one card and ask students who they think the nickname belongs to. I avoid asking them to explain why—nothing good can come of that! After a lot of guessing, I ask for the owner of the index card to stand up and claim the nickname. Then, I invite the student to share the meaning or reasoning behind the nickname or just talk a little about it.

3. After repeating this several times, I ask students if they feel like they learned a bit more about their classmates. I lead a discussion around the notion that knowing other names for things and people helps everyone to feel more connected and as if they better understand the person, idea, or event.

4. Finally, I connect this to writing. I explain that students can have this same effect on their readers if they make the *Also Known As (AKA)* move in their writing. I also ask students to think about some of the nicknames that they didn't understand earlier, and remind them that, as writers, they can use the *AKA* move to not only introduce another name but to explain it.

Guided Writing Practice Ideas

- Ask students to think about a sports team, celebrity, historical figure, school, neighborhood, or city that has a nickname. People and places that they know well will be the most helpful in this discussion. Then, ask students to use this move to explain the nickname. Share their sentences and discuss. If students struggle to find a topic, ask them to extend the activity from the introduction and write about themselves instead. The subject can really be anything you choose; the goal is to practice this move and test-drive how it works.

- Ask students to select a book character. Read Spinelli's example to the students and have them create their own nicknames for the book characters they've chosen, then explain them in an *Also Known As (AKA)* sentence. Prompt students to tell why the nickname would be appropriate and what it reveals about the character.

- Often students have extended family members that go by names other than their given names. Invite students to write a short paragraph describing that person, being certain to include their nickname (Figures 5.8 and 5.9). When students share their paragraphs, point out how the inclusion of the nickname makes the description seem more personal.

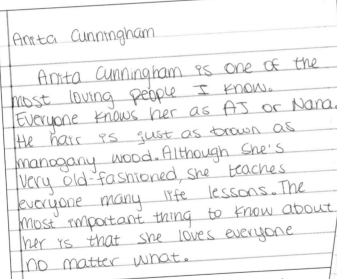

Anita Cunningham

Anita Cunningham is one of the most loving people I know. Everyone knows her as AJ or Nana. He hair is just as brown as mahogany wood. Although she's very old-fashioned, she teaches everyone many life lessons. The most important thing to know about her is that she loves everyone no matter what.

Figure 5.8 Xavier describes his grandmother by giving her a name, but then explaining that everyone calls her AJ or Nana.

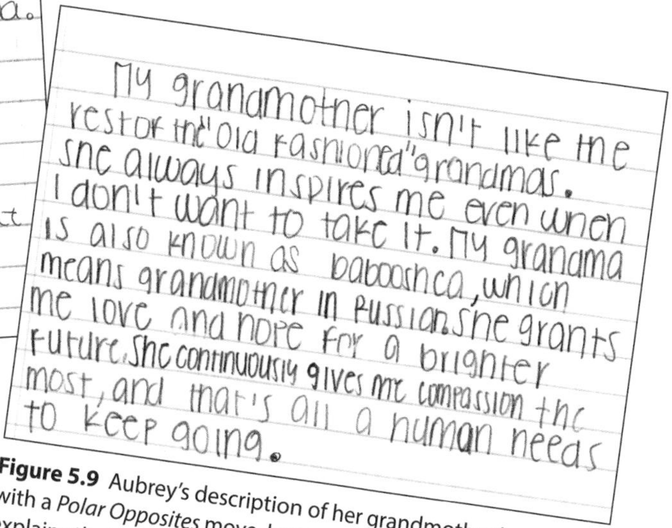

My granamother isn't like the restof the "old fashioned" granamas. she always inspires me even when I don't want to take it. My granama is also known as babooshca, which means grandmother in russian. she grants me love and hope for a brighter future. she continuously gives me compassion the most, and that's all a human needs to keep going.

Figure 5.9 Aubrey's description of her grandmother begins with a *Polar Opposites* move, but later in the paragraph she explains that her grandmother is known as Babooshca, and elaborates on why.

- Review the four examples from the What Does This Move Look Like in Writing? section. Then, challenge students to take each of the examples and structure them differently. Ask students to stick to the same alternative names, but encourage them to consider other ways to structure the sentences and organize the words. This activity helps students to think about multiple ways to make this move, rather than just pick one structure and decide to only use or emulate that in their writing. Share the revisions and talk about which ones they like better and why.

- Send students to research the nicknames of presidents online. There are many websites that list this information for you to bookmark for students. I use www.classroomhelp.com/lessons/Presidents/nicknames.html for a full list or www.biography.com to search individual presidents by name, see videos about each president, and learn lots of other facts as well. You can assign students to specific presidents, or ask them to select three or four to work with. Once students find the nicknames, they are to craft a *Also Known As (AKA)* sentence about each president. The only rule? No two sentences can be structured the same. The goal is to experiment with this move so that students feel comfortable and have a wealth of options for making this move. After students have gathered their information, they can share what they found about the presidents. When students share, deliberately offer responses that show that knowing that information makes you feel like you know the president better and how it piques your curiosity so that students connect that goal to this move. That way, when students write independently they will know when to make this move to achieve those effects.

Move 8

In Other Words

*i*n Other Words is when an author restates information in a different way. In some ways, it might feel like a version of the *Also Known As (AKA)* move, but it uses an explanation or a description rather than an alternate name.

What Does This Move Look Like in Writing?

Rube was a master. A brilliant man.
>—Kadir Nelson, *from* We Are the Ship: The Story of Negro League Baseball

Abuela is my grandma.
She is my mother's mother.
>—Arthur Dorros, *from* Abuela

By the end of the 1800s, people could travel from New York to California, or across the continent, by train.
>—John Perritano, *from* The Transcontinental Railroad

Although all of these examples follow the pattern of using other words to restate an idea, there is no one structure associated with this move. For example, these writers have used appositives, a fragment, and adjacent simple sentences.

When Writers Make This Move

In Other Words often clarifies information or clears up possible misinterpretations. It also supports the reader's comprehension of the ideas in the text. Writers use this move to either provide clarity by breaking something down into more familiar language or to help an idea to linger. If a complex concept or definition is explained, a writer will often follow up with a briefer, simpler explanation of the term. Similarly, if a writer wants to express that something is quite large, explaining that in two different ways is a great way to drive that point home.

This move is often overlooked during writing instruction because it seems redundant. In explanatory writing, however, this move is actually quite common. It works with this type of writing simply because of the purpose: explanatory writing aims to make something understandable to readers. Restating something in a different way is just one way to allow multiple entry points for readers.

Asking your students to make this move is a great way to see if they fully understand the concept that they are writing about. If they can only say something in one way, that is a red flag that they still need to learn more about their topic.

How I Introduce This Move

1. I write a sentence on the board about a term that my students may be unfamiliar with. Typically, I write something similar to this:

   > Hypertension can be life-threatening.

2. Then I ask: ***What does this mean? Who understands what I wrote? Raise your hand to explain it to the class.*** I call on students for suggestions, then I add a second sentence:

   > Hypertension can be life-threatening.
   >
   > In fact, high blood pressure claims the lives of many people.

3. Now, I ask the question again: ***Who understands what I wrote?*** I don't bother calling on students for meaning suggestions; instead I begin a discussion about how many more students seem to have a better understanding of my meaning when I added the second sentence. I point out that I renamed the disease using a name that more people might have heard of.

4. I lead students to the idea that sometimes we can say something in our writing very clearly, but add a second sentence to repeat the same idea in a different way to make it stand out or to help it make sense to more readers.

5. I repeat this conversation with different sentences and point out how the two-sentence combination helps readers to make meaning. Then, I introduce the name of this move and explain that although our examples have used the two-sentence format, *In Other Words* can use a variety of structures, as long as it restates information in different words.

Guided Writing Practice Ideas

- Write several sentences on the board. Invite students to rewrite each sentence in a different way. Share the sentences and discuss the changes and what they did. Did they use simpler or more commonly used language? Did they clarify the meaning? How did the rewording help readers?

- Consider using vocabulary words that students are currently studying. Write the definition of the word on a large sentence strip or large sticky note. Invite students to use the *In Other Words* move to revise the definition. Share the sentences and discuss how they helped readers make sense of the original definition. Consider posting the original definitions and some of the revisions around the room for an instant vocabulary study guide.

- Ask students to select a passage from a content-area book or an online news or magazine article and to revise one or two sentences from the passage using this move. (See Figure 5.10.)

- Bring in a few different newspaper and magazine articles with different headlines. Consider selecting headlines that relate to content that you will be studying in class or that relates to another subject that students have recently studied. Place the articles in different places around the room. Invite students to move around the room, revising each headline using this move. They can place their revisions on sticky notes next to the original article, then rotate to another article.

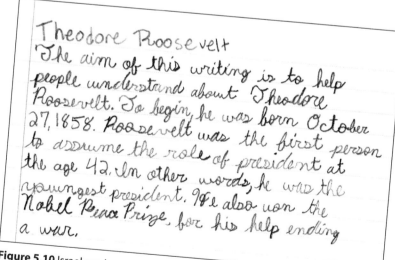

Theodore Roosevelt
The aim of this writing is to help people understand about Theodore Roosevelt. To begin, he was born October 27, 1858. Roosevelt was the first person to assume the role of president at the age 42. In other words, he was the youngest president. He also won the Nobel Peace Prize, for his help ending a war.

Figure 5.10 Israel read an online article about Theodore Roosevelt. He selected one paragraph from the article and revised it to include an *In Other Words* move. The addition of the sentence makes the paragraph more conversational in tone.

Move 9

So Important

*t*his move is possibly one of the easiest to explain and emulate. Authors directly tell the reader that the content of their writing matters. The author does not provide detailed information to explain why their topic is important. They simply use one sentence to affirm that it is important.

What Does This Move Look Like in Writing?

History is especially important for Americans.

—*Joy Hakim, from* A History of US: The First Americans: Prehistory–1600

Lincoln is an important man in America's history.

—*Caroline Crosson Gilpin, from* National Geographic Readers: Abraham Lincoln

Each part of the Tree of Life is important.

—*Rochelle Strauss, from* Tree of Life: The Incredible Biodiversity of Life on Earth

These authors created simple sentences that announced to the world that their topic is important. With limited fanfare they each managed to make it clear that the content of their writing matters and should be paid attention to.

When Writers Make This Move

Writers do this to help to establish context, to provide a simple reason why the reader should listen for what's to come, and to lay the groundwork for more extensive information. This move comes at the beginning of a section or at the beginning of a text. It serves to refocus the readers and signal that something that matters is soon to follow. Although *So Important* is useful in directing readers' attention, it's not as useful in helping readers to understand *why* something is important. Also, *So Important* is a move that writers use sparingly: the move becomes less helpful the more it is used.

How I Introduce This Move

1. I ask students to name things that are important for people their age to know. For example, I suggest that it is important to know contact numbers for parents in case of an emergency. Then, I write *contact numbers* on the board or on chart paper.

2. As students share, I record their ideas on the chart.

3. Finally, I point out that all of these things are important. I say, **Sometimes in writing, we need to let the readers know that something is important. We can simply tell our readers this. We don't have to cram all of our reasons to support that importance in great detail. Sometimes writers begin a section, paragraph, or even longer pieces by establishing that the topic matters and is very important.** So Important *sentences do just that.*

4. Then, I ask students to select one of the ideas from our chart and craft their own *So Important* sentences. We share the sentences and discuss.

5. Then, I take several of the students' *So Important* sentences and read them together as if they were a paragraph. I ask them to rate how the paragraph sounds. We discuss how overusing *So Important* makes writing sound more like a list of things to remember than text that is engaging or instructive.

Guided Writing Practice Ideas

- Talk with younger readers about the word *important*. Read the definition and ask students to verbally use the word in the sentence. Then, explain that even though this is the *So Important* move, we aren't tied to the word *important*. Together, brainstorm synonyms for *important*. Add the words to a large chart. This chart will come in very handy for writers as they attempt to use this move without sticking with the same exact wording. After you create the chart, invite students to brainstorm possible topics that are important to them. After they list the different topics, call on as many students as possible to read some of their topics. Then, challenge students to craft *So Important* sentences for each of their potential topics. The only catch?

They have to vary each sentence. Invite students to share the sentences and the challenges they faced creating these sentences. Store ideas in their writing folders for future writing project ideas.

- Reread the ideas that you added to the board when you introduced this move. Ask students to write a *So Important* detail for three or four of the ideas, encouraging students to add qualifying adverbs or adjectives and to consider synonyms for *important*.

- Visit the media center and send students on a scavenger hunt to find actual books that use this move. I like to do this in the media center so that students have a myriad of options and can move around, rather than sitting and searching for digital examples. If they find an example, they can tag the page with a sticky note. If they don't find an example, they can look for places in the book where they can add a *So Important* sentence. These can be recorded on a sticky note and placed on the book page. Gather students in small groups to share their findings.

- Read an excerpt that explains a process or a sequence of multiple events or steps. Many science textbooks feature writing like this. You can also consider introducing a process that students have just learned about in another subject area. Concepts like recycling, water cycle, moon phases, or historical events like the *Brown v. Board* case, the civil war, or a phase of exploration work well. Make sure it is a selection that they can read along with you, rather than just listen. After you read the piece, ask students to write two different *So Important* sentences that they could use to talk about the story. Discuss their sentences as a whole group, so that students can see a wide variety of alternatives. This is a challenging but rewarding activity because students have to make decisions about what is actually important and to consider more than one option.

Move 10

Share the Love

hare the Love is a move that is typically reserved for informational writing about a person. Research reports, biographies, or historical accounts commonly feature this move. For students this move is a simple way to include more information about a person by describing things that they feel strongly about—typically love or hate.

What Does This Move Look Like in Writing?

Ben found real joy in reading and writing—skills that could turn a lowly apprentice into a gifted printer.

> —Brandon Marie Miller, from Benjamin Franklin, American Genius: His Life and Ideas with 21 Activities

But Henry's greatest love was studying mechanical objects.

> —Michael Burgan, from Who Was Henry Ford?

From the very beginning little Jacques loved water—the way it felt on his hands, face, his body.

> —Jennifer Berne, from Manfish: A Story of Jacques Cousteau

These sentences are not structured in any consistent way. What is consistent is what they express: the passion of different historical figures.

When Writers Make This Move

Discussing a person's "real joy" or "greatest love" helps readers to see the subject as a real human being with a passion. Naming something that a subject loves (or despises) helps to pull back the curtain and offers a more intimate view of Henry Ford, Jacques Cousteau, and Benjamin Franklin. This move can help readers connect with nearly any subject: most people have a love (or an enmity) for something! This move can also be used to foreshadow other events in the life of that person. Perhaps the person despises war, but it will later be revealed that he leads a war. Revealing how a person feels toward something is a way to introduce readers to a person, not just to inform readers about the facts of a person's accomplishments and life.

How I Introduce This Move

1. I write a set of accomplishments on a chart.

2. I call on a student to read the list out loud. Then, I tell students that this list is about the life of a very important person and add the name.

3. Then, I explain that these facts are all important, but sometimes we want to show the person's feelings so that our reader can remember that they're reading about a real person.

4. Next, I rewrite each fact using *Share the Love*, adding a comment about something that the subject loved or hated. The goal is to make that same fact become charged with emotion.

5. We reread each one and discuss the differences. I lead students to the idea that we would never want to do this to every sentence, but one or two *Share the Love* sentences help bring a person alive in a more genuine way.

Guided Writing Practice Ideas

- Show students the three examples from the What Does This Move Look Like in Writing? section. Invite them to rewrite each one. This process is really about getting students to think about their own ways to structure a sentence. I do this to encourage them to explore myriad ways to organize sentences and not fall into the trap of just doing exactly what the mentor examples do. This is important for this move because this is very much about content, not sticking to a certain sentence structure.

- Project a paragraph about a person on the board. Ask students to select two sentences to revise with this move. Then, ask students to read the paragraph out loud, inserting their revised sentences into the text. As a class, discuss how this changed the writing.

- Have students read a biographical profile of a person. Then, have students write a paragraph about that same person. Encourage students to use this move at least once in their paragraph. When students finish, have them swap papers and let them read each other's work. When readers notice a *Share the Love* move, ask them to highlight or underline the sentence. Bring the pairs back together to talk about what they noticed and share how effective the move was.

- Invite students to write their own short, autobiographical profiles. Encourage students to think about how *Share the Love* moves can make them more accessible to their peers. When students read their writing, encourage the others to listen and signal when they notice this move. Select a signal that is fun, but not overly disruptive. I have asked students to snap their fingers, wiggle their fingers in the air, or clap when they notice the *Share the Love* move in each other's work.

Details that Speak

Conversation, Dialogue, and Speech

*S*ome dialogue never leaves you and can transport you back to very specific scenes. I can hear the witches' cackling and nearly smell what's inside the bubbling pot when I hear, "Double, double, toil and trouble; Fire burn and cauldron bubble." I can feel Dorothy's relief when she half-speaks, half-sighs, "There's no place like home."

We, adults and children, often read dialogue that sticks with us, that not only moves a plot along but also gives us insights about characters or a situation. But when the tables are turned and students are expected to include dialogue in their own writing, a common requirement on many writing rubrics, they often stumble. Instead of unfolding like a natural conversation, their dialogues can feel awkward, unnecessary, or dull. When dialogue is stilted, even the most exciting or heartfelt story can sound artificial.

A common response to poorly written conversations or dialogue is to tell students to switch out the word *said* for another word. We all have seen the abundance of lists that encourage students to write *exclaimed*, *shouted*, or *demanded* in lieu of *said*. Although well intentioned, this swap rarely yields more purposeful dialogue and is often just an exercise in synonyms, rather than writer's craft. Instead, students need to know the moves of writing dialogue and the impact of their choices so that they can apply the moves as they need them in their own writing. *Details That Speak* are the sentences, phrases, and paragraphs that do just that.

When Do Writers Make These Moves?

The Details That Speak move is most common in narratives, memoirs, and personal accounts. Although storytelling is where most dialogue shows up, it should not be considered a strategy reserved simply for the narrative genre. Dialogue can be used in an introduction to engage readers for any type of explanatory writing. Dialogue can be included in an informational piece to recap a conversation or hypothetical situation that supports the author's claims. Teaching students multiple ways to craft dialogue sentences should not be explored only during narrative units. Questions readers might ask themselves regarding *Details That Speak* include:

- What information do readers need to hear in a specific character or person's voice?

- Can I use speech to show the attitudes, traits, beliefs, or stances of the speaker(s)?

- Is the content of the conversation the most important thing?

- Does this conversation sound robotic or varied?

- Is this conversation taking up too much space and slowing down my story?

- What does the reader learn from this dialogue?

- Do I need the dialogue to help my piece? Is there a better way to make my point?

Modeling These Moves

When introducing any type of detail, begin with your own writing. As with any skill, students need to see how you use the *Details That Speak* move, the types of questions you wonder, and how and why you decide to make different choices in your own writing.

Students should have mastered several different writing moves by the time you introduce dialogue. I find that if I begin with dialogue, students always situate this as the most important type of detail. The result? They tend to use it more frequently. This results in dialogue, dialogue, and more dialogue in everything that they write. Although this may sound like a good thing, it is not. I want my students to see this as an addition to their already large writing toolkits, not the foundation to their writing. I begin by sharing a piece of dialogue that uses the word *said* for each person that is speaking. Here is an example from my class:

"What are you doing?" said Jessica.

"Nothing," Max said.

Jessica said, "I saw you. I saw you!"

"Huh? What?" Max said.

After we read it together I ask students if they like what I wrote. It usually takes a few moments for students to come to the conclusion that the dialogue is flat and a little repetitive. Then, I rewrite it and replace all of the *saids* with a different verb. I write:

"What are you doing?" questioned Jessica.

"Nothing," Max replied.

Jessica shouted, "I saw you. I saw you!"

"Huh? What?" Max retorted.

I ask students if this revision is better. Expect your student responses to be split. Many students will instantly decide that the second version is better because it does not include *said*. Once I have a student bring this up, others will start to agree, but when I ask students if this revision helps them to understand the events or the speakers better, they realize it doesn't. At this point, I draw a line through the whole passage and explain that using words other than *said* just for the sake of variety doesn't strengthen the writing. (Sadly, though, I've seen it help scores on state writing tests.) More importantly, I use this example to remind students that dialogue should have a purpose beyond just the content of the conversation. If the content is all the writer wants to communicate, an author can skip the quotation marks and just tell the reader what was said. Writers use dialogue for a reason. Then, I call on different students and ask, ***Why do you use dialogue? Why show speech in text?*** (See Figure 6.1.)

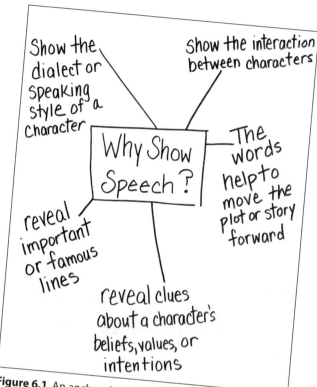

Figure 6.1 An anchor chart where we brainstormed reasons why writers show speech.

Then, I write the second revision on the board or chart.

Jessica slowly opened the door and hissed, "What are you doing?"

Max slid his hand out of Jessica's book bag. "Nothing."

Jessica's voice grew louder. "I saw you." She snatched the strap of her bag away. "I saw you!"

"Huh?" He stepped backward, looking toward the door. "What?" Then, he mumbled something.

At this point, I ask students to tell me why this revision is better. Often they respond by telling me that Jessica is suspicious of Max, perhaps sneaky, and certainly angry (she hissed at him, she opened the door slowly, her voice grew louder and she snatched her bag from him), that Max is not being truthful and is either unwilling or unable to explain himself (he said he was doing nothing while he was messing with her book bag and then moved away from the bag guiltily, he mumbled and didn't answer her questions). It's typically a very different response than the earlier versions received. After I hear ideas from the class, I begin to label the sentences and name the move that I made. I wrap this introduction up by explaining that writers use *Details That Speak* in many different ways. As a class, we are going to spend some time learning several different moves so that our writing will be more like the revision and have a purpose. We don't want to include dialogue for no reason; we want to be intentional and know why we make different writing choices.

Details That Speak: The Writing Moves

Each of the *Details That Speak* moves in this chapter is listed here. When you read students' writing and notice different things that you would like for them to elaborate on or revise, this chart provides direction to help move students to consider different possibilities.

Details That Speak

If you see this in the student's writing . . .		Try this . . .
Confusion about who is speaking	〉	*Ending Dialogue Tags* (page 184) *Beginning Dialogue Tags* (page 187) *Middle Tags* (page 194) *Action & Words* (page 198)
Repetitive sentence structure	〉	*Invisible Tags* (page 191) *Middle Tags* (page 194) *Action & Words* (page 198) *Mix It Up* (page 214)
Listing the speaker's name after every quote	〉	*Beginning Dialogue Tags* (page 187) *Say, What?* (page 203) *Tell Me About It* (page 206)
Including lengthy dialogue that slows down the writing	〉	*Action & Words* (page 198) *Tell Me About It* (page 206)
Boring conversation that confuses or loses the reader	〉	*Tell Me About It* (page 206) *Talking and Thinking* (page 210) *Mix It Up* (page 214)
Unrealistic conversation or conversation that doesn't fit the speaker	〉	*Say, What?* (page 203) *Tell Me About It* (page 206)
Flat characters	〉	*Say, What?* (page 203) *Talking and Thinking* (page 210)

This chart is a tool to help *students* think about different ways to use *Details That Speak* effectively in their writing. Based on student goals, this chart can direct students to some possibilities. This is not all-inclusive and moves can be used to meet lots of different writing goals. This chart just offers a beginning set of possibilities.

Details That Speak

If you want to . . .		Try this . . .
Show who is speaking.	〉	*Ending Dialogue Tags* *Beginning Dialogue Tags* *Middle Tags* *Action & Words*
Mix up your dialogue and try out lots of different styles.	〉	*Invisible Tags* *Middle Tags* *Action & Words* *Mix It Up*
Avoid repeating each speaker's name after his or her dialogue.	〉	*Beginning Dialogue Tags* *Say, What?* *Tell Me About It*
Skip long lines of dialogue.	〉	*Action & Words* *Tell Me About It*
Have a conversation that is really clear for your readers.	〉	*Tell Me About It* *Talking and Thinking* *Mix It Up*
Tell about a conversation without using quotation marks and exact quotes.	〉	*Say, What?* *Tell Me About It*
Show more about how the speaker feels and thinks.	〉	*Say, What?* *Talking and Thinking*

Move 1

Ending Dialogue Tags

*i*n most writing classrooms, *Ending Dialogue Tags* are the beginning and end of dialogue instruction. The basic structure begins with a quotation and ends with a synonym for *said* and the speaker's name or a pronoun for that speaker. Although this move has its place in writing, it should never be the primary or only type of dialogue included in a piece of writing. Variations may also include whom the speaker is directing their comments to and adverbs or adjectives to describe the speakers or their words.

What Does This Move Look Like in Writing?

"Where did you first get Sounder?" the boy asked.
　　—William H. Armstrong, *from* Sounder

"They're dumping us on her is what they're doing," Mary Alice said darkly.
　　—Richard Peck, *from* A Long Way from Chicago

"People live here?" I asked finally.
　　—Gary Paulsen, *from* Harris and Me

"Otis Spofford!" hissed Mrs. Gitler.
　　—Beverly Cleary, *from* Otis Spofford

"Thank you, ma'am," said a clear young voice.
—Lauren St. John, from The Last Leopard

"I'm coming," Omakayas called back to her grandmother.
—Louise Erdrich, from The Birchbark House

Each of these examples consistently begins with a quotation mark and includes punctuation before the end quote and at the end of the sentence. These are great examples to use to show the different punctuation options inside of the quotation mark. Many students skip this punctuation, or assume only commas can be included. Point out that question marks (like the examples from Armstrong and Paulsen) and exclamation marks (like the Cleary example) can also be used with *Ending Dialogue Tags*.

When Writers Make This Move

This is the most basic way to indicate who is speaking in a conversation. Writers often use this to keep the conversation moving forward by not slowing it down with too many extra details, descriptions, or actions. This is also used when a conversation involves lengthier text, when writers don't want readers to get lost or confused about who is speaking.

How I Introduce This Move

1. I list the names of generic but familiar people on the board: police officer, doctor, principal, middle school student, reality show star, tennis pro, and so on.

2. Then, I select two of the people. I ask students what these two people might say to each other. Using their suggestions, I begin to write lines of dialogue showing what each person might say to the other. I deliberately use only the quotations, not tags. After I finish, I point out how confusing this conversation is for readers. I say, **How do they know who is speaking? To make the conversation clearer, we need to add** Ending Dialogue Tags. Then, I go back and add a tag to each person's words.

3. I like to leave an anchor chart visible in the classroom as a reference for students (Figure 6.2).

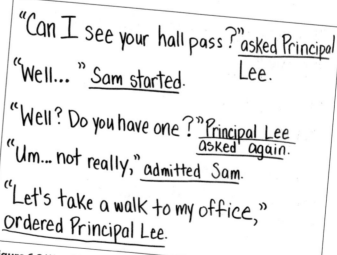

"Can I see your hall pass?" asked Principal Lee.
"Well..." Sam started.
"Well? Do you have one?" Principal Lee asked again.
"Um... not really," admitted Sam.
"Let's take a walk to my office," ordered Principal Lee.

Figure 6.2 We added the underlined *Ending Dialogue Tags* and kept the chart as a visual for students to reference.

Guided Writing Practice Ideas

- I list the names of book characters, superheroes, and celebrities on the board. Then, I pair students together and ask them to select two people from the list and to think about a conversation that they might have. Working as a team, students are to write down this conversation using ending dialogue tags. This is a great way to practice this skill. Students can revise this very simple conversation later as they learn more complex *Details That Speak*.

- Write a line of speech on the board or on a chart. Leave off the quotation marks and any punctuation. Ask students what type of *Ending Dialogue Tag* might match the quotation. Call on students for ideas, then add some to the line of dialogue. Then, ask students to consider how the *Ending Dialogue Tag* might be different if a different person was speaking. Rewrite the same quote underneath the first one, this time with the new dialogue tag. Discuss how different *Ending Dialogue Tags* feel different and show the speaker's attitude or feeling. Also, draw students' attention to the various ways that punctuation can be used with lines of dialogue. Repeat this a few times. Then, repeat with a new quotation. This time, challenge students to come up with two different *Ending Dialogue Tags* for the quotes. (See Figure 6.3.)

- Ask students to find a line of dialogue in a book that they are reading that has no dialogue tag. Students then write down the quotation and add their own *Ending Dialogue Tag* or use sticky notes to add dialogue tags to the text in their books. Have students read the whole conversation with and without the *Ending Dialogue Tag*. Ask students to write about and discuss how or why this move helped or hurt the conversation.

- List the names of characters from a book you are reading or have just finished in class. Discuss the character traits of each. Then ask students to have an imaginary conversation with the character. Students will use *Ending Dialogue tags* to write about this conversation. Keep these conversations to revise later when students study other *Details That Speak*.

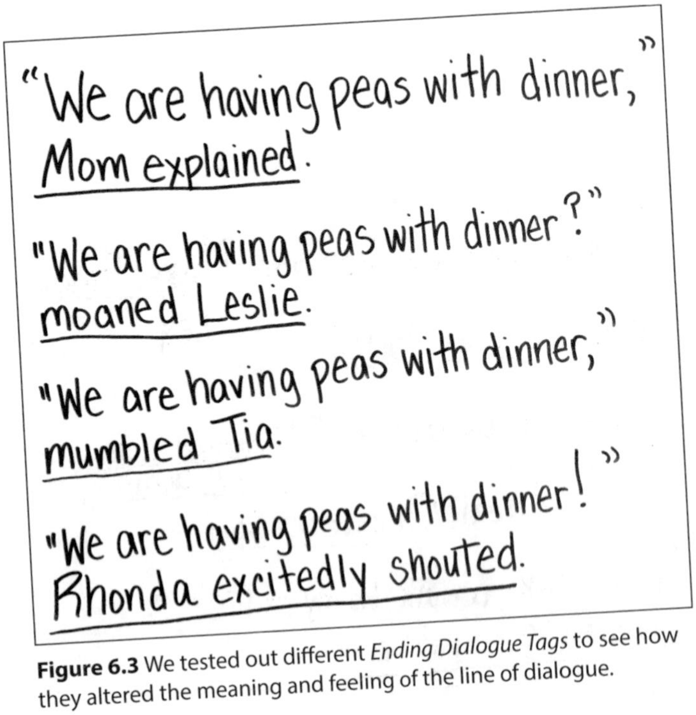

"We are having peas with dinner," Mom explained.

"We are having peas with dinner?" moaned Leslie.

"We are having peas with dinner," mumbled Tia.

"We are having peas with dinner!" Rhonda excitedly shouted.

Figure 6.3 We tested out different *Ending Dialogue Tags* to see how they altered the meaning and feeling of the line of dialogue.

Move 2

Beginning Dialogue Tags

*b*eginning Dialogue Tags are speech tags that name who is speaking *before* the actual direct quotation is written. Although this move might seem nearly identical to *Ending Dialogue Tags*, it's interesting that *Beginning Dialogue Tags* are used far less often in published texts than *Ending Dialogue Tags*. However, *Beginning Dialogue Tags* are common in student writing. Many students will recognize this move and have probably included it in their own writing before.

What Does This Move Look Like in Writing?

She told Pa, "I don't mind saying it, but this isn't right. Coming out to Idlewild and putting these girls on a plane so Cecile can see what she left behind. If she wants to see, let her get on an airplane and fly out to New York."
  —Rita Williams-Garcia, *from* One Crazy Summer

People sometimes say, "You can't compare apples and oranges."
  —Ken Robbins, *from* Food for Thought: The Stories Behind the Things We Eat

They answered, "Why be scared of a hat?"
  —Antoine de Saint-Exupery, *from* The Little Prince

Webb squawked, "Yeah!"
  —Jerry Spinelli, *from* Crash

Each of these authors structured their *Beginning Dialogue Tags* very similarly. They name the subject(s) speaking, followed by a comma, and a quotation with ending punctuation. The focus here is on the content of what the speaker is saying. Unlike some other *Details That Speak*, rarely is an action or character attribute embedded into this type of detail. The goal is to communicate the actual quote without confusion about who said it. Writers want readers to know what was said and often little more.

When Writers Make This Move

Writers rely on *Beginning Dialogue Tags* to identify a speaker, typically within an established conversation, when it may be unclear who is speaking and the writer wants to establish ownership of the words right away. For example, if there are multiple characters or speakers have been mentioned and the writer wants to clarify who is talking right away, or when a speaker unexpectedly enters the conversation, *Beginning Dialogue Tags* can help writers to clarify who is speaking

Beginning Dialogue Tags can be used not only for conversation in fiction, but also in informational or argument writing, such as content-area texts, biographies, or memoirs. It can help writers establish well-known or notable things that have been said before, as shown in the example from Ken Robbins. At times, the subject is not even a singular person. Common *Beginning Dialogue Tags* may include "Many people . . ." or "People say . . ." or simply a collective pronoun. In this way, the *Beginning Dialogue Tag* often stands alone and simply situates information for the reader.

How I Introduce This Move

1. I ask students to raise their hands if they have ever known or been a tattletale. Then, I ask, **What is the first thing that a tattletale does when they start talking?** I invite students to respond, leading them to the idea that the first thing that a tattletale says is the name of the person that they are telling on. If they don't lead with their name, they use a pronoun or description of the person. I write several sentence starters on the board:

   Kim said . . .

   Everyone . . .

   That boy over there . . .

2. I explain that the *Beginning Dialogue Tag* feels a bit like a tattletale. Just like a tattletale, the *Beginning Dialogue Tag* wants readers to know *who* is doing the talking. This is upfront and in your face from the very beginning. Unlike other *Details That Speak*, this move is about simply identifying the source of the information from the start. After that is done, the content will follow.

3. I share examples from mentor texts with the students. I am careful to point out that this move is about making sure that the person or people

responsible get recognized right away but that it doesn't do much work in giving readers details about the speaker, other than who the speaker is and what the speaker said.

4. Then, I call on students to create some of their own *Beginning Dialogue Tags* about their real or imagined interactions throughout the day.

Guided Writing Practice Ideas

● Select a wordless picture book to share with your students. Display a two-page spread. Ask students to test out *Beginning Dialogue Tags* by writing one sentence that represents what the characters or people are saying. Call on students to share or post their writing. Continue through the book until students have had several opportunities to practice writing *Beginning Dialogue Tags*. Fun wordless picture books that work well for this activity are *The Arrival* by Shaun Tan, *The Red Book* by Barbara Lehman, and *The Lion and the Mouse* by Jerry Pinkney.

● In teams or small groups, ask students to look through magazines. I typically gather a few from the media specialist or an older collection in my reading center. Ask teams to locate a picture and write a *Beginning Dialogue Tag* for that picture. If you are using your own magazines, consider letting students cut out their pictures and write their sentences on paper, index cards, or sentence strips below the picture, like a caption. To save time, consider selecting specific pictures in advance and letting students choose among those pictures.

● Share examples of dialogue that do not include a *Beginning Dialogue Tag*. This can be from a mentor text, a set of examples that you write, or student samples. Invite students to revise the dialogue using the *Beginning Dialogue Tag* move. Once students have revised the original text, ask students to think about whether they prefer the original or the revision. In small groups, students should share the two versions and discuss how they feel about each. This is an important step because *Beginning Dialogue Tags* shouldn't be used all of the time. They can easily feel awkward or out of place if they're misplaced or overused. Encourage students to think about the move in terms of its effect and not view this as an easy way to insert dialogue into their writing.

● Post a list of life lessons on the board (Figure 6.4). Lead a discussion about the lessons. Ask students to select two of the sentences. Once students have selected their lessons, ask students to add *Beginning Dialogue Tags* to each one. These sentences can serve as the introduction or hook for a brief constructed response or possibly a longer piece explaining the lesson and the meaning it has in their lives. This is a great way to show students the connection between dialogue tags and informational text.

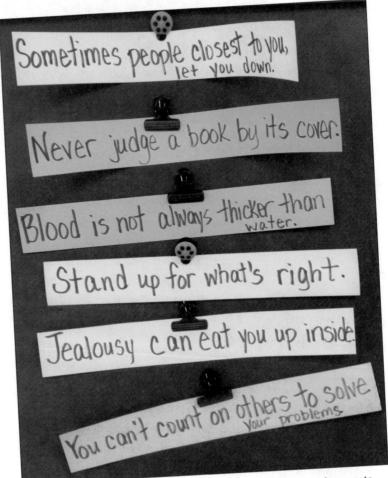

Figure 6.4 A life lesson board created using sentence strips and magnets.

Move

3

Invisible
Tags

*i*nvisible Tags are quotations that have no speaker directly named. The quotation stands alone and the reader is left to decide who is speaking. The information includes no speech tags or identifiable labels. *Invisible Tags* are used to keep the text succinct and to simply let readers "hear" the content.

What Does This Move Look Like in Writing?

"Little Man, would you come on? You keep it up and you're gonna make us late."

> —Mildred D. Taylor, *from* Roll of Thunder, Hear My Cry

"It belonged to your grandpa. Would've belonged to you anyhow sooner or later. Might as well be now."
"You mean—it's mine?"
"Aye, it's yourn. Be kind of company, hearing it tick."

> —Elizabeth George Speare, *from* The Sign of the Beaver

"And they take out for taxes and stuff, so I really don't take home all that much."
"Eight hundred?"
"I don't know, maybe."

> —Louis Sachar, *from* Small Steps

Each of these quotations probably seems wrong in some way. This is because they have been lifted out of context. Unlike the other moves, *Invisible Tags* feel incomplete on their own. This is because they are! *Invisible Tags* complement other *Details That Speak.* Without other details, it is challenging to know who is speaking. Point this out to your students as well.

When Writers Make This Move

I consider *Invisible Tags* "partners" to other *Details That Speak*. When an author uses *Invisible Tags*, he or she has left enough other clues in the text for the reader to determine who is speaking. This move is often a great accompaniment to more sophisticated or complex moves: it provides a balance, breaking up lengthier dialogue and providing the reader with a break from ornate description.

How I Introduce This Move

1. Of all the *Details That Speak,* this move is structured in the easiest and most straightforward manner. Because of this, I focus my lesson on students recognizing when and how to use this move, rather than how to structure it.
2. I divide a large piece of chart paper into three columns. I label each one: All *Invisible Tags*, Some *Invisible Tags*, and No *Invisible Tags.*
3. I add a few lines of dialogue under each column. In the first column, I don't add any tags at all. I ask students to tell me who is speaking. Typically they will respond that readers can't tell.
4. I rewrite the same lines of dialogue in the second column, but this time adding tags when they are necessary to introduce each character. This time, I ask students who is speaking and they can identify the names of the speakers.
5. In the final column, I add a speech tag to the end of each quotation. I ask students to compare the three different styles. Which do they like better? Which flows best? Which makes sense? Typically, the students come to two conclusions: (1) *Invisible Tags* are great in moderation and (2) *Invisible Tags* work best when the speakers have been clearly named early in the conversation. (See Figure 6.5.)

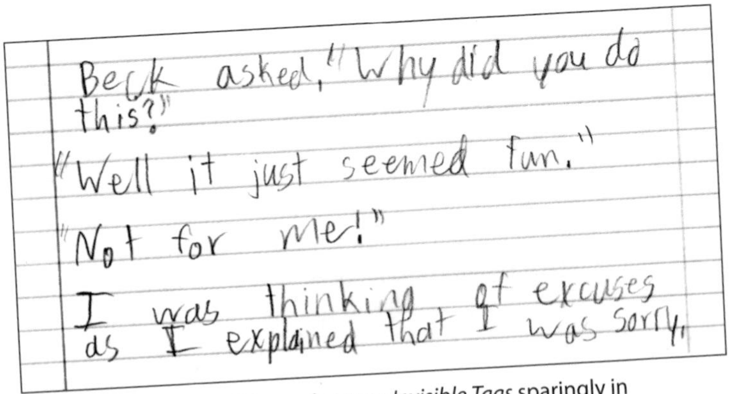
Beck asked, "Why did you do this?"
"Well it just seemed fun."
"Not for me!"
I was thinking of excuses as I explained that I was sorry.

Figure 6.5 Vincent, a fifth grader, uses *Invisible Tags* sparingly in his writing in between other types of dialogue moves to keep the conversation flowing.

Guided Writing Practice Ideas

- For many students, this will be the first time that they have been conscious of *Invisible Tags* in their reading. Many will be ready to ignore this as a viable option for their own writing. Let students spend some time on a scavenger hunt, exploring books in the class library or media center. Each time they notice an *Invisible Tag*, have them record it in their writing notebook. When I work with young writers, we spend a full writing period collecting examples. This time is essential because it moves this strategy from being hypothetical to being something that is tangible.

- Write the names of famous (or infamous) movie or book characters on sentence strips. Select two and write a conversation between the two using all *Invisible Tags*. Ask students which character is talking. Repeat with different character combinations, releasing the responsibility for creating the content of the conversations to the students. Finally, let students create one individually using the characters of their choice.

- Pair students with a partner. Ask pairs to write their own conversations between any two book characters. To make this more challenging, encourage students to mix up characters from different stories. As students write these conversations, encourage them to use *Invisible Tags* in their writing. To share their writing, have students pass their writing to other groups and let each group have an opportunity to read at least one other group's writing. Ask students to consider who is speaking and how they can tell who is speaking. Then, have students perform their conversations for the class. Students usually find these performances hilarious, but they can also use them to check their comprehension: Were there any lines that they misattributed as they read? Were there any points that were clearer in the performance than on the page? What does this tell them about when *Invisible Tags* work best and when they need support from other moves?

- Pass out different texts to students. Invite students to find examples of conversations that include a good balance of *Invisible Tags*. Build a class list showcasing these examples. If you can make photocopies of the examples, capture the surrounding text in the dialogue, as well, and let students note how the author has used other moves or dropped other hints in the section that help readers to understand the conversation even without dialogue tags. This will be a great shared resource for students to reference and take joint responsibility for creating.

Move
4

Middle *Tags*

*m*iddle Tags are one of the most popular methods among professional writers. Go ahead, pick up your favorite book. You will notice that this move is used about half of the time when published authors write a conversation into their books. Oddly, this is rarely taught to students. Much of our focus is on using just ending and beginning speech tags. The whole point of learning from our favorite authors is to see what works in real life, not just for school. This move results in ~~dialogue that feels authentic~~ and familiar to both readers and writers.

What Does This Move Look Like in Writing?

"Oh, Nell, even when I try my best, they don't care," he whispered. "Now that Mama's gone, you and Uncle Silas are all I have."

—*Deborah Hopkinson, from* From Slave to Soldier: Based on a True Civil War Story

"Well, we can't stand here all summer," said Grandma. "C'mon, Nicky, it's time for supper."

—*Jim LaMarche, from* The Raft

"Sit," I said to Charles. "Here."

—*Anthony Browne, from* Voices in the Park

"Trying to," Eva answered, "but nothing ever happens on 90th Street!"

—*Roni Schotter, from* Nothing Ever Happens on 90th Street

Notice the variety of ways that writers can structure their sentences when making this move. Deborah Hopkinson and Jim LaMarche quoted the character and added a tag. Then, after the tag, they continued on with the very next sentence. Anthony Brown identifies the speaker and listener in the middle of the talking, and Roni Schotter splits one sentence up, adding the speech tag in the middle of the sentence.

When Writers Make This Move

Like other dialogue tags, *Middle Tags* help writers to show who is speaking and even to provide a hint of detail (the speaker "whispered" in the example above from Hopkinson). Middle tags can also help the writer to vary the way he or she tags dialogue, which helps to keep the text from feeling robotic. The *Middle Tags* move's special feature is that it can be used to isolate or emphasize certain parts of what a speaker is saying. This makes the two sections of speech stand on their own. In Roni Schotter's example, placing that dialogue tag in the middle of the sentence highlights the title of the book (*Nothing Ever Happens on 90th Street*) that is embedded in Eva's statement. Here's what the sentence would look like if the tag were in a different location:

> *"Trying to, but nothing ever happens on 90th Street!" answered Eva.*

This structure puts the focus on the idea that Eva is trying rather than the notion that 90th Street is pretty boring, at least from her perspective. Writers can divide their sentences up in a similar fashion to focus on different parts of the speaker's words.

How I Introduce This Move

1. I select a long paragraph or excerpt of text to read aloud. I read it without stopping. Good choices for this include sections from content-area textbooks. Sadly, much of this writing goes on and on, with limited sentence variety.

2. After reading, I ask for volunteers to explain what I just did. As they share ideas, I prompt students toward the idea that I just read a lot of information without stopping, pausing, or interacting with anyone. Then I ask, **Would you like for me to teach like this all of the time?** Students immediately respond with a resounding *no*! I ask students to tell me why, listing the different reasons on the board. Terms like *boring*, *too long*, and *confusing* will more than likely be named.

3. At this point, I stand back and look at the list quizzically. Then I ask, **So you guys want people to say this about your writing?** I connect students to the notion that any type of talking that just goes on and on will feel like this to readers. Boring dialogue happens when writers just focus on words in a long stretch. These words need to be broken up. One way to break up a string of dialogue, long or short, is to add a speech tag in the middle.

4. Then, I explain that although *Middle Tags* are great tools to break up lengthy dialogue, they also have another superpower. *Middle Tags* cause your readers to focus on where the words are broken. At this point, I share the examples from the What Does This Move Look Like in Writing? section. We read each one and talk about what parts of the dialogue we focus on. I point out that where the *Middle Tag* is inserted can focus the readers on different words.

5. Next, I write two or three examples of dialogue that have speech tags at the end or beginning. I revise one or two of the sentences in front of the students, thinking out loud. I deliberately ask myself, **Where should I break this sentence up?** I verbalize a few possibilities, finally settling on a revision that uses this move. (See Figure 6.6.)

6. After revising these sentences, I write two new sentences of dialogue that include only ending or beginning tags. I ask students to talk with partners to revise the sentence using *Middle Tags*. We share the revisions and repeat with a new sentence.

7. After all of the sentences have been revised, I review the reasons that we use this move. I emphasize that the move can be used by writers to focus the reader on specific words while also being a great tool to develop more varied sentences. Sentence variety is a pretty constant request that we ask students to be conscious of. Then, I ask students to create their own lines of dialogue, using this move. (See Figure 6.7.)

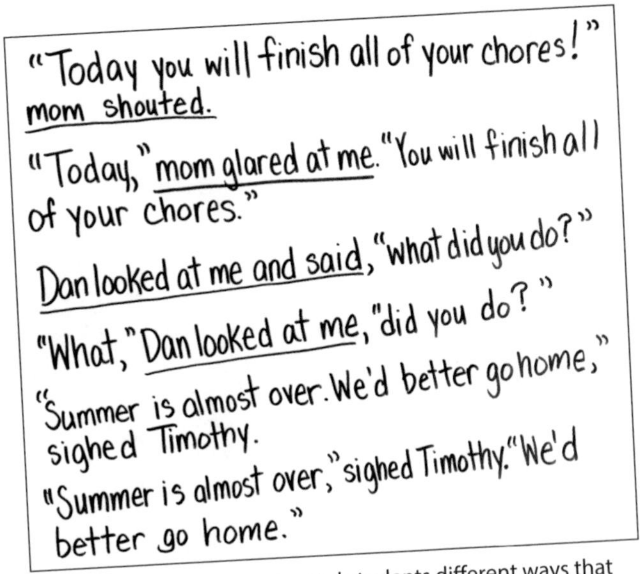

"Today you will finish all of your chores!" mom shouted.

"Today," mom glared at me. "You will finish all of your chores."

Dan looked at me and said, "what did you do?"

"What," Dan looked at me, "did you do?"

"Summer is almost over. We'd better go home," sighed Timothy.

"Summer is almost over," sighed Timothy. "We'd better go home."

Figure 6.6 My revisions showed students different ways that *Middle Tags* can be used to revise dialogue.

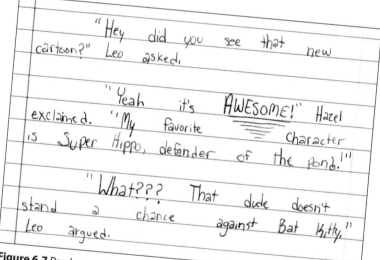

"Hey did you see that new cartoon?" Leo asked.

"Yeah it's AWESOME!" Hazel exclaimed. "My favorite character is Super Hippo, defender of the pond."

"What??? That dude doesn't stand a chance against Bat Kitty," Leo argued.

Figure 6.7 Presley used an *Ending Dialogue Tag* and a *Middle Tag* to write an exchange between two students.

Guided Writing Practice Ideas

- Type up as many sentences of dialogue as there are students in your class, printing each on a separate strip of paper. Ask students to cut their sentences apart at the point where they would like to insert a *Middle Tag*. Have them glue the first part to a piece of light-colored construction paper, write a *Middle Tag* in the middle, and glue the rest of the sentences onto the page. This is a great opportunity to reinforce punctuation and quotation placement rules. Display the new sentences as exemplars for this writing move.

- Pass out highlighter tape and sticky notes. Tell students that they are going to search for examples of fun *Middle Tags* that they find in classroom books. When they find an example, they can add highlight tape to the book and tag it with a sticky note. Display all of the books on one table and invite students to browse the examples. Then, copy five or six examples onto a larger chart. This can be a great reference for students. Some teachers take photographs of large charts like these and print out smaller versions. Slip these into a notebook and build a reference book for different writing strategies.

- Share mentor text examples from professional writers who have used this strategy. Challenge students to rewrite the mentor examples differently while still using a *Middle Tag*. This is a fun opportunity for students to see that there are numerous possibilities for how words can be arranged. Throughout the lesson check for understanding by circulating and asking students why they are selecting certain words or organizing their text in specific ways.

- *Middle Tags* can be arranged in lots of different ways. To help students see this, create what I call a *Middle Tag* assembly line. The goal is to create a conversation together. Begin by writing one line of conversation on the board. After you write, pass your marker to a student. They have the option of revising your line of text or adding in a response. This continues, with each student adding to the conversation, or revising a *Middle Tag*. The only rule? Only *Middle Tag* details can be added. The result? A crazy long (possibly nonsensical) conversation, lots of smiling faces, and a class full of students who "get" how to make this move.

Action & *Words*

*t*his move paints a picture of the speaker and/or the listener just before or just after the dialogue is spoken. This move relies on specific description, but always in the form of physical movement. Common approaches include showing a character repositioning themselves or adjusting to the speaker or listener. Readers get to "see" the action and "hear" the words.

What Does This Move Look Like in Writing?

Suddenly a large hand descended on his shoulder. "Well, m'boy, you're on your way home," a gruff voice said, with a decidedly English accent.
Alec looked up into the captain's wrinkled, wind-tanned face. "Hello, Captain Watson," he answered.

　　—Walter Farley, *from* The Black Stallion

He pushed his face so close that Rob could smell his breath. It smelled metallic and rotten. "You ain't a Kentucky star," Billy said, his eyes glowing under the brim of his John Deere cap.

　　—Kate DiCamillo, *from* The Tiger Rising

"Get outta here! Beat it!" She repeated, raising a yardstick and slapping it against the refrigerator.

　　—Gary Soto, *from* Local News

"Then when you know who lives there, you make up what they do. For instance, Mr. Charles Hanley runs the filling station on the corner." Harriet spoke thoughtfully as she squatted next to the big tree, bending so low over her notebook that her long straight hair touched the edges.

    —Louise Fitzhugh, *from* Harriet the Spy

"All I want to do is live my life in peace. I'm calling your grandmother," he shouted as he wagged his finger in Stewart's face.

    —Patricia Polacco, *from* Chicken Sunday

Each example tells the reader what action happens just before or just after the direct speech. Many of these examples include action that is relevant to how the speaker positions themselves physically. Notice that DiCamillo offers an up close picture of the speaker, his movements, and his breath. Students can focus on intentionally including sensory language to help paint a picture of the speaker. Notice that with this move writers do not add *said* or a synonym for *said* before the direct quote: the speech tag comes after the quotation, not before.

When Writers Make This Move

Writers use this move when they want readers to understand the body language of the character who is speaking. When they lead with the action (as in the Farley and DiCamillo examples), they lay out what one or both of the people involved in the conversation are doing before the content of their words is revealed. This helps readers contextualize the relationship between the speaker and listener. When writers lead with the words and then follow up with the description (as Soto, Fitzhugh, and Polacco do in the examples), the actions show the emotions of the speaker, without ever naming the emotions directly.

How I Introduce This Move

1. This move is an excuse to break out the toys and have some fun. Invite students to bring in their favorite action figures, childhood toys, or other small toy or doll. Specify that students can only bring two and that they must fit into a shoe box. Have a few extra on hand, claiming two for yourself.

2. Announce that today students will write about action! To model the activity, introduce your two figures. I typically use toys that are polar opposites. A Barbie and a Batman figure typically work well.

3. Explain that we will be writing a conversation between our two toys. The conversation can be about anything that you want. This usually results

in cheers from elementary-aged students and silent smirks from middle schoolers. *But . . .* I explain. *You have to stick to two rules! You must write a clear action just before or just after the words or dialogue. Let me show you how.*

4. I begin by writing an action on the board:

    A shadowy figure came closer.

    Then I say to students, *This is the action. What comes next?*

5. Once students respond that the words must follow, I continue writing and add this:

    A shadowy figure came closer and closer. "I'm here to save you!" the brave voice whispered.

6. I point out that I have an action, followed by a direct quotation (words). This is the model for writing about action today.

7. *Now it's time for my other character to talk back. What's my one rule?* I ask students. When they repeat that I need to have a physical action as well as the speaker's words, I add the response:

    A shadowy figure came closer. "I'm here to save you!" the brave voice whispered.

    "Thank you for saving me!" Batman gushed. A smile of relief spread across his terrified face. He reached up to hug Barbie and then broke into tears.

8. Students are typically surprised that Barbie is rescuing Batman—sometimes even confused. I explain that I can write whatever I want to. As long as it follows the *Action & Words* pattern! This tends to spark a bit of creativity among students, so be prepared for lots of outlandish conversations. Don't let it bother you. The point is that students internalize how to use this move and are willing to try it out. With that final statement, I set a timer for 5–10 minutes and invite students to create their own dialogues between their two characters. Students will likely be eager to share their writing with the class.

9. At the end of the lesson, I announce the name of this move. *What you guys have been doing is crafting* Action & Words *details. Was it fun? Pretty easy?* I like to do this at the end to keep the focus on the *fun* of this writing time, not just the name of the move.

Guided Writing Practice Ideas

- This move is great for revising dialogue that already exists. Ask students to look at an older piece of writing that contains dialogue. Look for places where they could replace the direct quotations or other types of dialogue with an *Action & Words* detail. For reluctant writers, consider assigning partners or using shared class writing as a starting point.

- Read a picture book where characters speak often in the text. When you reach a line of dialogue, stop and point out that any dialogue can be followed with a description of what the character is doing or how they are responding. Tell students to freeze, think about the dialogue, then rewrite the dialogue using the *Action & Words* move. Call on a volunteer to share their sentences and move on to the next section of the book. I situate this activity as an exercise in taking a "little kids" book and making the dialogue move from simple structures to more complex "big kid" dialogue. Picture books that work well with this activity: *That Is NOT a Good Idea* by Mo Willems, *Chrysanthemum* by Kevin Henkes, or *No, David!* by David Shannon.

- Write a list of different emotions (happiness, anger, fear, bravery, nervous, sadness) on slips of paper. Pair students with a partner and invite each pair to draw one slip of paper. Then, ask students to work with their partner to use *Action & Words* to write a few lines of dialogue that help to communicate the emotion that they've chosen. Call on students to share their examples with the class. Repeat several times, swapping slips to give students a wider variety of experiences. I like to record some of the examples, with the attributes, on an anchor chart for students to reference later (Figure 6.8).

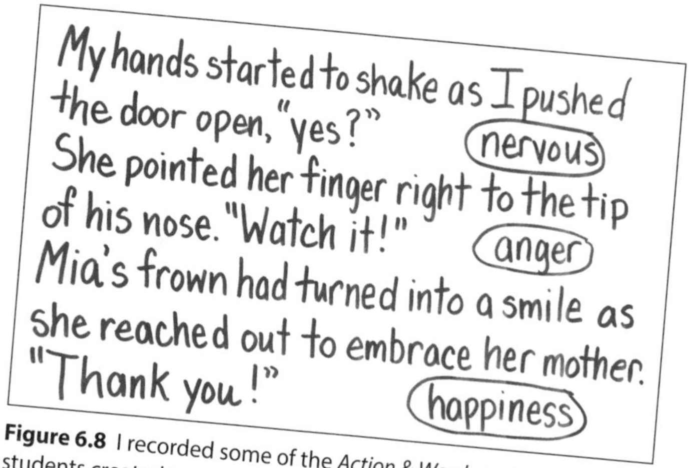

My hands started to shake as I pushed the door open, "yes?" (nervous)
She pointed her finger right to the tip of his nose. "Watch it!" (anger)
Mia's frown had turned into a smile as she reached out to embrace her mother. "Thank you!" (happiness)

Figure 6.8 I recorded some of the *Action & Words* sentences that students created to match their emotions.

- Ask students to review earlier writing to select a piece to revise. Students should select a piece that features two or more characters speaking. Students should revise the conversation to integrate action and movement. If students don't have text that features conversation (some won't), ask them to do the opposite. Students can find a place where there is a physical action or movement and add a line or two of dialogue. The goal here is for students to think about intentionally using a move in their own writing. You want students to consider places where this move might enhance or tell more about the character or scene.

- Pair students in teams. Ask each team to test out this move by writing a conversation between two characters that "shows" the feelings of their two characters. Be flexible and let students select or invent their own characters. The goal is not to create conversations that can extend into longer pieces of text. The goal is to give students more practice intentionally choosing words that reveal the characters' feelings or attitudes. Circulate and talk with students about what they are considering and why they have made different choices.

- Choose a video clip of someone talking to play for your students. Political or historical speeches (www.americanrhetoric.com/ is a good source), clips from television shows, documentaries, or even infomercials are great starting points. Preview the clip to find a fifteen- to thirty-second segment that includes lots of motions, hand movements, or shifts in positions (morning news shows are good sources for this). Or, to make this more challenging, select a clip where the speaker seems to be less active. Let students watch the clip and select any quotation from the clip and write it as a line of dialogue using the *Action & Words* move.

Move
6

Say, What?

*t*his move is used to tell the reader the main point of what someone said without telling the reader the exact words that were said. The actual direct quote is irrelevant.

What Does This Move Look Like in Writing?

Leo's father grumbled something about turtle soup, but Leo's mother was sympathetic toward turtles, so Leo was allowed to pick it up off the highway and bring it home.

> —Cynthia Rylant, *from* Every Living Thing

Mrs. Mason screamed like a banshee and ran from the house shouting about lunatics.

> —J. K. Rowling, *from* Harry Potter and the Chamber of Secrets

The teacher droned on with the lesson, about the Arabic language.

> —Linda Sue Park, *from* A Long Walk to Water: Based on a True Story

Each author used *Say, What?* in a similar fashion. They all wanted the reader to know that a speaker was talking about a certain subject. Park's character talked about the Arabic language; Rowling's character talked about lunatics; Rylant's character talked about turtle soup. Notice that each of these authors used verbs that offer clues about how the listener feels about the speaker's words. *Droned on* indicates a lack of interest. *Grumbled* reveals an unhappy attitude. *Screamed like a banshee* paints a picture of fear. When writers skip the actual words, the verbs and adverbs must be specific to offer a clue about the content. *Say, What?* details may leave out the content, but not the feelings toward the content.

When Writers Make This Move

This move is used to ~~avoid slowing down a story, allowing the author to communicate that someone is speaking without taking the time to build the back-and-forth dialogue that would normally be associated with a conversation~~. This is used when the actual words don't really add to the story, but the nature of the words does. Writers also often use *Say, What?* when the speaker is praying or repeating familiar words (like the Pledge of Allegiance or a common song).

How I Introduce This Move

1. Do you remember those moments in the Peanuts cartoons when an adult speaks, but all you can hear is *wah-wah-wah*? Find a clip of one of these moments online. (An Internet search for a video clip of "Charlie Brown adult speaking" will turn up abundant resources.) Most clips are between five and eight seconds long.

2. Show students one or two clips. Ask students what the adult (usually the teacher) said. Then, ask how they think the listeners (Charlie Brown and friends) felt about what the adult was saying.

3. Lead a discussion about how we know that the kids are not really interested in what the adult is saying. Students will mostly point out the expressions that Charlie Brown and friends have when the teacher is speaking.

4. Tell students that sometimes there will be times when they want to write about someone speaking, but don't really care about the words that the person is saying, just the topic and the way that the speaker feels about it.

5. I let them know that when this happens, they can use a *Say, What?* detail. I write a few examples and we discuss them, highlighting that although we don't get the details of what was said, the verbs that writers use give us a clear idea of what the listener is thinking or feeling. Examples from my class:

   The teacher babbled on incessantly about fractions.

   Mom whined about the state of my bedroom and bathroom.

   My brother mumbled something under his breath about hypocrisy and unfairness.

6. Then, I replay one of the Charlie Brown clips and ask students to write their own examples from the clip. I ask students to share the sentences and we repeat this activity as often as time allows.

Guided Writing Practice Ideas

- Create a bank of verbs that are often used with the *Say, What?* move (Figure 6.9). Ask students to rewrite each of the mentor text examples using a different *Say, What?* verb. Talk with students about how the sentences "felt." Did they make sense? Did they seem stronger? Did they help readers to visualize the conversation better?

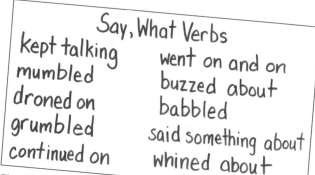

Figure 6.9 *Our bank of Say, What? verbs*

- Gather a few picture books that your students are familiar with. I typically pull books from Mo Willems for my youngest students and Jacqueline Woodson or Cynthia Rylant for older students. Sit with your students in a whole group and tell them that they are going to get to work on reading aloud and writing today. Explain that you will be the first reader. Select one of the passages and read it with an extreme emotion. Consider reading it in an extremely shy, frightened, or angry voice. Ask students to use the *Say, What?* move to write about what you just said. Call on a few students to share what they wrote. Then, invite students to take turns being the readers, while everyone else tries to craft a *Say, What?* sentence about each spotlighted student. After several students have had a chance to read, break students into small groups to continue to practice. Circulate and redirect as needed.

- Group students in pairs or small groups. Invite students to craft two or three *Say, What?* sentences that represent dialogues or conversations they have heard or could hear around the school. When you reconvene the class to share, ask groups to share one of their sentences and tell about the process of coming up with the sentences and the choices they made, particularly in regard to their verbs. Although these practice sentences are in isolation, they require students to verbalize why they would make specific word and style choices and to defend their use of this move. Without realizing it, students are having a discussion about writer's craft and when and where it makes sense.

- Share dialogue written using other *Details That Speak*. This can come from your own modeled writing, earlier drafts of text, or mentor texts. Challenge students to revise the conversations using this move. Use the same initial text for everyone in the beginning. Then, after students have all revised the same piece of text, talk about how this impacted the text. Did it make it more confusing? Was it clearer? Did the reader lose important information?

Tell Me *About It*

*t*his move is similar to *Say, What?* in that it lets a character recount a conversation that the reader does not get to hear, but the similarity ends there. In the *Tell Me About It* move, a speaker does not try to summarize an entire conversation. Instead, he or she recounts a particular, salient comment from another character, often in the words in which it was said. No quotation marks are used to communicate a conversation.

What Does This Move Look Like in Writing?

Mama says it's okay to be on the quiet side—if quiet means you're listening, watching, taking it all in.

> —Jacqueline Woodson, *from* From the Notebooks of Melanin Sun

My best friend, Tracy Wu, says I'm really tough on people. She says she wonders sometimes how I can like her.

> —Judy Blume, *from* Blubber

They asked the clerk in the shop. He said that the plane was built from a kit. It cost ten cents.

> —Montrew Dunham, *from* Neil Armstrong: Young Flyer

She overheard Cirone and me as we unloaded crates, and she asked what we were speaking. She said Sicilian was pretty, like music.

> —Donna Jo Napoli, *from* Alligator Bayou

He said he was from Pittsburgh, so he was a Pennsylvanian, too. And he was going to be a pro football player, just like me. I found out all of this stuff in the first five minutes.

　　—Jerry Spinelli, *from* Crash

I asked Mother if I could cut off my hair, which hung in a dense swelter all the way down my back. She said no, she wouldn't have me running about like a shorn savage.

　　—Jacqueline Kelly, *from* The Evolution of Calpurnia Tate

Each writer recounted some notable bit of a conversation. In the lines from Woodson and Blume, we don't get a feel for the entire conversations in which Mama and Tracy made their comments—the comments themselves are all that is passed on to the reader. The other examples give a sketch of the conversations that the speakers are recounting, but the focus is on just a few telling details, not a summary of the entire conversation.

When Writers Make This Move

Tell Me About It helps authors to share a character's insights without having to write entire dialogues that might be extraneous or distracting. Writers use this move not only to tell readers what another character has said previously, but also to give the reader clues about what the speaker (who is recounting the comment) values or finds interesting.

How I Introduce This Move

1. I ask students to tell me their favorite television shows. As students name different shows, I send them to the board to write down the name of the show and at least two characters from that show. It gets a little busy as students move to and from the board, but they're glad for a chance to stretch, and they'll soon put these character names to good use.

2. After we have several shows listed, I ask if anyone wants to tell me about one of their favorite scenes or characters in the show. After several students have shared, I explain that they all just recounted an experience. They told me about what happened. I didn't see it, or read it, I just listened to their summary of what happened. I am careful to point out that their summaries didn't tell me everything that happened; that would be impossible! Point out that summaries capture the big parts, not everything, just the salient details.

3. Just like we recount experiences, we can also recount conversations. Sometimes writers don't want to take up a lot of space crafting a long quotation filled conversation. It is easier to just tell readers about a conversation.

Deciding to recount a conversation is exactly what writers do when they decide to use a *Tell Me About It* detail.

4. Then, I share a mentor text example with students. Typically, I use one of the examples featured in this section or create my own. Regardless of the type of example you use, make sure that you write it down, rather than just read it. You want students to see the text, not just hear about it.

Guided Writing Practice Ideas

- Read a few lines from a script together. I usually select an excerpt from Roald Dahl's *The BFG: A Set of Plays* or *The Witches: A Set of Plays*. You can also search online for reader's theatre to find several options. Ask students to work with a partner to use this move to tell what one of the speakers said that was important. Challenge them to do it in the least number of sentences possible. Allow students to share their revisions in small groups. Then, select several to share with the class.

- Select a conversation from a text to share with students. Read the conversation aloud and ask students to use this move to summarize the conversation. When students share their versions, point out the differences. Question students about why they left out some parts that others chose to include. Lead students to the idea that even though everyone read the same conversation, we all summarized it differently. This can even open up a discussion about how a narrator or character's retelling of a conversation is colored by his or her own perspective.

- Invite students to find an excerpt of dialogue that they are interested in. Typically, I set a timer for ten minutes to help the kids stay focused. When the timer goes off, call on students to read the conversations that they found to the class. If you have a document camera, use it to project the text for the class to see. Then, set another timer and tell the class to revise this conversation using the *Tell Me About It* move, focusing on the salient point in the conversation. Have students share their revisions in small groups and circulate around the room. Periodically, read a few examples aloud and discuss how the *Tell Me About It* move shows the perspective of the person citing the conversation as well as the perspective of the person who made the initial comment. Continue this with a few more book passages as long as time allows.

- Tell students that they will revise the work of some great authors. Project the text from a book written by an author that students know and love. Ask students to use this move to replace a conversation that uses direct quotes.

- More experienced students can also read plays and scripts to practice this move. Working individually, ask students to select one conversation from the play of their choice (most reading anthologies contain at least one) and to identify which line or lines are the most important to the plot or to another character. Then, ask students to use the *Tell Me About It* move using the conversation as their raw material. I like to post the name of the plays that they selected around the room with their *Tell Me About It* sentences displayed underneath as a "sneak peek" into that play. I always notice students walking and reading what others have written and growing curious about the play. This is a great way to encourage students to read more plays! If you need a place to start when looking for plays consider Jennifer Kroll's *Simply Shakespeare: Readers Theatre for Young People* or Elizabeth Weinstein's *Shakespeare with Children: Six Scripts for Young Players*.

Talking
AND
Thinking

*t*alking and Thinking is a detail move that not only shows what a speaker is saying, but reveals the thoughts that the speaker is having. These thoughts can be related to what the speaker is saying, a response to another speaker, or simply an expression of the author's feelings or thoughts.

What Does This Move Look Like in Writing?

I didn't know what to say except, "Where?"
> —Jerry Spinelli, *from* Knots in My Yo-Yo String

"Did you hear what I said? Otha Vance is building hisself a hog house . . ."
Him. Himself, honey. Not hisself, Tut thought.
Doesn't Maylene of that school teach you a thing?
> —Virginia Hamilton, *from* Cousins

"Not if I could help it," she laughed. Did she think anyone would stay in that stuffy cabin by choice?
> —Elizabeth George Speare, *from* The Witch of Blackbird Pond

"I can wait." The truth is I've eaten an entire bag of Cheez Doodles. After school junk food is another fundamental right of the latchkey kid.
> —Rebecca Stead, *from* When You Reach Me

Each author uses this move a bit differently. Notice what they are thinking about. Spinelli is explaining the author's feelings about how to respond to another speaker. George Speare and Hamilton are making judgments about what the other speaker is saying, and Stead is letting the reader know a bit of information that the character's mother doesn't know yet—that she has devoured a bag of Cheez Doodles—and her stance on her rights as a latchkey kid.

When Writers Make This Move

Talking and Thinking is used when the author wants the reader to know something that the other characters do not know. Typically, this is the speaker's reaction to something, his true feelings (often showing that the speaker feels the opposite of what his or her words are communicating), or the evolution of his thinking. Because an author is sharing a private, unedited thought, this move almost always adds a clear sense of the author's (and speaker's) voice and style. This move is frequently used in nonfiction memoirs.

How I Introduce This Move

1. I begin showing images to my students. Typically, I find images of visually unappealing foods, odd fashion choices, or humorous images. When I project the first one, I say something about the image that is obviously the opposite of what I mean.

2. For example, for a picture of a man eating a raw egg with his bare hands, I might say, "That looks so delicious. I cannot wait to do that at lunch today." For an image of several clowns packed in a small car, I would say, "Comfortable ride there!" For an image of a complicated mathematical problem, I might say, "Well, that's pretty obvious."

3. After each image, I ask students to write my words in quotation marks. Then, I reveal that I may have said that, but that I was thinking something quite different. I ask if anyone wants to guess what I was really thinking.

4. Students always love to offer suggestions here. I record their different ideas after the quotation to show just how knowing what a character is thinking can impact how a reader interprets their words. (See Figure 6.10.)

5. After this, I explain that this move is called *Talking and Thinking*. This is a fun way not only to offer a block of speech, but also to

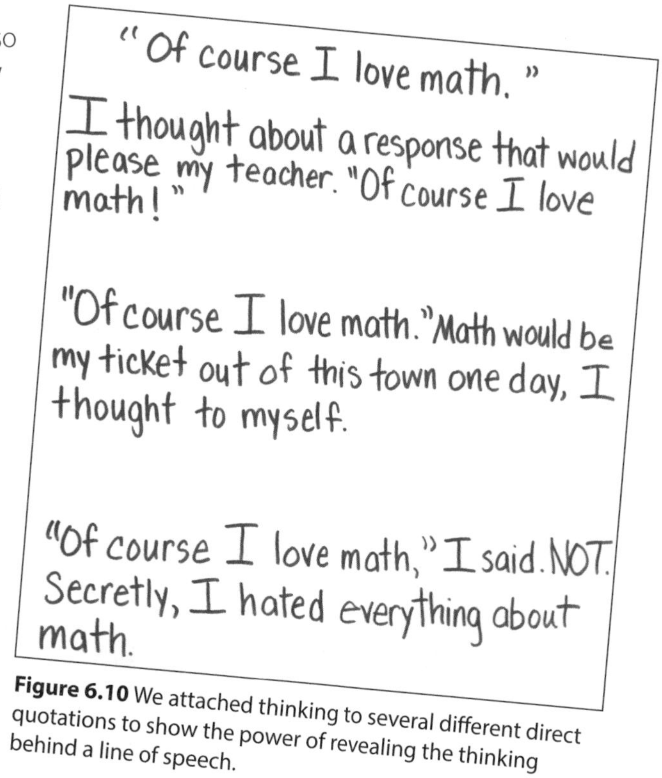

" Of course I love math. "
I thought about a response that would please my teacher. "Of course I love math! "

"Of course I love math." Math would be my ticket out of this town one day, I thought to myself.

"Of course I love math," I said. NOT. Secretly, I hated everything about math.

Figure 6.10 We attached thinking to several different direct quotations to show the power of revealing the thinking behind a line of speech.

show readers what you or the speaker is thinking. I continue to project different pictures and ask students to craft their own *Talking and Thinking* sentences with partners. Typically, we share our different sentences and repeat the exercise two or three times.

6. Once I feel comfortable that students understand this move, I share the examples from the What Does This Move Look Like in Writing? section. Because this lesson tends to center around sarcasm and humor, I make a special point to examine each of the examples and look at the different ways that authors use this move. We end the introduction by talking about each example and what we can learn from the characters talking and from their thinking.

Guided Writing Practice Ideas

* Draw a large thought bubble in advance and photocopy one for each student (or have them quickly draw their own). Tell students that you want them to become the pigeon from Mo Willems' *Don't Let the Pigeon Drive the Bus*. Read a few pages, then freeze, holding up the last page of dialogue, and ask students to write what the pigeon is really thinking when he says those lines. Ask students to read the dialogue bubble and their thought bubble together as an example of *Talking and Thinking*. Repeat as you read the rest of the book. *Don't Let the Pigeon Drive the Bus* works well because the majority of the book is made up of speech bubbles. This makes it easy to pair the thought bubbles and the speech bubbles. Students are able to "see" the pairing between talking and thinking.

* Select a few comic strips to read to your students. Deliberately choose ones with thought bubbles and speech bubbles. Then, ask students to create their own short cartoon strips. They can draw dialogue bubbles to show what the characters are thinking and thought bubbles to reveal their thoughts, considering what the characters would want to say publicly and what they might be thinking privately. For writers who need more guidance, consider creating comic strips with only one line of dialogue and one thought bubble.

* Show students examples of Family Circus comic strips from the 1970s and 1980s (they are still funny). These comics (http://familycircus.com/strip-archives/) are great because they typically feature one image and a line of dialogue in quotations under the picture. Challenge students to select one of the images and add a thought bubble showing what the characters are actually thinking while they are speaking. Next, have students exchange completed images. Once they have a peer's picture, each student should read what the character said and thought, then write *Talking and Thinking* sentences to communicate that on lined paper. Extend this by asking

partners to share what they wrote with one another or simply continue swapping images in small groups.

- On the board, write one or two examples of someone speaking in a way that requires a response. A few examples that have worked for me:

> The principal shouted at us, "Clear the building!"

> Suddenly Melanie rolled her eyes at me and hissed, "Leave me alone!"

> The new kid on the team turned to me and whined, "I hate soccer. I never win."

The more emotional the prompts, the more accessible this assignment is for students. I ask the class, **If this was happening to you, would you have some thoughts racing through your mind?** I call on a volunteer to share what the character who is hearing these people might be thinking and how his or her thoughts might differ from what he or she might say in response to any of these comments. Then, I record a few students' responses on the board. I ask students to work with partners to suggest situations and then write responses using *Talking and Thinking*. Let students share their sentences and talk about why they added their specific thought. (See Figure 6.11.)

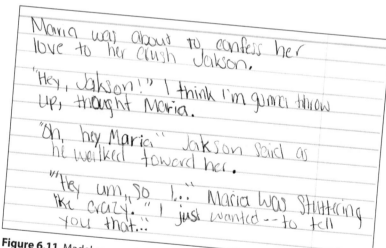

Figure 6.11 Madelyn uses the *Talking and Thinking* move to showcase a nervous conversation where a girl tries to confess her feelings to a crush.

Mix It Up

mix It Up is the last *Details That Speak* move that I teach students. I do this intentionally because *Mix It Up* relies on students being able to integrate multiple *Details That Speak* into their writing. When I first began teaching *Details That Speak*, I made the assumption that students would vary the different moves within the context of one conversation. The opposite happened. Students fell in love with a few favorites and relied solely on those to write dialogue. This resulted in a variety of strategies in our classroom, but still individual papers that felt monotonous and tiresome.

When students go to craft a conversation, they want to avoid relying solely on one or two moves. *Mix It Up* names this concept and draws students back to mentor texts, not to examine individual moves but to notice how authors mix up multiple types of moves to weave rich conversations. *Mix It Up* reminds students to intentionally include multiple styles.

What Does This Move Look Like in Writing?

"The sea is smooth," Ramo said. "It is a flat stone without any scratches."
My brother liked to pretend that one thing was another.
"The sea is not a stone without scratches, "I said. "It is water and no waves."

> —Scott O'Dell, *from* Island of the Blue Dolphins

"Yesterday," Sam nodded. "It was a good book.
I liked the bears."
"Where is it now?" asked Stella.
"I left it on the front porch," Sam answered,
"by the mailbox."
   —Lisa Campbell Ernst, *from* Stella Louella's Runaway Book

I heard his voice saying, "What's up, chief?" before
I knew it he was in the room.
I sat up. "Dad, can we go to the Phillies game on Saturday?"
   —Jerry Spinelli, *from* Crash

"Winifred! That is DISGUSTING."
Winnie smiled. "It's sugarless gum Mom. No cavities!"
"I was talking about the noise, not the gum." Mrs. Barringer
reached into the pocket of her skirt. "Here's a letter from
your brother. As soon as I clean up I'm going to fix lunch.
I expect you to join me in ten minutes. And please Winnie,
do SOMETHING about that hair."
Mrs. Barringer made a military turn and left the room.
   —Judy Blume, *from* Iggie's House

Notice how each of these authors combines multiple moves to share a conversation. None of the authors relies on one single move. By mixing it up, these authors craft conversations that seem to naturally unfold.

When Writers Make This Move

Published authors do this regularly. Flip open any book and you will identify and notice the collection of different moves in one simple conversation. I teach students that this move indicates the skill level of a writer. For students, this move allows them to vary their sentence structures and show their ability to write with style.

How I Introduce This Move

1. This move is introduced after I have taught students the other *Details That Speak* moves. I like to use this day to enjoy ice cream with my students. I begin by adding a scoop of vanilla ice cream into a plastic bowl. I hold up the bowl and ask students what they think of my dessert. Responses

vary, but I lead students to the idea that the dessert is just fine, but not very interesting.

2. I drizzle chocolate sauce on top and hold it up for students to see, asking if this is more interesting. Then, I add miniature marshmallows and sprinkles. As I add more toppings, I point out that the dessert becomes a bit more interesting. I also point out that if I dumped ten more toppings on top, it might get to be too much. Adding a bit of variety with two or three toppings is enough to make it interesting.

3. Then, I explain that bowls of ice cream are a lot like *Details That Speak*. A plain scoop of vanilla has little interest, just like always using one type of *Detail That Speaks* is also boring and will lose readers.

4. On the board, I write:

   Mom said, "Hi, James."

   I responded, "Hey, mom!"

   She asked, "Are you ready for dinner?"

   I yelled back, "Sure thing!"

   I walked into the kitchen.

5. While I write, I encourage students to think about which one move I am using. When I finish, I call on a student to name that I only wrote with *Beginning Dialogue Tags*. I ask, **Is this interesting? Does it show sentence variety? This is just like our plain scoop of ice cream. It is okay, but it has no variety. Readers will be bored!**

6. I ask students to name different ways that writers can write *Details That Speak*. What moves do writers make? While they are naming different moves and adding the names of the moves to the board, I begin scooping ice cream into bowls. After students have named each of the different moves, I explain that writers want to mix up these details. To build an effective conversation, quote speakers, or retell a conversation, writers should rely on multiple moves, just like I relied on multiple toppings to add variety to my ice cream.

7. At this point, I ask who wants to revise my conversation to include at least three different *Details That Speak*. **Who can rewrite this so that it has variety?** Each volunteer grabs a bowl of ice cream and the instruction to return to their desk and revise this. I make sure that everyone gets a bowl and that all students create their own revision. There is always at least one student who turns down my revision request and refuses ice cream. I still ask them to revise the conversation at their desk.

8. As students finish their revisions, they add toppings and enjoy their ice cream. When most students have finished their revisions, we share them and name what moves we noticed.

9. I have tried this without a sweet treat. Sadly, I never have the same level of active participation, nor the same level of eagerness to revise. Don't want the mess of ice cream? Consider Skittles, jelly beans, or M&M's. Begin with only one color and add others to represent the variety.

Guided Writing Practice Ideas

- Search online for two or three movie clips or commercials that feature a conversation. After students watch the clip, have them write down the dialogue. I typically let them name the characters and use as much imagination as possible. I find that younger students will need to watch the clip multiple times to do this. Some teachers even offer students a typed-up version of just the words that the characters say. When students share their writing, even they will be surprised at how differently they wrote about the same conversation.

- Select a page of dialogue and display it for students to see. Read the conversation once in its entirety. Then, read it again. This time stop at different points to think out loud. I say things like, **_Hey! I noticed that they began with a speech tag. I know what this author is doing. On the next line, they showed what the speaker was thinking!_** Go through and name the different _Details That Speak_. Afterward, project another passage for students. This works well with a document camera and a favorite novel. My go-to author for this is Jerry Spinelli. He uses a wide variety of dialogue in his writing. For nonfiction consider _Knots in My Yo-Yo_; for fiction consider _Crash_ or _Fourth Grade Rats_.

- Take a trip to the media center. Ask students to spend time looking through autobiographies or novels to select one conversation. Students are to revise that conversation using different _Details That Speak_ than the author did. Students can share the originals and the revisions with the class the next day.

- Ask students to recall a conversation that they have had in real life. Then, ask them to record that conversation on paper, using a variety of _Details That Speak_. Invite students to share their writing in small groups. (See Figure 6.12.)

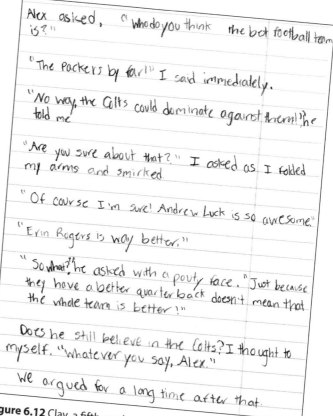

Alex asked, "Who do you think the best football team is?"

"The Packers by far!" I said immediately.

"No way, the Colts could dominate against them!" he told me

"Are you sure about that?" I asked as I folded my arms and smirked

"Of course I'm sure! Andrew Luck is so awesome."

"Erin Rogers is way better."

"So what?" he asked with a pouty face. "Just because they have a better quarterback doesn't mean that the whole team is better!"

Does he still believe in the Colts? I thought to myself. "Whatever you say, Alex."

We argued for a long time after that.

Figure 6.12 Clay, a fifth grader, writes about a conversation that he had with a friend about whether the Colts or Packers are the better football team. Notice he has used _Ending Dialogue Tags, Invisible Tags, Middle Tags, Say What?_, and _Talking and Thinking_ moves to build his conversation.

- Ask students to think about a memorable conversation from their past. Suggest moments where they learned something, changed as a person, or accepted new truths or beliefs. Ask students to write about that conversation, using the *Mix It Up* move. Although students are welcome to share, for this activity I let students know in advance that no one will read their conversations but me. This expected privacy helps students to share more meaningful moments. I have been moved to tears with some of the conversations and moments that students have shared. I typically write a heartfelt response to each student as feedback.

7

Moving Forward

WITH *Lesson Clusters and Classroom Ideas*

*n*ow that you have all of these great ideas—how do you dig in and use them? How do you make sense and decide what fits where?

Our goal as teachers is not to teach every lesson or move in this book. You will need to organize and select lessons to meet your classroom goals and your students' instructional needs. I typically determine which lessons to teach based on students' writing needs, which I notice during small-group work or conferences. Although that is most effective for me, I have also organized lessons to teach specific genres or even to prepare for writing assessments.

Lesson Clusters: Detail Moves for Targeted Writing Goals

A lesson cluster is a group of specific moves that work together to target a specific goal, such as writing in a particular genre, writing for a high-stakes assessment, or writing to address common rubric-driven goals. You can teach these lessons to your entire class, or develop a series of small-group lessons to work with students who struggle with certain types of writing or specific goals. You can even use these lesson clusters to reteach specific skills or crafts during writing conferences.

Genre-Driven Writing Goals

Although this is a book about crafting details, the heart of writing, these moves can also help students to write strong introductions and conclusions across all genres.

Writing Goals	*Moves*

Narrative Beginnings

Since I began teaching in the 1990s, narrative writing has always been a part of my writing instruction. In my elementary classes, we focused on crafting imaginative stories or recreating events in our lives. When I worked with older students, we focused more on memoirs and realistic fiction. Regardless of the type of narrative, the goal of crafting narrative hooks, leads, or beginnings was always front and center. How can writers develop text that engages readers? How do writers build context or situate their stories? These lesson clusters feature writing moves that all lend themselves to creating narrative beginnings that do just that.

Action Clues (page 27)
Zoom In (page 36)
Set It Up (page 51)
Time Marker (page 71)
Location Marker (page 75)
INGS Up Front (page 83)
Explain That Sound (page 92)

Narrative Conclusions

THE END. We have all experienced the disappointment, or dare I say horror, of reading a student's work and suddenly being slapped in the face with those two words. THE END is the crutch for students who have run out of ideas, finished describing the events, or simply grown tired of writing. The lessons here represent possibilities to move students away from this and toward richer, more meaningful narrative endings.

Zoom In (page 36)
Repeaters (page 40)
Thought Bubbles (page 55)
Adverb Comma (page 79)
INGs Up Front (page 83)
EDs Up Front (page 88)

Opinion and Argument Beginnings

When students are beginning any type of writing where they are establishing a claim, they tend to write in formulaic, stiff language. In real-life, arguments are rarely written in this manner. In fact, arguments are often the more passionate type of writing. This lesson clusters offer multiple moves that students can consider when beginning an argument.

Opposite Side (page 107)
Imagine This (page 116)
Very Complicated (page 120)
Now and Then (page 126)
We the People (page 129)

Informational Beginnings

Narratives tend to begin in ways that are much different from informational text. Often students attempt to apply the same strategies to both types of writing. An attempt to establish a setting or describe a character within the context of informational or opinion writing results in beginnings that feel artificial or just plain awkward. When explaining events or arguing a particular viewpoint, students need ways to establish context and situate their topics, but they also need a wide range of possibilities so that they can craft beginnings that make sense and fit the type of writing that they are crafting. This lesson cluster offers multiple moves that students can make when beginning an explanatory/informational or opinion/argument text.

Numbers Game (page 123)
What's Next? (page 146)
Sweet and Sour (page 150)
Big Deals and Famous Firsts (page 154)
Define It (page 158)
So Important (page 172)

Informational and Argument Conclusions

Just as stories can begin differently than informational and opinion writing, they can also end in different ways. This lesson cluster offers students a variety of moves that work well with both explanatory/informational and opinion/argument endings.

If . . . Then (page 102)
Good Question (page 112)
Call to Action (page 133)
In Other Words (page 169)

Rubric-Driven Writing Goals

Many scoring guides are aligned to six traits of writing: sentence fluency, word choice, organization, voice, conventions, and ideas. More recently, presentation has even been added to popular writing rubrics. Numerous writing rubrics and instructional programs are arranged around some or all of these areas. As a result of the popularity of these traits and the frequent embedding into scoring guides and assessment rubrics, teachers often set instructional goals around these traits and develop instruction to reinforce or teach competency in these areas. This section outlines writing moves that help to strengthen student writing in the five traits that are most clearly related to the content of writing.

Writing Goals	*Moves*
Sentence Fluency Sentence fluency is about the flow of the language. How do the word patterns impact the rhythm and movement of the text? How are sentences structured to flow smoothly for the eye and the ear?	*Right in the Middle* (page 31) *Repeaters* (page 40) *Adverb Comma* (page 79) *INGs Up Front* (page 83) *EDs Up Front* (page 88) *Explain That Sound* (page 92)
Word Choice Word choice is about the precise language that an author selects. How do the words present the ideas? Are they rich, colorful, and appropriate for the type of writing?	*Action Clues* (page 27) *Right in the Middle* (page 31) *Personify It* (page 48) *Set It Up* (page 51) *Good Question* (page 112) *We the People* (page 129) *In Other Words* (page 169)
Organization Organization is about how students present and arrange their ideas. How are ideas grouped? This is about the structure or pattern of ideas.	*Time Marker* (page 71) *Location Marker* (page 75) *Opposite Side* (page 107) *Very Complicated* (page 120) *Now and Then* (page 126) *What's Next?* (page 146) *So Important* (page 172)
Voice Many people consider the voice to be the feeling of the individual writer coming through the page. Can we sense the magic, feelings, or conviction of the author? How is this communicated through the text?	*Just Like That* (page 23) *Pop Culture References* (page 44) *Thought Bubbles* (page 55) *Imagine This* (page 116) *Call to Action* (page 133) *Polar Opposites* (page 142) *Also Known As (AKA)* (page 165)
Ideas Ideas are about the content of the writing. What is at the core or the focus of the writing? What is the heart of the text? These are the foundational ideas that students build their entire piece around.	*State the Obvious* (page 19) *Act & Think* (page 65) *But, Why?* (page 68) *Opposite Side* (page 107) *Sweet and Sour* (page 150) *Define It* (page 158) *Name an Example* (page 161) *So Important* (page 172)

Students' Charts: Fostering Writing Independence

Ideally, we would have sufficient instructional time to guide students through enough moves that they develop a toolkit of details to elaborate and write independently. Students would know the moves and choose what worked best and when. However, we know that doesn't always happen as often as we'd like. To help students to make the moves their own, you can offer students the If You Want to . . ./Try This . . . charts that you'll find in the early pages of Chapters 2–6, which are similar to the teacher charts in those same sections of each chapter, or you can create your own versions of these charts that are tailored to your students' needs. Students can keep these charts in their writing folders and refer to them when they are planning and revising their writing.

Classroom Ideas: Making Detail Moves "Sticky"

I never want my students just to complete a task or write a piece for me. I want them to take these writing moves and internalize them so that they can apply the moves to any type of writing or communication that they choose. The goal is to make my writing instruction "stick" with students. I want them to hold on to these ideas and moves for good. This sticky instruction builds agency among my students by teaching them moves that they can take away from my classroom and apply to anything that they do. Each of the suggestions that follow can help you make your writing instruction stickier.

The Writing Moves Clipboard: Transforming Writing Conferences

When I first began to hold writing conferences with my students, I was beyond frustrated. I watched videos by well-known writing gurus and read everything I could get my hands on about conferring, but when it came to implementation, it was terrible. Most of my students had trouble verbalizing what they wanted to do in their writing. I also struggled with quick ways to reteach or redirect students. The most upsetting part was that all of my conferences took way too long. I am not a math whiz, but at five minutes a conference, with about twenty minutes to conference, in a classroom of thirty kids, I couldn't confer with most of my class!

Once I began teaching my students explicit moves for their writing, conferences took on a new life. First of all, we had a new, common language. We were able to name what we were doing. We were able to talk about intentionality and why specific sentences were developed. Our conversations became specific and started to reflect a shared understanding that we had lots of bite-size goals for each piece that we crafted.

To realize this shift, I added one thing to my writing classroom: a moves clipboard. The clipboard had all of my students' names and a column for each move that I introduced. During guided practice, I circulated and recorded plus and minus marks for each student. If a student struggled with a move, I recorded a minus. If a student showed mastery and could use a move skillfully, I recorded a plus mark. After several days of observation, I had lots of data on what my students could and could not do. Next, I looked at my clipboard and started to see patterns. Instead of creating an artificial conference schedule or just conferring with students who requested conferences, I began to organize small-group conferences. These conferences were driven by the data collected on my clipboard. (See Figure 7.1.)

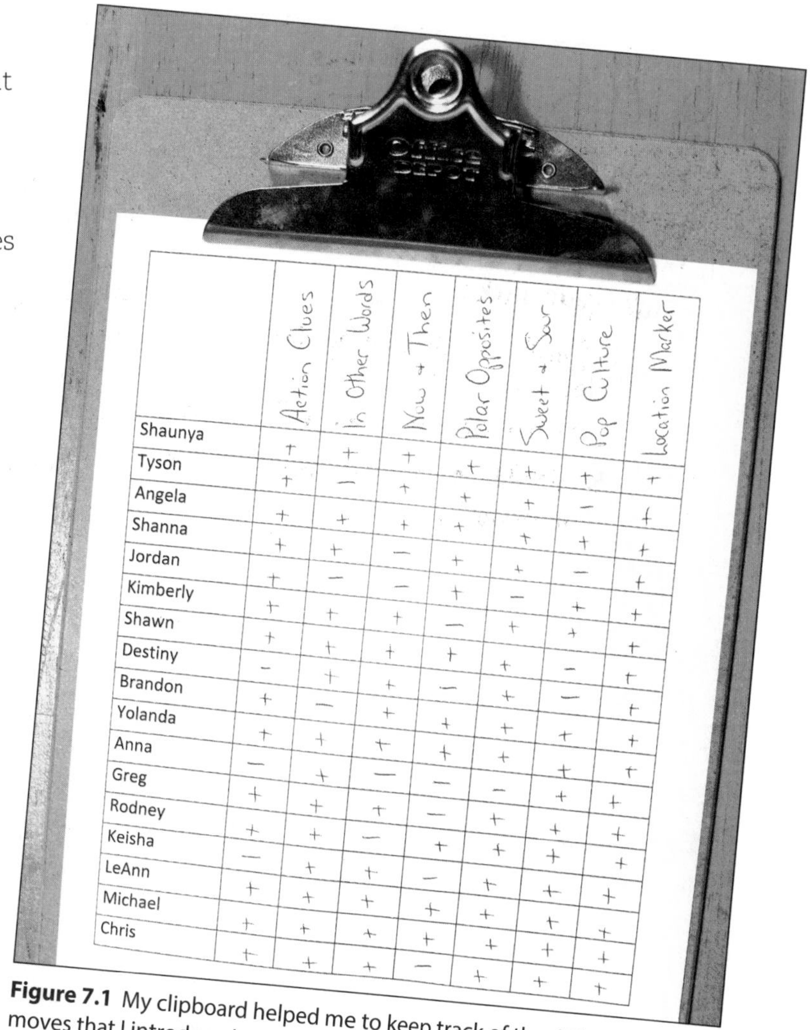

When we sat down to confer, I already knew what we needed to discuss. This way, I could gather tools for quick reteaching ahead of time and have very targeted conversations with students.

Figure 7.1 My clipboard helped me to keep track of the different writing moves that I introduced and plan small groups and conferences based on the data.

This strategy also helped me to reach more students throughout the week. By using the data collected during our guided practice activities, I was able to stop going through the motions of a conference and start talking about real craft issues.

Quick Writes: Keep the Practice Going

While writing should be authentic and meaningful, students still need practice opportunities that are not about crafting an authentic, lengthy piece of writing. Students need multiple opportunities to try out writing strategies. *Quick Writes* are short (one or two paragraphs) writing assignments where students are asked to try out several writing moves at once.

I like to do my *Quick Writes* outside of the writing workshop. I typically assign these as bell ringer activities at the start of the day or as exit slip activities at the end of the day. For my *Quick Writes*, I select one or two moves that have already been introduced and challenge students to test-drive those moves in a short, written response. Typically, students have five or ten minutes to respond to a question. (See Figures 7.2 and 7.3.)

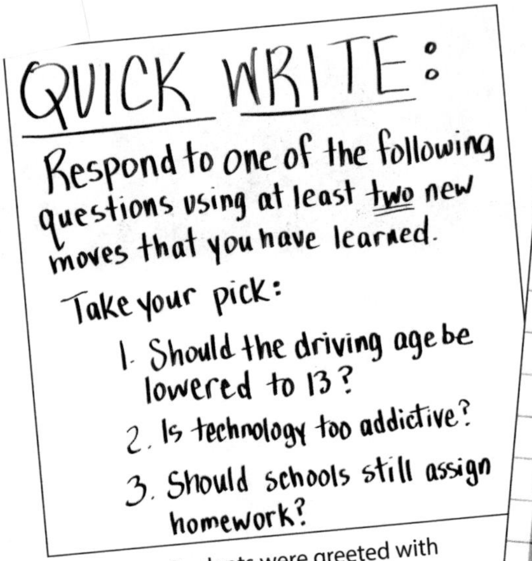

QUICK WRITE:

Respond to one of the following questions using at least __two__ new moves that you have learned.

Take your pick:

1. Should the driving age be lowered to 13?
2. Is technology too addictive?
3. Should schools still assign homework?

Figure 7.2 Students were greeted with a *Quick Write* question as they entered the classroom.

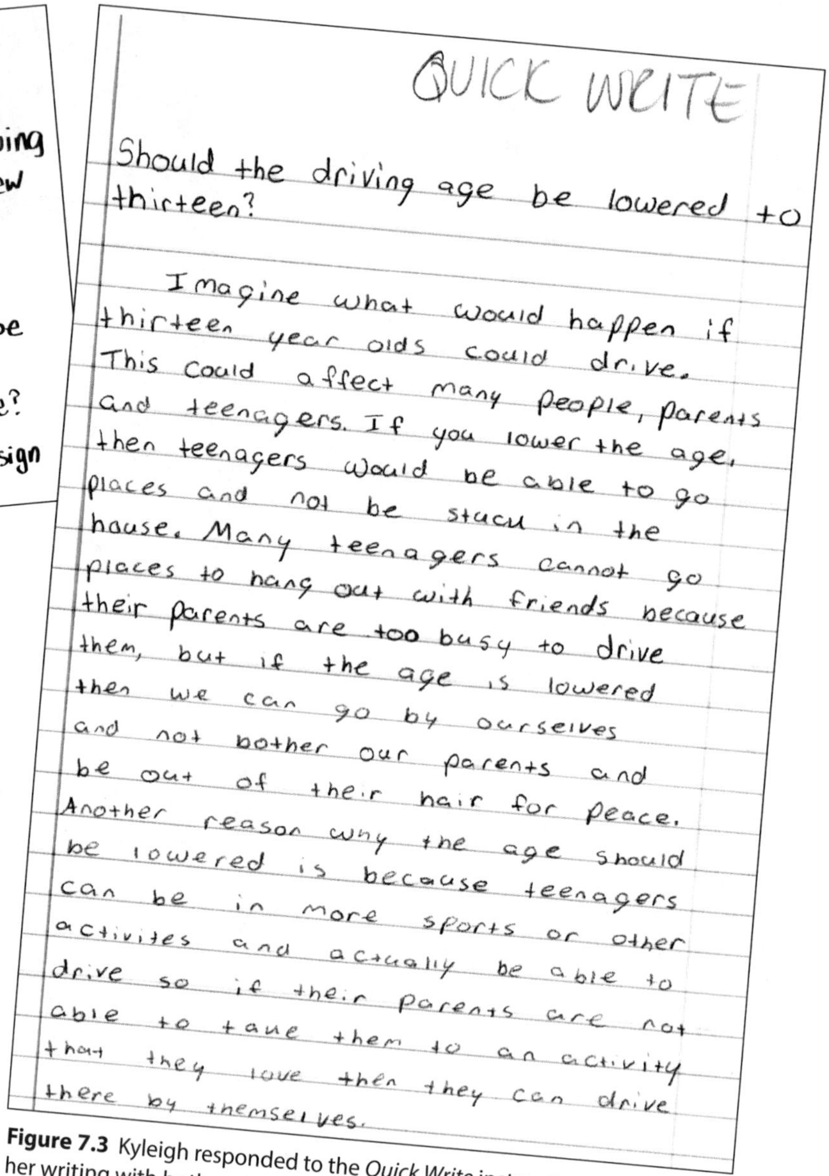

QUICK WRITE

Should the driving age be lowered to thirteen?

Imagine what would happen if thirteen year olds could drive. This could affect many people, parents and teenagers. If you lower the age, then teenagers would be able to go places and not be stuck in the house. Many teenagers cannot go places to hang out with friends because their parents are too busy to drive them, but if the age is lowered then we can go by ourselves and not bother our parents and be out of their hair for peace. Another reason why the age should be lowered is because teenagers can be in more sports or other activites and actually be able to drive so if their parents are not able to taue them to an activity that they love then they can drive there by themselves.

Figure 7.3 Kyleigh responded to the *Quick Write* instructions by beginning her writing with both an *Imagine This* and an *If... Then* move.

Spiral Writing Journal: Modeling Writing Moves

Write with your students each day! Whenever my students have a guided practice activity or any type of writing, I make sure that I model that type of writing as well. It doesn't matter if this is the first or fifth time that we have discussed a move, I want to model how I use the move.

To make this practice even more powerful, I keep a large spiral writing journal of all of the writing that I model for my students throughout the year. For my writing, I like to use an easel and large spiral chart paper. I dedicate at least one large chart to my writing each year. Sometimes, I need multiple charts. Each day that I write, I record the date on the chart. The next day, I either continue writing on that same page (but add the new date) or simply flip the page the next day to continue writing. I like to build this collection of my own writing. When students are frustrated or need help with a strategy, it is a great resource to flip back to the day when the strategy was first introduced and revisit my own writing. I also find that students will walk over to the chart during independent writing and flip through the pages looking for something significant that they remember or want to revisit.

Annotated Writing

We tend to associate annotation with reading. When you teach writing moves, annotation can be a powerful strategy to focus on specific and intentional moves in writing. There are several ways to use annotation in writing. The first way that I depend on is to share a piece of writing with my students on a large chart or on the whiteboard (Figure 7.4). I read the text and go through and underline different sentences and words. Then, in the margin I name what move I notice. The second way to do this is to have students annotate their own writing. Ask them to underline what they have done and name the moves in the margin. Another way to use annotation is to ask students to annotate each other's writing. They can do this by writing on sticky notes and placing them directly on the text, naming what they notice. This can even be extended to textbooks and novels.

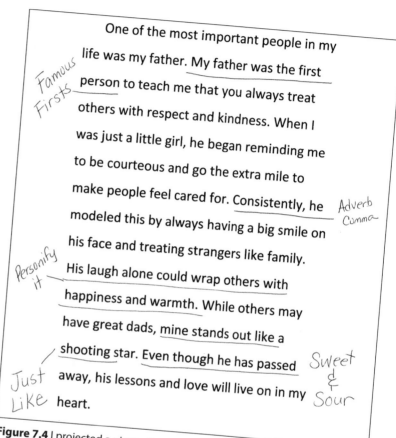

Figure 7.4 I projected a piece of my own writing for students to see. Then, we read it together and stopped to mark different moves that we noticed.

Individual Strategy Notebooks

Most teachers are familiar with writing journals, notebooks, or folders to keep track of student work. Those types of notebooks simply house students' drafts. Although these types of notebooks can be used strategically and powerfully in classrooms, if students don't see these notebooks as tools, they won't reach for them when they need help with a particular writing dilemma. Strategy notebooks are different. These types of notebooks are filled with different writing moves. Students refer to their own notebooks just as they would any type of reference tool.

I usually have students decorate the cover of a spiral-bound notebook at the beginning of the school year. We title the notebook *My Strategy Notebook* and leave three or four pages in the front blank. These pages serve as the table of contents. Each time we add a new move, we write the name of the move at the top of a page, write a definition describing the move, and record several mentor text or student-created examples of the move. Throughout the year, we may revisit the pages to add more examples or tips for using the move.

At the end of the school year, this is typically one of the only things that students make sure that they take with them. In fact, I get more emails and calls from other teachers asking about the strategy notebooks than about anything else. Usually, the teachers I hear from have first encountered the strategy notebooks when one of my former students pulled out his or her notebook to reference during a writing assignment.

Class Strategy Notebooks

The class strategy notebook serves as a master version of the individual strategy notebooks. This notebook is typically maintained by me at the beginning of the year. As the year progresses, I begin to call on volunteers to add the new moves we learn to the class strategy notebook. Students who have been absent know to visit this notebook to see what new moves might have been introduced while they were out, and parents like to look through the notebook during open house or on parent nights.

Some teachers I have worked with use technology to create their classroom strategy notebooks. A common practice is to create one PowerPoint presentation and add a slide to represent each move after it has been taught. This allows for space to add a picture of any anchor charts or visuals from the lesson. Some teachers make these files available on their classroom website or through email as well.

Anchor Charts and Visuals

I cannot say enough about the powerful impact that visuals have on student retention. Although space will never allow us to always display every anchor chart we create all year, it is important to create them with your students and keep them up when you are introducing a skill. Charts offer a visual reminder of what is expected, how to get there, and ways to troubleshoot. Most students will not come to you and readily admit that they need some help or cannot remember a writing move. Anchor charts and visuals provide a consistent visual reminder for all students.

To save space, consider hanging retired charts on pants or skirt hangers. You can snag these from a discount store for a few bucks. Once they are attached to hangers, use a garment stand to house multiple charts. If you or your students want to revisit a chart, you can quickly access it from the garment stand, but you don't have the clutter associated with dozens of charts.

Get Messy! Make Some Mistakes!

As a teacher, I wanted my kids to have the best instruction possible. If this meant late nights planning at the school, summer days filled with lesson planning, or weekends camped out at the local Starbucks to stay caffeinated and brainstorm new ways to teach a new writing move, I was game. This also meant I took it personally when I didn't get the results I wanted. Back to the drawing board I would go, disappointed that things didn't go exactly as I planned.

Eventually, I learned not to be so tough on myself. Writing is an art—it takes time to get it just right. I am going to make mistakes. I am going to have lessons that fall flat. I am going to have moments where I am unsure of the best way to help a student. It happens. After all these years of teaching, I have finally learned to let go of the desire for perfection and just get in there and give it my all. I have learned to simply enjoy both my students and their steps toward honing their own writing craft. Just like we tell our kids: learning is a process, not a destination. Enjoy the journey!

—Roz

Mentor Texts Referenced in This Book

Alexie, Sherman. 2009. *The Absolutely True Diary of a Part-Time Indian*. New York: Little, Brown Books for Young Readers.

Allard, Harry. 2014. The Miss Nelson Collection. Boston: HMH Books for Young Readers.

Allman, Toney. 2014. *Food in Schools*. Chicago: Norwood House Press.

Anderson, Laurie Halse. 2005. *Thank You, Sarah: The Woman Who Saved Thanksgiving*. New York: Simon & Schuster.

Armstrong, William. 2002. *Sounder*. New York: HarperCollins.

Asher, Jay. 2011. *Thirteen Reasons Why*. New York: Razorbill.

Atwater Richard, and Florence Atwater. 1992. *Mr. Popper's Penguins*. New York: Little, Brown Books for Young Readers.

Avi. 2003. *The Secret School*. Boston: HMH Books for Young Readers.

———. 2013. *Sophia's War: A Tale of the Revolution*. New York: Beach Lane Books.

Babbit, Natalie. 2007. *Tuck Everlasting*. New York: Square Fish.

Balliett, Blue. 2015. *Pieces and Players*. New York: Scholastic.

Banks, Lynne Reid. 2004. *The Mystery of the Cupboard*. New York: HarperCollins.

Bartoletti, Susan Campbell. 2005. *Black Potatoes: The Story of the Great Irish Famine, 1845–1850*. Boston: HMH Books for Young Readers.

Baum, Frank. 1996. *The Wizard of Oz*. Mineola, NY: Dover.

Becker, Aaron. 2014. *Journey*. Somerville, MA: Walker Books Ltd.

———. 2015. *Quest*. Somerville, MA: Walker Books Ltd.

Berne, Jennifer. 2015. *Manfish: A Story of Jacques Cousteau*. San Francisco: Chronicle Books.

Blume, Judy. 2007. *Tales of a Fourth Grade Nothing*. New York: Puffin.

———. 2014. *Blubber*. New York: Atheneum Books for Young Readers.

———. 2014. *Deenie*. New York: Atheneum Books for Young Readers.

———. 2014. *Iggie's House*. New York: Atheneum Books for Young Readers.

Brallier, Jess. 2002. *Who Was Albert Einstein?* New York: Grosset & Dunlap.

Bridges, Ruby. 1999. *Through My Eyes*. New York: Scholastic.

Browne, Anthony. 2001. *Voices in the Park*. New York: DK Children.

Bruchac, Joseph. 1998. *A Boy Called Slow*. New York: Puffin Books.

Buckley, James. 2013. *Who Was Milton Hershey?* New York: Grosset & Dunlap.

Burgan, Michael. 2014. *Who Was Henry Ford?* New York: Grosset & Dunlap.

———. 2014. *Who Was Theodore Roosevelt?* New York: Grosset & Dunlap.

Burns, Loree Griffin. 2010. *Tracking Trash: Flotsam, Jetsam, and the Science of Ocean Motion*. Boston: HMH Books for Young Readers.

Burton, Virginia Lee. 1977. *Mike Mulligan and His Steam Shovel*. Boston: HMH Books for Young Readers.

Bush, George H. W. 1988. Acceptance Speech at the Republican National Convention. August 18. http://millercenter.org/president/bush/speeches/speech-5526.

Carroll, Lewis. 2015. *Alice's Adventures in Wonderland*. Princeton, NJ: Princeton University Press.

Chall, Marsha Wilson. 1992. *Up North at the Cabin*. New York: HarperCollins.

Cherry, Lynne. 2000. *The Great Kapok Tree: A Tale of the Amazon Rain Forest*. Boston: HMH Books for Young Readers.

Chin-Lee, Cynthia. 2008. *Amelia to Zora: Twenty-Six Women Who Changed the World*. Watertown, MA: Charlesbridge.

Christopher, Matt. 1986. *The Kid Who Only Hit Homers*. New York: Little, Brown Books for Young Readers.

Cleary, Beverly. 2008. *Otis Spofford*. New York: HarperCollins.

———. 2013. *Beezus and Ramona*. New York: HarperCollins.

———. 2014. *The Mouse and the Motorcycle*. New York: HarperCollins.

Clement-Moore, Rosemary. 2013. "Monster Recognition for Beginners." In *Demigods and Monsters: Your Favorite Authors on Rick Riordan's Percy Jackson and the Olympians Series*, edited by Rick Riordan, 1–12. Dallas: Smart Pop.

Clements, Andrew. 1998. *Frindle*. New York: Atheneum Books for Young Readers.

Coad, John. 2009. *Reducing Pollution*. Chicago: Heinemann-Raintree.

Collins, Suzanne. 2010. *The Hunger Games*. New York: Scholastic.

Criswell, Patti Kelley. 2009. *Stand Up for Yourself and Your Friends: Dealing with Bullies and Bossiness and Finding a Better Way*. Middleton, WI: American Girl.

Curtis, Christopher Paul. 2000. *The Watsons Go to Birmingham—1963*. New York: Laurel-Leaf Books.

———. 2004. *Bud, Not Buddy*. New York: Laurel-Leaf Books.

———. 2006. *Bucking the Sarge*. New York: Laurel-Leaf Books.

Dahl, Roald. 2007. *The BFG: A Set of Plays*. New York: Puffin Books.

———. 2007. *The Witches: A Set of Plays*. New York: Puffin Books.

David, Laurie, and Cambria Gordon. 2007. *The Down-to-Earth Guide to Global Warming*. New York: Scholastic.

Davies, Jacqueline. 2009. *The Lemonade War*. Boston: HMH Books for Young Readers.

De La Peña, Matt. 2010. *Mexican Whiteboy*. New York: Ember.

de Saint-Exupery, Antoine. 2000. *The Little Prince*. Boston: Mariner Books.

Demuth, Patricia Brennan. *What Was Ellis Island?* New York: Grosset & Dunlap.

Denenberg, Barry. 1990. *Stealing Home: The Story of Jackie Robinson*. New York: Scholastic.

DiCamillo, Kate. 2002. *The Tiger Rising*. Somerville, MA: Candlewick.

———. 2015. *Flora and Ulysses: The Illuminated Adventures*. Somerville, MA: Candlewick.

Dorion, Christiane. 2010. *Earth's Garbage Crisis*. Independence, KY: National Geographic School Publishers.

Dorros, Arthur. 1997. *Abuela*. New York: Puffin Books.

Draper, Sharon. 2015. *Stella by Starlight*. New York: Atheneum Books for Young Readers.

Dunham, Montrew. 1996. *Neil Armstrong: Young Flyer*. New York: Alladin.

Erdrich, Louise. 2002. *The Birchbark House*. New York: Disney-Hyperion.

Ernst, Lisa Campbell. 2001. *Stella Louella's Runaway Book*. New York: Simon & Schuster Books for Young Readers.

Farley, Walter. 1991. *The Black Stallion*. New York: Random House.

Fitzhugh, Louise. 2001. *Harriet the Spy*. New York: Yearling.

Fleischman, Sid. 2003. *The Whipping Boy*. New York: Greenwillow Books.

Fletcher, Ralph. 2014. *Guy-Write: What Every Guy Writer Needs to Know*. New York: Square Fish.

Freedman, Russell. 1990. *Cowboys of the Wild West*. Boston: HMH Books for Young Readers.

Gardiner, John Reynolds. 2010. *Stone Fox*. New York: HarperCollins.

George, Jean Craighead. 2004. *My Side of the Mountain*. New York: Puffin Books.

Giff, Patricia Reilly. 1999. *Lily's Crossing*. New York: Bantam Doubleday Dell.

Gifford, Clive. 2005. *Pollution*. Chicago: Heinemann-Raintree.

Gilpin, Caroline Crosson. 2012. *National Geographic Readers: Abraham Lincoln*. Independence, KY: National Geographic Children's Books.

Grabenstein, Chris. 2014. *Escape from Mr. Lemoncello's Library*. New York: Yearling.

———. 2015. *The Island of Dr. Libris*. New York: Random House Books for Young Readers.

Griffey, Harriet. 2013. *DK Readers: Secrets of the Mummies*. New York: DK Children.

Gutman, Dan. 2009. *Recycle This Book: 100 Top Children's Book Authors Tell You How to Go Green*. New York: Yearling.

Hakim, Joy. 2007. *A History of US: The First Americans: Prehistory–1600*. New York: Oxford University Press.

Hamilton, Virginia. 2011. *Cousins*. New York: Scholastic.

Harrison, Geoffrey C., and Thomas F. Scott. 2014. *Great Debates: Church and State*. Chicago: Norwood House Press.

Haugen, Hayley Mitchell. 2014. *Video Games*. Chicago: Norwood House Press.

Henkes, Kevin. 2008. *Chrysanthemum*. New York: HarperCollins.

Hicks, Deron. 2013. *Secrets of Shakespeare's Grave*. Boston: HMH Books for Young Readers.

Hopkinson, Deborah. 2007. *From Slave to Soldier: Based on a True Civil War Story*. New York: Simon Spotlight.

Hughes, Langston. 1995. "April Rain Song." In *The Collected Poems of Langston Hughes*, edited by Arnold Rampersad, 595. New York: Vintage.

Hunt, Lynda Mullaly. 2015. *Fish in a Tree*. New York: Nancy Paulsen Books.

Jankeliowitch, Anne. 2014. *Kids Who Are Changing the World*. Naperville, IL: Jabberwocky.

Johnson, Jr., John. 2010. *Living Green*. New York: Flash Point.

Kamkwamba, William, and Bryan Mealer. 2015. *The Boy Who Harnessed the Wind: Young Readers Edition*. New York: Dial Books.

Kanefield, Teri. 2014. *The Girl from the Tar Paper School: Barbara Rose Johns and the Advent of the Civil Rights Movement*. New York: Harry N. Abrams.

Kelly, Jacqueline. 2011. *The Evolution of Calpurnia Tate*. New York: Square Fish.

Kennedy, John F. 1961. Inaugural Address. January 20. www.ushistory.org/documents/ask-not.htm.

Kessler, David. 2012. *Your Food Is Fooling You: How Your Brain Is Hijacked by Sugar, Salt, and Fat*. New York: Roaring Brook Press.

Konigsburg, E. L. 1998. *The View from Saturday*. New York: Atheneum Books for Young Readers.

———. 2007. *From the Mixed-up Files of Mrs. Basil E. Frankweiler*. New York: Atheneum Books for Young Readers.

Koscielniak, Bruce. 2013. *About Time: A First Look at Time and Clocks*. Boston: HMH Books for Young Readers.

Kroll, Jennifer. 2003. *Simply Shakespeare: Readers Theatre for Young People*. Santa Barbara, CA: Libraries Unlimited.

Krull, Kathleen. 2000. *Wilma Unlimited: How Wilma Rudolph Became the World's Fastest Woman*. Boston: HMH Books for Young Readers.

Kumar, Aanchal Broca. 2014. *Why Should I Recycle? A Smart Kids Guide to a Green World*. New Delhi, India: The Energy and Resources Institute.

LaMarche, Jim. 2002. *The Raft*. New York: HarperCollins.

Lehman, Barbara. 2004. *The Red Book*. Boston: HMH Books for Young Readers.

L'Engle, Madeleine. 2007. *A Wrinkle in Time*. New York: Square Fish.

Lewis, C. S. 1994. *The Lion, the Witch, and the Wardrobe*. New York: HarperCollins.

Loewen, Nancy. 2011. *Believe Me, Goldilocks Rocks!* North Mankato, MN: Picture Window Books.

London, Jonathan. 1998. *Hurricane*. Boston: Lothrop, Lee & Shepard.

Lowry, Lois. 2011. *Number the Stars*. Boston: HMH Books for Young Readers.

———. 2014. *The Giver*. Boston: HMH Books for Young Readers.

Macaulay, David. 1998. *The New Way Things Work*. Boston: HMH Books for Young Readers.

MacLachlan, Patricia. 2015. *Sarah, Plain and Tall*. New York: HarperCollins.

Mass, Wendy. 2011. *The Candymakers*. New York: Little, Brown Books for Young Readers.

McDonough, Yona Zeldis. 2002. *Who Was Harriet Tubman?* New York: Grosset & Dunlap.

Miller, Brandon Marie. 2009. *Benjamin Franklin, American Genius: His Life and Ideas with 21 Activities*. Chicago: Chicago Review Press.

Montgomery, Sy. 2009. *Quest for the Tree Kangaroo: An Expedition to the Cloud Forest of New Guinea*. Boston: HMH Books for Young Readers.

Mooney, Carla. 2011. *Explorers of the New World: Discover the Golden Age of Exploration with 22 Projects*. White River Junction, VT: Nomad Press.

———. 2013. *Forensics: Uncover the Science and Technology of Crime Scene Investigation*. White River Junction, VT: Nomad Press.

———. 2014. *Recycling*. Chicago: Norwood House Press.

Moore, Kay. 1998. *If You Lived at the Time of the American Revolution*. New York: Scholastic.

Murphy, Frank. 1949. *Always Inventing: The True Story of Thomas Alva Edison*. New York: Cartwheel Books.

Napoli, Donna Jo. 2010. *Alligator Bayou*. New York: Wendy Lamb Books.

Nelson, Kadir. 2008. *We Are the Ship: The Story of Negro League Baseball*. New York: Jump at the Sun.

Nixon, Richard. 1973. Press Conference at the Annual Convention of the Associated Press Managing Editors Association, November 17. www.emersonkent.com /speeches/i_am_not_a_crook.htm.

O'Dell, Scott. 2010. *Island of the Blue Dolphins*. Boston: HMH Books for Young Readers.

Orwell, George. 1950. *1984*. New York: Signet.

Palacio, R. J. 2012. *Wonder*. New York: Knopf Books for Young Readers.

Paratore, Coleen. 2009. "The Swap Shop." In *Recycle this Book: 100 Top Children's Book Authors Tell You How to Go Green*, edited by Dan Gutman, 107–108. New York: Yearling.

Park, Linda Sue. 2010. *Keeping Score*. Boston: HMH Books for Young Readers.

———. 2011. *A Long Walk to Water: Based on a True Story*. Boston: HMH Books for Young Readers.

Parks, Peggy. 2014. *Matters of Opinion: Smoking*. Chicago: Norwood House Press.

Paterson, Katherine. 2004. *Bridge to Terabithia*. New York: HarperTeen.

Paulsen, Gary. 2006. *Hatchet*. New York: Simon & Schuster Books for Young Readers.

———. 2007. *Harris and Me*. Boston: HMH Books for Young Readers.

Peck, Richard. 2004. *A Long Way from Chicago*. New York: Puffin Books.

Pinkney, Jerry. 2011. *The Lion and the Mouse*. New York: Walker & Company.

Perritano, John. 2010. *The Transcontinental Railroad*. New York: Scholastic.

Polacco, Patricia. 1998. *Chicken Sunday*. New York: Puffin Books.

Ritter, John. 2005. *The Boy Who Saved Baseball*. New York: Puffin Books.

Robbins, Ken. 2009. *Food for Thought: The Stories Behind the Things We Eat*. New York: Flash Point.

Rochelle, Belinda. 1997. *Witnesses to Freedom: Young People Who Fought for Civil Rights*. New York: Puffin Books.

Roehm, Michelle, and Marianne Monson-Burton. 1998. *Boys Know it All: Wise Thoughts and Wacky Ideas from Guys Just Like You*. Hillsboro, OR: Beyond Words Publishing.

Roosevelt, Franklin Delano. 1933. "Inaugural Address of the President." March 4. http://historymatters.gmu.edu/d/5057/.

Roth, Veronica. 2014. *Divergent*. New York: Katherine Tegen Books.

Rothschild, David. 2011. *Earth Matters: An Encyclopedia of Ecology*. New York: DK Publishing.

Rowling, J. K. 2000. *Harry Potter and the Chamber of Secrets*. New York: Scholastic.

Ryan, Pam Munoz. 2002. *Esperanza Rising*. New York: Scholastic.

———. 2015. *Echo*. New York: Scholastic.

Rylant, Cynthia. 1988. *Every Living Thing*. New York: Modern Curriculum Press.

———. 2000. *The Old Woman Who Named Things*. Boston: HMH Books for Young Readers.

———. 2001. *Scarecrow*. Boston: HMH Books for Young Readers.

Sachar, Louis. 2000. *Holes*. New York: Yearling.

———. 2004. *Sideways Stories from Wayside School*. New York: HarperCollins.

———. 2008. *Small Steps*. New York: Ember.

Schlitz, Laura Amy. 2013. *The Hero Schliemann: The Dreamer Who Dug for Troy*. Somerville, MA: Candlewick.

Schotter, Roni. 1999. *Nothing Ever Happens on 90th Street*. New York: Scholastic Inc.

Schwartz, Alvin. 2010. *Scary Stories to Tell in the Dark*. New York: HarperCollins.

Scieszka, Jon. 1996. *The True Story of the Three Little Pigs*. New York: Puffin Books.

———. 1998. *The Stinky Cheese Man and Other Fairly Stupid Tales*. New York: Puffin Books.

Selden, George. 2008. *The Cricket in Times Square*. New York: Square Fish.

Selznick, Brian. 2007. *The Invention of Hugo Cabret*. New York: Scholastic.

Seredy, Kate. 1990. *The Singing Tree*. New York: Puffin Books.

Seuss, Dr. 1960. *Green Eggs and Ham*. New York: Beginner Books/Random House.

Shakespeare, William. 2003. *Macbeth*. New York: Simon & Schuster.

Shannon, David. 1998. *No, David!* New York: Scholastic.

———. 2004. *A Bad Case of the Stripes*. New York: Scholastic.

Shaskan, Trish Speed. 2011. *Seriously, Cinderella Is So Annoying*. North Mankato, MN: Picture Window Books.

Shurtliff, Liesl. 2015. *Jack: The True Story of Jack and the Beanstalk*. New York: Knopf Books for Young Readers.

Sidman, Joyce. 2010. *Ubiquitous: Celebrating Nature's Survivors*. Boston: HMH Books for Young Readers.

Smith, David. 2011. *This Child, Every Child: A Book About the World's Children*. Toronto, Canada: Kids Can Press.

Solheim, James. 2001. *It's Disgusting and We Ate It! True Food Facts from Around the World and Throughout History*. New York: Aladdin.

Solway, Andrew. 2008. *Designing Greener Vehicles and Buildings*. Chicago: Heinemann-Raintree.

Soto, Gary. 2003. *Local News*. Boston: HMH Books for Young Readers.

Speare, Elizabeth George. 2011. *The Sign of the Beaver*. Boston: HMH Books for Young Readers.

———. 2011. *The Witch of Blackbird Pond*. Boston: HMH Books for Young Readers.

Spilsbury, Richard. 2008. *Managing Water*. Chicago: Heinemann-Raintree.

Spinelli, Jerry. 1997. *Crash*. New York: Yearling.

———. 1998. *Knots in My Yo-Yo String*. New York: Ember.

———. 1998. *The Library Card*. New York: Scholastic.

———. 1999. *Maniac Magee*. New York: Little, Brown Books for Young Readers.

———. 2012. *Fourth Grade Rats*. New York: Arthur A. Levine Books.

St. John, Lauren. 2010. *The Last Leopard*. New York: Puffin Books.

Stanley, Jerry. 1993. *Children of the Dust Bowl: The True Story of the School at Weedpatch Camp*. New York: Crown Publishers.

Stead, Rebecca. 2010. *When You Reach Me*. New York: Yearling.

———. 2013. *Liar & Spy*. New York: Yearling.

Stone, Tanya Lee. 2009. *Almost Astronauts: 13 Women Who Dared to Dream*. Somerville, MA: Candlewick.

———. 2013. *Courage Has No Color, The True Story of the Triple Nickles: America's First Black Paratroopers*. Somerville, MA: Candlewick.

———. 2013. *Who Says Women Can't be Doctors? The Story of Elizabeth Blackwell*. New York: Henry Holt and Company.

Strand, Rebecca. 2015. *Goodbye Stranger*. New York: Wendy Lamb Books.

Strauss, Rochelle. 2013. *Tree of Life: The Incredible Biodiversity of Life on Earth*. Toronto, Canada: Kids Can Press.

Sullivan, Otha Richard. 2011. *Black Stars: African American Inventors*. Hoboken, NJ: Wiley.

Szumski, Bonnie. 2014. *Cheating*. Chicago: Norwood House Press.

Tan, Shaun. 2007. *The Arrival*. New York: Arthur A. Levine Books.

Taylor, Mildred. 2004. *Roll of Thunder, Hear My Cry*. New York: Puffin Books.

Thimmesh, Catherine. 2002. *Girls Think of Everything: Stories of Ingenious Inventions by Women*. Boston: HMH Books for Young Readers.

Thompson, Ruth. 2013. *Terezin: Voices from the Holocaust*. Somerville, MA: Candlewick.

Tolkien, J. R. R. 2012. *The Hobbit*. Boston: Houghton Mifflin Harcourt.

Twain, Mark. 1998. *The Adventures of Tom Sawyer*. Mineola, NY: Dover.

Ullman, James Ramsey. 1988. *Banner in the Sky*. New York: HarperTeen.

Ursu, Anne. 2013. *Breadcrumbs*. New York: Walden Pond Press.

Van Allsburg, Chris. 1984. *The Mysteries of Harris Burdick*. Boston: Houghton Mifflin Harcourt.

Viorst, Judith. 1987. *Alexander and the Terrible, Horrible, No Good, Very Bad Day*. New York: Atheneum Books for Young Readers.

———. 1993. *Earrings!* New York: Atheneum Books for Young Readers.

Weinstein, Elizabeth. 2008. *Shakespeare with Children: Six Scripts for Young Players*. Hanover, NH: Smith and Kraus.

White, E. B. 2012. *Charlotte's Web*. New York: HarperCollins.

Wiesel, Elie. 2006. *Night*. New York: Hill and Wang.

Willems, Mo. 2003. *Don't Let the Pigeon Drive the Bus!* New York: Hyperion Press.

———. 2014. *That Is NOT a Good Idea*. Somerville, MA: Walker Books Ltd.

Williams-Garcia, Rita. 2011. *One Crazy Summer*. New York: Amistad.

Wilson, Charles, and Eric Schlosser. 2007. *Chew on This: Everything You Don't Want to Know About Fast Food*. Boston: Houghton Mifflin Harcourt.

Wishinsky, Frieda. 2012. *Profiles #4: Freedom Heroines*. New York: Scholastic.

Woodson, Jacqueline. 2001. *The Other Side*. New York: G. P. Putnam's Sons Books for Young Readers.

———. 2010. *From the Notebooks of Melanin Sun*. New York: Puffin Books.

———. 2012. *Each Kindness*. New York: Nancy Paulsen Books.

Wulffson, Don. 1999. *The Kid Who Invented the Popsicle*. New York: Puffin Books.

———. 2014. *Toys! Amazing Stories Behind Some Great Inventions*. New York: Square Fish.

Yolen, Jane. 1997. *Welcome to the Green House*. New York: Puffin Books.

Zusak, Markus. 2007. *The Book Thief*. New York: Alfred A. Knopf.

References and Recommended Reading

Teachers are always helping others to learn. More importantly, as teachers, we never stop learning. This list of resources represents just a fraction of the amazing books that I have referenced, relied on, and regarded as my go-to resources for the teaching of writing. I hope that they can inspire you as well.

Atwell, Nancie. 1987. *In the Middle: Writing, Reading, and Learning with Adolescents.* Upper Montclair, NJ: Boynton/Cook.

Beers, Kylene and Robert E. Probst. 2012. *Notice & Note: Strategies for Close Reading.* Portsmouth, NH: Heinemann.

Bernabei, Gretchen. 2005. *Reviving the Essay: How to Teach Structure Without Formula.* Shoreham, VT: Discover Writing Press.

Bernabei, Gretchen S., and Dorothy P. Hall. 2012. *The Story of My Thinking: Expository Writing Activities for 13 Teaching Situations.* Portsmouth, NH: Heinemann.

Bernabei, Gretchen S., Jayne Hover, and Cynthia Candler. 2009. *Crunchtime: Lessons to Help Students Blow the Roof off Writing Tests—and Become Better Writers in the Process.* Portsmouth, NH: Heinemann.

Burke, Jim. 2010. *What's the Big Idea? Question-Driven Units to Motivate Reading, Writing, and Thinking.* Portsmouth, NH: Heinemann.

Calkins, Lucy. 1986. *The Art of Teaching Writing.* Portsmouth, NH: Heinemann.

Culham, Ruth. 2004. *Using Picture Books to Teach Writing with the Traits: An Annotated Bibliography of More Than 200 Titles with Teacher-Tested Lessons.* New York: Teaching Resources.

———. 2004. *The Writing Thief: Using Mentor Texts to Teach the Craft of Writing.* Newark, DE: International Reading Association.

———. 2010. *Traits of Writing: The Complete Guide for Middle School.* New York: Scholastic.

Daniels, Harvey, Steven Zemelman, and Nancy Steineke. 2007. *Content-Area Writing: Every Teacher's Guide.* Portsmouth, NH: Heinemann.

Fletcher, Ralph J., and JoAnn Portalupi. 1998. *Craft Lessons: Teaching Writing K–8.* York, ME: Stenhouse Publishers.

———. 2001. *Writing Workshop: The Essential Guide.* Portsmouth, NH: Heinemann.

Fletcher, Ralph J. 1993. *What a Writer Needs.* Portsmouth, NH: Heinemann.

———. 2011. *Mentor Author, Mentor Texts: Short Texts, Craft Notes, and Practical Classroom Uses.* Portsmouth, NH: Heinemann.

Graham, Steve, Charles A. MacArthur, and Jill Fitzgerald. 2013. *Best Practices in Writing Instruction,* 2d ed. New York: Guilford Press.

Harvey, Stephanie. 1998. *Nonfiction Matters: Reading, Writing, and Research in Grades 3–8.* York, ME: Stenhouse Publishers.

Heard, Georgia. 2002. *The Revision Toolbox: Teaching Techniques That Work*. Portsmouth, NH: Heinemann.

———. 2013. *Finding the Heart of Nonfiction: Teaching 7 Essential Craft Tools with Mentor Texts*. Portsmouth, NH: Heinemann.

Hillocks, George. 2011. *Teaching Argument Writing, Grades 6–12: Supporting Claims with Relevant Evidence and Clear Reasoning*. Portsmouth, NH: Heinemann.

Hoyt, Linda. 2011. *Crafting Nonfiction. Lessons on Writing Process, Traits, and Craft*. Portsmouth, NH: Firsthand Heinemann.

Killgallon, Don and Jenny. 1997. *Sentence Composing for Middle School: A Worktext on Sentence Variety and Maturity*. Portsmouth, NH: Boynton/Cook.

———. 2000. *Sentence Composing for Elementary School: A Worktext to Build Better Sentences*. Portsmouth, NH: Heinemann.

———. 2013. *Paragraphs for Middle School: A Sentence-Composing Approach: A Student Worktext*. Portsmouth, NH: Heinemann.

———. 2014. *Paragraphs for Elementary School: A Sentence-Composing Approach: A Student Worktext*. Portsmouth, NH: Heinemann.

Lane, Barry. 1993. *After the End: Teaching and Learning Creative Revision*. Portsmouth, NH: Heinemann.

———. 1999. *Reviser's Toolbox*. Shoreham, VT: Discover Writing Press.

———. 2008. *But How Do You Teach Writing? A Simple Guide for All Teachers*. New York: Scholastic.

Lehman, Christopher. 2012. *Energize Research Reading and Writing: Fresh Strategies to Spark Interest, Develop Independence, and Meet Key Common Core Standards, Grades 4–8*. Portsmouth, NH: Heinemann.

Leograndis, Denise, and Pam Allyn. 2008. *Launching the Writing Workshop: A Step-by-Step Guide in Photographs*. New York: Scholastic.

McGregor, Tanny. 2007. *Comprehension Connections: Bridges to Strategic Reading*. Portsmouth, NH: Heinemann.

Overmeyer, Mark. 2005. *When Writing Workshop Isn't Working: Answers to Ten Tough Questions, Grades 2–5*. Portland, ME: Stenhouse Publishers.

Ray, Katie Wood. 1999. *Wondrous Words: Writers and Writing in the Elementary Classroom*. Urbana, IL: National Council of Teachers of English.

———. 2002. *What You Know by Heart: How to Develop Curriculum for Your Writing Workshop*. Portsmouth, NH: Heinemann.

Ray, Katie Wood, and Lester L. Laminack. 2001. *The Writing Workshop: Working Through the Hard Parts (and They're All Hard Parts)*. Urbana, IL: National Council of Teachers of English.

Routman, Regie. 2005. *Writing Essentials: Raising Expectations and Results While Simplifying Teaching*. Portsmouth, NH: Heinemann.